Water Politics

Water Politics

Governing our most precious resource

DAVID L. FELDMAN

polity

First published in 2017 by Polity Press

Polity Press
65 Bridge Street
Cambridge CB2 1UR, UK

Polity Press
350 Main Street
Malden, MA 02148, USA

ISBN-13: 978-1-5095-0461-9
ISBN-13: 978-1-5095-0462-6 (pb)

A catalogue record for this book is available from the British Library.

Library of Congress Cataloging-in-Publication Data
Names: Feldman, David Lewis, 1951- author.
Title: Water politics : governing our most precious resource / David L.
    Feldman.
Description: Cambridge, UK ; Malden, MA : Polity Press, 2017. | Includes
    bibliographical references and index.
Identifiers: LCCN 2016028561 (print) | LCCN 2016043496 (ebook) | ISBN
    9781509504619 (hardback) | ISBN 9781509504626 (pbk.) | ISBN 9781509504640
    (mobi) | ISBN 9781509504657 (Epub)
Subjects: LCSH: Water-supply–Political aspects. |
    Water-supply–Co-management. | Water security. | Water resources
    development.
Classification: LCC HD1691 .F454 2017 (print) | LCC HD1691 (ebook) | DDC
    333.91–dc23
LC record available at https://lccn.loc.gov/2016028561

Typeset in 9.5/13 Swift light by
Servis Filmsetting Limited, Stockport, Cheshire
Printed and bound in the UK by CPI Group (UK) Ltd, Croydon, CR0 4YY

For further information on Polity, visit our website:
politybooks.com

Contents

Figures

Preface

A familiar adage of our time is that water is to the twenty-first century what oil was to the twentieth – a contested resource for which the fate of entire nations hangs in the balance. Strategic and other comparisons between oil and water are somewhat problematic, however. While disputes over water are growing due to climate change, demands for food and energy that are increasing, and with the advent of mega-cities, nations rarely resort to violence to resolve water conflicts. Moreover, unlike petroleum, which can be exhausted, there is no upper bound to available fresh water *if* we manage it well.

In many regions of the world such as the Indus, Mekong, or Colorado basins, the need to share over-stressed supplies and to cooperatively manage water infrastructure often leads to collaboration, however precariously. In fact, there are long-standing approaches to conjoint management of water arising out of needs for food, hydropower, and domestic supply (Harrington 2014).

This book analyzes the *processes* that determine how water issues get the attention of decision-makers, and how disputes over water arise within and between countries. We also examine how varied sources of *power*: economic, legal, and expert, determine its governance – how we allocate, use, and protect it. Finally, we consider the *purposes* that direct decisions over cost, availability, and access to water. In this wide-ranging analysis, we also provide timely examples from every continent.

Most of all, we consider appropriate arrangements to equitably address water problems. By "governance arrangements," we mean combinations of public agencies and civil society entities that cooperate to manage water problems. Among these problems are the challenge of water pollution, one of the world's gravest health and environmental threats, and that is aggravated by poverty, rapid industrialization, efforts to produce more food, and by newer "contaminants of concern" that are often beyond the reach of law and regulation.

Special agreements to govern water, such as river basin compacts and confidence building efforts to resolve trans-boundary disputes, are also assessed. And, attention is paid to controversies surrounding desalination, wastewater reuse, rainwater harvesting and other non-conventional supply alternatives. Finally, we examine growing threats to established governance arrangements posed by drought and flood.

Chapter 1 introduces a framework for understanding water politics: anchored by process (the interaction of agencies and groups), power (the ability to influence decisions), and purpose (the goals of participants). These are the major factors that determine how water politics is conducted, by whom, and toward what ends.

Chapter 2 discusses the political challenges of water supply. We begin with this issue because it is arguably the basis for all other aspects of water politics. Finding, acquiring, and delivering water is of paramount urgency, especially in the world's burgeoning mega-cities where a plurality of the planet's population now resides. These cities are grappling with the means to provide ample, safe drinking water supplies through leveraging resources to improve infrastructure on one hand, while facing the resistance of city residents who are asked to pay for these improvements on the other. It is also an urgent priority for feeding growing populations, especially in developing nations. To comprehend these issues, in urban and rural areas alike, requires that we first understand debates over control, ownership, and marketing of water for all needs.

As important as water supply is, degradation of that supply can undermine efforts to make it readily available. Thus, chapter 3 examines why, despite some 40 years of progress, water quality remains one of the world's most serious environmental challenges. Following a discussion of quantity with one on quality also makes logical sense, we feel, especially since pollution is a ubiquitous global issue. Cases from the US, France, Russia, and China, as well as recent efforts to remove "microbeads" from the water environment, utilize natural means of pollution attenuation, and trade pollution rights, are also discussed. In the past half-century, nations have extended water quality protection beyond human health to encompass the environment itself.

Chapter 4 discusses the so-called water, food, and energy nexus. Some of the most important debates over water politics revolve around making energy and food more plentiful and affordable, and balancing these goals against the desire to protect water quality; achieve integrated management of these resources; and use hydraulic techniques for energy extraction or "fracking." This nexus amplifies many of the political controversies first discussed under water supply and quality.

Climate change and variability is taken up in chapter 5. We discuss flood abatement, drought alleviation, and recent efforts to manage climate extremes. A growing political challenge is the effort to span local and expert knowledge in managing water and climate. Illustrations from Latin America, the US, and Australia illuminate the effectiveness of this effort. As we will see, it has been complicated by ideologically motivated debate over climate change that impedes long-term collaboration.

Chapter 6 focuses on water law as an evolving set of practices and institutions. Fresh water has long been managed through codified or common law – it is the oldest form of water governance. Law may also take the form of river basin compacts that divide water between provinces or states. Moreover, these arrangements are generally quite durable, even if parties periodically engage in contentious negotiations over how to re-allocate drought-stricken flows.

Chapter 7 examines international collaboration to manage shared waters. Because water is irreplaceable by any other substance, countries must share it. Attempts to monopolize it would generate wars fought to suicidal desperation. This is why chronic water shortages among states sharing watersheds, especially in arid regions, lead to some form of cooperation. By establishing rules over permissible withdrawals and diversions, as in the Tigris-Euphrates basin, or over water infrastructure as between Israel and Palestine, violence can be averted.

Whereas chapter 7 focuses on avenues for transnational collaboration, chapter 8 examines intractable sources of disputes – within and between countries. Debates over hydropower generation; protests over permitting of beverage plants that draw down local groundwater; relocation of populations to make room for large dams or diversion projects; and continued degradation of water bodies – such as the Aral Sea in central Asia, Ojos Negros Valley in Mexico, or Han River in China – are among the most serious of such conflicts. And, these disputes engage many levels of governance.

In Chapter 9, we examine the impacts and implications of alternative sources of water supply, as well as innovative ways to temper or reduce demands. These are topics infrequently discussed in water politics texts, despite the fact that these unconventional methods to augment supply – including wastewater reuse, rainwater harvesting, desalination, and demand management – are growing in significance across the globe. While there has been much discussion about their technical feasibility for quenching the world's growing thirst, far too little attention has been paid to their public acceptability, perceived risk, and professed fairness (i.e., who pays for, and benefits from, them?). These *political* factors affect long-term prospects for their implementation.

Finally, chapter 10 considers the future of water governance and prospects for better democratizing water politics in order to amicably resolve disputes. We also weigh the likelihood of sharing power among diverse groups, and of broadening purpose to better encompass issues of inclusiveness and public engagement – especially at the local community level.

This text also explores other issues not commonly addressed elsewhere. One example is debate over water as a commodity. In addition to the advantages and disadvantages of privatization, there is growing interest in the impacts of so-called "virtual" water trades – the buying and selling of products whose manufacture depends on water. These trades raise nagging questions regarding the capacity of developing countries to engage in import substitution and industrialization. They also prompt us to inquire whether the dependence of water-short countries on others for water-intensive products retards their development, denies them equal access to resources, encourages the building of large water projects, and is unfair (Hoekstra & Chapagain 2007).

Water wars – as implied earlier – are rare. Nevertheless, an issue of growing concern in global water politics is the fact that, should war erupt for other reasons, water infrastructure may become a prime military objective. Germany's Ruhr dams were effectively targeted during World War II, for example, while attacks on water supply and treatment facilities have occurred in parts of the Middle East since 1948 (Oren 2003; Holland 2012). More recently, Islamic State has "weapon-ized" water as a means of securing control over contested territory, and internecine wars in Iraq and Syria have led protagonists to do the same.

The arenas where water politics play out encompass formal governance arrangements at various jurisdictional levels, overseen by agencies charged with managing water and other resources. The tools these agencies employ include laws and regulations governing water supply and its quality; treaties negotiated among countries for sharing or conjointly managing river and groundwater basins; and partnerships between public (i.e., governmental) and non-governmental entities to advise and set standards for managing pollution.

Water politics is further composed of a vast array of interests; informal and formal organizations; and diverse venues where debate, dialogue, discussion, and decision-making occur. Corporate boardrooms, science and engineering labs, and religious gatherings serve as political venues for water when they prescribe objectives water policies should achieve – such as recommending standards for clean water, determining what new or innovative methods for providing additional supply are fair or equitable (e.g., desalination, wastewater re-use), and suggesting what roles public participation should play in setting water rates paid by users. Although their procedures and methods of decision-making differ from those found in, say, legislative chambers, law courts, or regulatory agencies, these diverse venues exercise power over policy outcomes. They also clearly engage in purposeful action. We touch upon these venues.

In recent years, water politics has become somewhat synonymous with *environmental politics*: an arena where questions regarding how to protect nature while satisfying society's need for natural resources intersect in complex ways. This has been true in a variety of cases: from cleaning up polluted rivers in Cologne or Cleveland; supplying water for growing food or producing hydropower in China or India; providing clean water to residents of Mexico City or Dublin, Ireland; mitigating the impacts of climate change, drought, and flood in Australia or Brazil; or building desalination plants in California or Israel.

Actions we take to enhance society's access to water can sometimes degrade the natural environment. By the same token, choices we may make to protect nature from engineered intrusions designed to enhance publically useable water supplies may limit our ability to meet societal demands (e.g., choosing *not* to dam a river). We often accept such trade-offs because powerful interests demand that we preserve pristine streams for the enjoyment of future generations. These groups also try to demonstrate the benefits in doing so: not only for ourselves but also for our progeny.

Across the planet, there are growing demands to treat fresh water as an amenity as opposed to a purely economic commodity. There also are growing demands to rethink how we value, allocate, and prioritize its use, particularly in light of major drought and serious apprehensions about the long-term impacts of climate change.

Both sets of demands have become linked in larger calls to manage fresh water more *equitably* – a word that has multiple, and even conflicting meanings: fairness toward people and their welfare, or toward nature and its sustainability. In cases where certain groups seek to develop large dams or diversion projects, for instance, there may be fervent pressure to ensure that under-represented groups living adjacent to these proposed projects share in their benefits. To others, however, equity with respect to building dams may mean protecting fauna and flora that might be driven to extinction if such projects are built without regard to their ecological impact.

With regard to the last of these issues, we pay special attention to *global* competition over water and its impacts on available supply and quality – in places as diverse as the Middle East, Africa, Latin America, and South and Southeast Asia. Disputes over water are not limited to developing nations. They are found in many parts of the developed world, especially Europe and the US. In the latter, water has long been a focal point of dispute, and is becoming more critical as a result of extreme weather – frequent, long-term droughts punctuated by sudden and destructive flooding.

While sole authored, the issues this book covers are the product of an inherently collaborative effort. I have drawn upon a career-long association with many distinguished colleagues, here in California and elsewhere, whose conversation and inspiration are – I hope – reflected here. My colleagues at the University of California, Irvine and in other parts of the US, as well as Australia, Russia, and Europe, have immensely enhanced my understanding of the politics of water through our work together on many of the questions and problems taken up in this volume. Most importantly, their ideas and support continue to reinforce a message that I hope resonates throughout this book: that every academic discipline, field of study, and intellectual domain is important for understanding the politics of water.

I especially thank several colleagues, students, and former students for their inspiration and ideas. At the University of California these include: Amir AghaKouchak, Victoria Basolo, Peter Bowler, Tim Bradley, Wing Cheung, Jean Fried, Silvia Gonzalez, Stan Grant, Travis Huxman, Helen Ingram, Sunny Jiang, Richard Matthew, Valerie Olson, Meg Rippy, Brett Sanders, Soroosh Sorooshian, Lindsey Stuvick, and Jinsuhk Suh.

I have also immensely benefitted from the insights of other US and Australian colleagues including Ashmita Sengupta and Eric Stein with the Southern California Coastal Water Research Project, and Vin Pettigrove and Meenakshi Arora from the University of Melbourne. I also thank Louise Knight, my editor at Polity, for her encouragement and patience throughout the process of writing this book. While I owe a great debt to all these colleagues for furthering my knowledge of these problems, all errors of fact, interpretation, or judgment are solely my own.

Finally, to my family who have patiently put up with me throughout this project – and whose support makes it all worthwhile – this book is dedicated to Justin, and most of all, to Jill.

CHAPTER 1

Why Water Politics Matters

A tale of two cities

Despite receiving an average of 63 inches of rain annually, 25 inches more than Seattle, Washington, Sao Paulo is in the throes of a severe drought that has led city leaders to adopt water rationing and undertake other emergency measures in this metropolis of 21 million – Brazil's largest, and the most populous city in the Southern hemisphere. Systematic removal of forest cover and subsequent sedimentation has severely reduced the capacity of the city's reservoirs, including the Guarapiranga, Rio Grande, and Billings. In some cases, reservoirs are also severely polluted.

Compounding this crisis, much of the city's largest source of freshwater, the Cantareira system, first came on-line in 1976 when the city had a little over half the population it has today. Infrastructure improvements have not kept up with growth. Moreover, when it does rain, the fast-growing city has been paved over with so much asphalt that, as Pedro Jacobi, an environmental scientist at the University of Sao Paulo notes, a storm dropping two inches of rain can result in massive flooding. Without adequate means to abate floods or harvest them for later use, floodwaters simply flow to the sea.

Not surprisingly, alternation between too little and too much water has contributed to a policy landscape that belies the severity of the current drought, and a skewed public perception that complicates voluntary conservation efforts. On top of this skewed outlook is a general sense of public distrust exacerbated by lackadaisical government responses to the crisis over the past three years. Residents first began complaining of dropping water pressure in their homes as early as May 2014, but officials did not commit to rationing or other actions until March 2015: stubbornly clinging to the hope that rain would refill the reservoirs, alleviating the need for more drastic measures and allowing officials to spend public funds on solving other problems.

The local water utility, Companhia de Saneamento Basico do estado de Sao Paulo, or "Sabesp," initially exercised expedient measures, including laying extra pipe to the Cantareira reservoir system. Later, it decided to increase water rates to encourage conservation and help pay for emergency measures. Further negating the credibility of officials was their belated admission of the seriousness of the drought, and the need for more expensive mitigation measures. Late concessions increased distrust of officials' competence and worsened protests (Borrell 2015; Kozacek 2015). Sabesp, together with the state regulator that is empowered to approve rate hikes, are mindful of the protests that accompanied bus and train ticket increases in Rio and Sao Paulo in 2013. Not surprisingly, they are reluctant to institute possibly unpopular measures that could cause civil unrest.

Experts like Professor Jacobi hope the drought is an opportunity to improve the city's future water security. "You have to think about the way of dealing with a crisis that has not just come in the short-range, but has come to stay . . . You have to look at it as permanent [and] . . . to learn that you cannot only depend on the government. You have to organize yourselves, developing more social learning to engage people into doing something . . . because it is the way we develop as a city" (Kozacek 2015).

If distrust and cynicism have pervaded Sao Paulo's responses to its drought, by contrast the recent experiences of Melbourne, Australia, during the so-called Millennium Drought (1996–2010) led to a number of measures that were based on a widely shared perception of crisis, and a set of responses that garnered a comparatively high level of public trust. Home to some four-and-a-half million people, one-fifth the size of Sao Paulo, but comprising one-fifth of Australia's entire population, Melbourne is almost entirely dependent on locally-sourced surface supplies that dwindled to less than 24 percent of total capacity during the heart of the drought. Faced with few options, the city turned to a number of unconventional approaches to ensure long-term resilience.

Melbourne Water – the city's utility – and the state of Victoria pursued a wide range of approaches, including construction of a controversial desalination plant which, while built, has yet to be used, several household conservation measures, as well as small-scale projects to harvest rainwater. Most crucial to Melbourne's dramatic reductions in water use during the drought, however – household water consumption fell by some 50 percent on average – is the fact that adoption of these measures was facilitated by governmental arrangements that: mandated cross-jurisdictional and coordinated policy response; permitted regional oversight of local utility operations (thus assuring such coordination took place); and delegated authority to localities to impose water use restrictions, implement conservation measures, fund rainwater harvesting projects, and employ direct public outreach via mass-media messaging.

Various layers of government were given authority to institute changes, and exercise of this authority was legitimized to a great extent by local citizen confidence in the capacity of these governments to act responsibly. In part, this confidence was brought about by Victoria's efforts to engage citizens in an extensive dialogue about water demand, possible supply options, and long-term changes in urban design.

In 2002, the Victorian Government announced a recycled water target of 20 percent of sewage inflows by 2010, an additional 6,200 ML by 2015, and an additional 10 GL by 2030. To meet Victoria's reuse targets and the exigencies imposed by the Millennium Drought, a rapid increase in the use of recycled water occurred between 2005 and 2009. In 2005, the government launched two major recycled water schemes that remain the anchors for water supply for the region. These so-called "Class A" (suitable for home and agriculture irrigation use) recycled water schemes include the Werribee Irrigation District and the Eastern Irrigation Scheme – and cover much of the Melbourne region.

Moreover, the drought severely reduced flows and increased the salinity of local river water, resulting in low river water allocations. In response, farmers in the Werribee District turned to groundwater until that source was banned by the Victorian government over concerns that rapid drawdown of groundwater could lead to seawater intrusion. This made the use of recycled wastewater especially attractive and practical, leading to its expansion beyond use as a stopgap measure.

Starting in 2005, three more urban recycled water schemes were added to ensure that precious drinking water would not have to be used for landscaping, parks, or golf courses, and in 2006 the first residential recycled water dual pipe system became operational in Melbourne.

Melbourne's experience suggests that major droughts can create windows of opportunity for decision-makers to engage the public constructively – somewhat at variance to the experience of Sao Paulo. While these cases share in common an attempt to respond to crisis – in this case drought – both also reveal much about the politics of water management in the early twenty-first century. In essence, decision-makers – and not just in cities – must be willing to pursue multiple remedies – and to engage various publics in adopting these possible remedies – in order to build confidence in their competence to deal with drought crisis (Grant et al. 2013; Low et al. 2015).

Moreover, both crises remind us that, while challenges posed by water availability will always arise, and can be exacerbated by human activity, especially in the case of drought, the capacity of societies to effectively respond to these crises depends on three things. First, do these societies' decision-making processes afford inclusive participation to those affected by decisions, and is this process transparent? If not, can they reform these processes to make inclusion and transparency possible? Second, are officials charged with managing and providing water willing to share power and authority for decisions with affected groups? And, how is this power exercised in deciding how to respond to a crisis – is it concentrated in the hands of a few, or widely shared among many? And third, can participants agree – whether they are the decision-makers or the people affected by decisions – on consensus-based principles for managing water problems based on common or shared purpose? Are these principles narrowly confined to a few objectives – say, economic prosperity – or do they also embrace social equity and environmental justice?

A framework for water politics

The theme of this book is that the provision and management of water are not merely technical problems whose resolution hinges on hydrological principle, economic cost, or engineering feasibility. They are and have always been products of decisions made by institutions that exercise control over access to water, that determine who gets it as well as prescribing the condition people receive it, and that define the goals for its use.

The allocation, protection, and use of water are influenced by a complex array of statutes, rules, and norms of exchange. This is not only true for megacities like Sao Paulo, or metropolises such as Melbourne, but it is true for entire countries such as modern day Kuwait, for instance, where bureaucrats appointed by the royal family determine how desalinated freshwater is distributed to citizens. Moreover, the centrality of politics to water management was no less true in the distant past when Egyptian pharaohs allotted Nile floods to farmers, and later, when Roman emperors built aqueducts to deliver water to burgeoning cities in Italy, Spain, and Gaul (today's France).

Likewise, water provision is partly determined by deeply held values that shape approaches viewed as legitimate for governing its quality and availability (Swyngedouw 2007; Linton 2010; Phillips et al. 2011). These values may be rooted in tradition and influenced by religious practice, as was true in nineteenth-century New Mexico, for example, where farmers paying homage to the patron saint of water, San Isidro, shared community supplies by cooperatively managing *acequias* – elaborate irrigation ditches maintained by the villages where they resided. Conversely, the values animating water management may be shaped by scientific observation and assessment – as many recent reports on the condition of the world's water contend. The rules, norms, and values of water politics, as well as the institutions that engage in decision-making, are rarely wedded to only one approach. They usually blend many values and types of knowledge.

Water politics matters because it determines the outcomes of issues vital to our well-being and survival. These include: our ability to balance the needs of nature and society without severely compromising one or the other; how to manage threats to water supply and quality in the face of a world that is increasingly urbanized and challenged by climate change; and what constitutes a fair price to pay for clean water – and who should be able to decide on this price? In seeking solutions to these and other problems, this book draws on a unique analytical framework.

Moreover, water politics comprises more than the actions of government. It embraces the activities of private businesses that treat, distribute and sell water for a profit; civil society groups that avidly defend the rights of people who demand access to affordable water; and entire nations that covet and compete for shared river- or groundwater basins. We employ a three-fold structure for understanding water politics: the *process of decision-making*, the *exercise of power*, and the *purposes governance aims to achieve*. This framework is depicted in figure 1.1.

Process

A key to understanding water politics is the *process* by which issues get the attention of officials (i.e., what political scientists call agenda setting), and the means by which policies are formulated and applied through law, rule, treaty, or common everyday practice. Process encompasses negotiation, bargaining, and accommodation among various interests that use, manage, and provide water and includes such entities as corporations; scientific, legal, and other experts; large user groups (e.g., farmers, industrial and commercial sectors, urban utilities); as well as environmental groups and citizen organizations. Individual decision-makers holding formal positions are also involved: from emperors, kings, chieftains, presidents, and prime ministers, to governors, mayors, legislators, bureaucrats, judges, and diplomats.

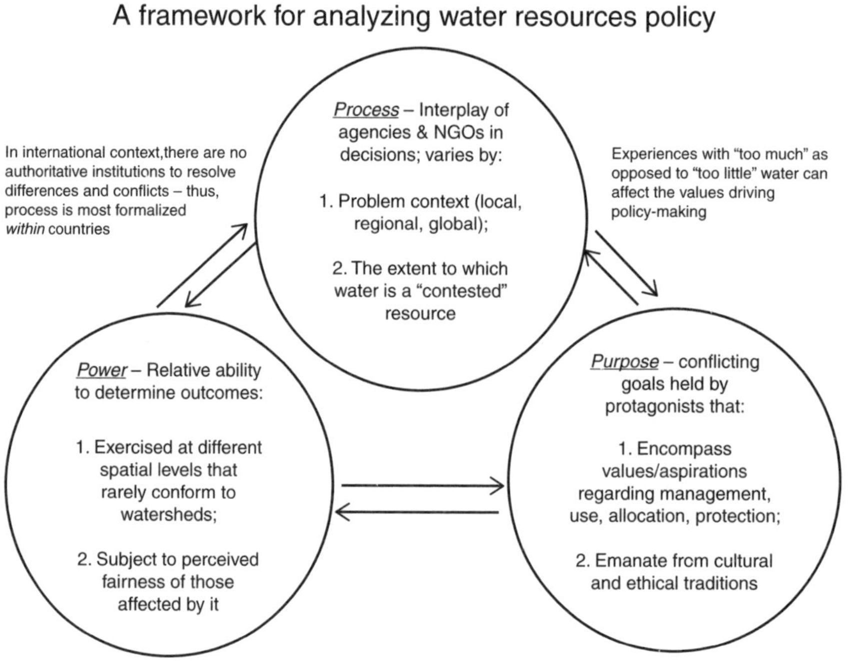

A framework for analyzing water resources policy

In international context,there are no authoritative institutions to resolve differences and conflicts – thus, process is most formalized *within* countries

Process – Interplay of agencies & NGOs in decisions; varies by:

1. Problem context (local, regional, global);

2. The extent to which water is a "contested" resource

Experiences with "too much" as opposed to "too little" water can affect the values driving policy-making

Power – Relative ability to determine outcomes:

1. Exercised at different spatial levels that rarely conform to watersheds;

2. Subject to perceived fairness of those affected by it

Purpose – conflicting goals held by protagonists that:

1. Encompass values/aspirations regarding management, use, allocation, protection;

2. Emanate from cultural and ethical traditions

Figure 1.1　*A conceptual framework for water politics*

Studies of the role of process in water politics have identified two important characteristics of decision-making. First, in every polity, decision-making usually involves a complex interplay of forces and participants that vary according to: the problem context (local, regional, national, or international); and the nature of water as a contested resource. Second, the "playing field" of water politics is dynamic, not static. A participant who loses a policy debate in one venue may try and change the outcome in another. These facts have long been known and studied by students of water politics since at least the 1960s, and their implications have been tied to efforts to better understand policy outcomes (Fox 1966; Ingram et al. 1980; Mann 1985).

In many cases, controversies regarding the provision of, say, public water supplies might engage the efforts of local elected officials, private companies, citizen groups, and even courts who might weigh in on appropriate ways to resolve a dispute over eminent domain, or the rates a water company can legally charge consumers. Questions guiding this process might include: how do private corporations and public distributors provide domestic supplies to municipalities; how much should people have to pay; and, should special measures be taken to treat – and otherwise protect – drinking water in poor communities to ensure it is safe from contaminants, even if it is expensive to do so? Finally, do providers confer with local citizens in making decisions?

Process doesn't stop there, however. If a private corporation manages local water supplies, for instance, or if a local groundwater basin is being used for the production of bottled water, or for use in production of energy, there may be international actors involved who control production, own or control a water source, or operate under license to a government. Local political authorities may have less influence over the operation of such enterprises than the countries in which these enterprises are based. An example of this is the important debate in Bolivia sparked by privatization many years ago.

In most cases, the better organized a group or interest, the more leverage and influence it has on this process of decision-making. This is one reason why the process of water politics often produces diverse outcomes, even when the process is initiated by one set of interests. For example, while a group or set of agencies may initiate efforts to divert water from a basin, other groups may be able to eventually reverse such actions – and even influence the decision-making process at critical junctures to restore the basin. This happened in the Aral Sea, for instance, and while not entirely successful, it does represent a change in decision-making.

Likewise, these factors also explain the leverage of various groups and interests in water management decisions and how this leverage can vary over time as certain groups slowly acquire access to junctions where critical decisions are being made. As we will see, water supply provision in rural areas tends to benefit well-organized farm groups while urban water supplies are often first provided to the wealthier classes who can afford the infrastructure through which it's provided. Likewise, while well-endowed energy interests may eventually succeed in harnessing water supplies for energy extraction (as in fracking, for example, a practice for extracting oil and gas using water), those who oppose such practices can find points-of-access to contest them.

Many issues reveal the importance – and the complexity – of process. One current controversy that aptly captures the challenges emanating from the interplay of diverse interests and jurisdictions is bottled water – especially its effects on local communities where the water is sourced. The latter has become a lightning rod for debate over the potential health impacts of its manufacture and bottling. The production, distribution and transportation of bottled water produce an enormous carbon footprint, and some three million tons of polyethylene terephthalate (PET) are annually produced for water bottles – consuming the equivalent of some 50 million barrels of petroleum.

Much of this PET finds its way into landfills, streams, rivers, and lakes – and the ocean – while another contaminant commonly found in plastic bottles, phthalate DEHP, has been linked to male infertility, hormonal imbalance and obesity. The source for much bottled water is pristine springs often located in rural areas – making its manufacture a source of geopolitical friction.

Multinational corporations such as Evian, Perrier-Nestle, Coca Cola, and PepsiCo have, over time, bought up and secured local water rights across the globe. Yet, despite concerted public opposition over actual (or possible) threats to springs, headwater streams, and groundwater, in very few instances has local resistance been successful in stopping these efforts. One reason is that while bottled water enterprises may pose local environmental risks, they also create jobs (see box 1.1).

Box 1.1   To bottle or not to bottle water – Northern California

Siskiyou County, in drought-stricken northern California, suffers from too little water and too few jobs. In 2013, Crystal Geyser announced plans to re-open an idled bottling plant near Mt. Shasta to produce bottled water, teas, and flavored soft drinks. A former logging community with high unemployment (in 2010, Coca Cola, which also operated a bottling plant, closed up its operations, worsening local economic conditions), the community has few opportunities.

County officials initially welcomed Crystal Geyser's plans, but many local residents are not so sure these plans are widely beneficial. The plant has no cap on how much snowmelt generated groundwater it can pump. And, despite nearby residents' concerns over truck traffic, noise, and the risk of compromising the shallow well supply of homeowners, local officials say they have no legal authority to actually halt or even modify the project. The California Environmental Quality Act requires an environmental impact assessment for large public-permitted projects that may have an effect on groundwater levels or other adverse impacts. However, local officials insist that they have no legal authority to require a report because the plant's site was zoned for heavy industry when it was a lumber mill, and water bottling is a prior and permitted use.

In effect, the process of decision-making with respect to bottling operations is fragmented and arbitrary – a fact conceded by one policy analyst who insists that reaction to the bottled water industry, in this instance and others, might be disproportionate to the problem at hand. Rather than "arbitrarily deciding that one particular use . . . is not good, it would be better to put in place a groundwater management plan because who's to say that the combined uses aren't causing a problem?" In other words, without a broadly inclusive process of decision-making, such arbitrary decisions are likely to be commonly made.

Source: Romney 2015

As contentious as debates over the twin objectives of economic development and environmental protection can be in local settings, when these disputes occur on an international stage, they face even greater process hurdles. There are no authoritative institutions at the international level that make binding decisions when choosing between job creation and protection of the environment. At that level, negotiation and accommodation require a commitment by autonomous nation-states to an independent process for problem solving. Furthermore, these nation-states must voluntarily comply with agreements they choose to ratify, and with the institutions charged with their enforcement (Mitchell 2009; Bakker 2013).

Other international issues regarding water confront us with similar process dilemmas. For instance, polities often permit water withdrawals for irrigation during drought, or continued deforestation threatening water quality – even in light of transnational agreements to restore water bodies. Sometimes such transnational agreements are ratified by international organizations which promise to provide aid to improve water supply systems: as with Haiti and the Dominican Republic, for instance. The more layers of governance involved in such decisions, the more complex the process. Inequalities of power and influence are also important in such cases – as we'll discuss in the next section.

Finally, process is strongly influenced by the overall scarcity (or relative abundance) of the resource, the quality of existing supplies, and the varying demands – especially for food and energy – we place on them. In parts of China, for example, too much (as opposed to too little) water (i.e., periodic flooding), or the need to harness the amount available for agriculture, is a major concern. For thousands of years, rural labor was employed in water control and irrigation – reinforcing, some argue, autocratic political control (Shaughnessy 2000). Since 2005 – Three Gorges Dam, a potent symbol of national engineering pride, has prevented severe flooding, enhanced navigation on the Yangtze River, and become the world's single largest generator of hydroelectricity.

The building of Three Gorges occurred in a contested political process. Dissidents and many others opposed its construction due to loss of ancestral homes and communities. Because of limited opportunities for participation in official forums, they fought its construction through demonstration and direct action. Environmental impacts on fisheries, wetlands, and water quality due to flooding of mines, waste sites, and siltation led, in some cases, to massive protests. Allegations of corruption in residential relocation efforts even led to high-level judicial investigations (Economy 2010).

More recently, in Iran, a large saltwater lake has become a focal point for a contested process for managing drought. Lake Urmia, located on a steppe bounded by Turkey and Azerbaijan, was once a thriving tourist haven which, as a result of irrigation practices, the damming of feeder streams by the state, and protracted drought has declined to the point where it now holds only 5 percent of the water it did in the 1990s. Environmentalists charge that the government has failed to protect and restore Urmia. Ethnic Azeris, affected by the lake's decline, claim that its conditions are a harbinger of long-term drinking water shortages, mandatory water rationing schemes for cities like Tehran, and threats to agricultural stability and food security.

Threats of rationing have led to public protests and clashes with police in Esfahan province due to government plans to divert available water to other, more needy, regions (Mostaghim & Sandels 2014). In this case, the process of water politics is not only fragmented but also reactive. As opposed to taking steps to avert crisis, governance processes have sought to impose the simplest methods available to forestall deeper problems, but not – in the view of critics – to prevent them from worsening.

Worldwide, growing population, rapid urbanization, rising demands for food and energy, and climate change will make freshwater increasingly contested. Nonetheless, there will remain important variations across regions, with parts of Africa, South and Southeast Asia, and the Middle East most likely to experience competition over water supply. The latter is particularly likely to experience a contested process for water politics in the future, as it has in the past. And, there are novel networking opportunities possible for local governments to share innovations across national boundaries.

Power

All water politics involves *power*. While "power" sometimes connotes manipulation, cajoling, or undue pressure exerted by a few individuals over decisions, these are only the most visible examples of its exercise in water politics. Strategically-positioned groups are able to successfully advocate for water policies because they own or control capital needed for investing in water infrastructure, possess legally-enshrined rights to water, have "spiritually-endowed" authority in its management – or, lastly – are able to physically coerce others.

While power has had an important role in shaping water politics in modern industrialized countries and developing countries alike during our present era, its importance has also been recognized in accounts of water decision-making in the distant past. Many scholars have chronicled connections between power, interest group dynamics, decision-maker access, and coalition building for generations (Pomeroy 1955; Hart 1957; Wittfogel 1957; Freeman 1965; McConnell 1966; Ferejohn 1974; Worster 1979, 1985; Weber 2001; Crow & Sultana 2002).

More recently, important work has been done on the special problems of power in collaborative governance arrangements – the kind commonly found in the trans-boundary management of water (Zeitoun 2007; Purdy 2012; Mumme 2016). This scholarship points to the continuing importance of legally enshrined authority in legitimizing certain kinds of power relationships; the continuing importance of resources as levers of influence, and "discursive legitimacy" – the ability of a group or other formal entity to represent and speak on behalf of some issue. The latter requires that these entities "act on behalf of the values or norms of a society, such as the rule of law, the logic of economic rationality, or principles such as democracy or respect for diverse cultures" (Purdy 2012: 410).

This work also holds special relevance for understanding water conflicts – discussed later in this book – by addressing institutionalized expressions of power such as: national sovereignty; the authority vested in entrenched user groups, regulatory agencies, or public works bureaucracies; and even international treaties and their guarantees of "water security." The latter phenomenon has been examined in the context of Mexico and the US, and Israel and Palestine, among other places (Zeitoun & Warner 2006; Zeitoun 2007; Mumme 2016). While legal arrangements established by treaties are designed to ensure equality among states, in fact, they often allow more powerful states to impose solutions accruing to their advantage.

All sources of power – authority vested in law or norms, discursive legitimacy, and asymmetrically (i.e., unequally) held resources – are exercised in subtle ways. It is often assumed that many water problems are technical issues that can be resolved by merely understanding the "facts" surrounding their management. Thus, if we had a clear understanding of the limits imposed on water supplies by drought, for instance, decision-makers could better meet the needs of farmers and thirsty cities. Likewise, if we fully understood the threats to water quality posed by contaminants found in, say, prescription drugs, we could convince the public to be more careful in how they use and dispose of them.

In fact, knowledge and expertise (as resources for power) may contribute to certain kinds of political inequalities over water in various contexts. Some people are invested with greater authority for decisions because they possess greater knowledge about technical issues than do others. However, they may not be accountable to those affected by these issues or sensitive to the latter's concerns. Moreover, while knowledgeable on some facets of problems, they may be ignorant about others. As a result, reliance on technical expertise alone can lead to unanticipated and even negative consequences. A recent illustration of these elements of power – and their consequence – is the water crisis in Flint, Michigan (see box 1.2).

As the Flint example illustrates, the wrongful exercise of expert power may result in abuses. However, demands for reform of both the process of decision-making and the power of influential protagonists may occur *if* water policies result in palpable harm to groups who are able to organize, and appeal to their own sources of power (such as other sources of expertise, or the legal power inherent in regulation) as a counterbalance. As a footnote, Michigan's governor has appointed a review panel comprised in part of expert critics of the state's early response to the crisis. Other examples of this phenomenon can be seen in the growing debate over the privatization of urban water supplies worldwide.

Conflicts among participants may cause shifts in the *context* (or political framework) in which power is exercised. Thus, power – like process – is subject to the structure of decision-making for water, which often straddles local, regional, national, and even international jurisdictions simultaneously (Swyngedouw 2004; 2005).

While multiple jurisdictions and interests complicate efforts to find amicable solutions, differences in power wielded by groups, as well as structural impediments to engagement by every citizen, can impede participation in decisions of those directly affected by them, but who lack access to pertinent levels of governance. Again, the Flint water crisis illustrates this.

Moreover, shared responsibility for resolving problems may also lead to interminable debates over where "sovereignty" for decisions ultimately lies (Bakker 2009). Many political debates over the management of drought, flooding, and other weather-related water management issues exemplify this problem, as we will see. Disputes over water allocation among states sharing the same river basin also are subject to debates regarding the "locus of control" for decisions.

In these and other water politics disputes, each level of political jurisdiction may add its own concerns to the mix of issues, complicating settlement of conflicts over water allocation or quality – especially in large river basins. For example, trans-boundary streams such as the

Box 1.2   Lead, water, expert power, and a city's degraded politics – The saga of Flint

In April 2014, Flint, Michigan – an industrial city that had been in economic and, subsequently, population decline for decades – cancelled a longstanding agreement with Detroit's municipal water supply system and decided to join a newly-formed regional authority that planned to build a pipeline to Lake Huron. The decision was undertaken to save some $18 million over eight years, once the pipeline was completed around 2016. To meet its interim water needs, the city's state-appointed emergency manager, the fourth such official appointed by the governor of Michigan since late 2011 to run the city and restore its fiscal solvency, decided to temporarily switch its supply source to the Flint River.

Almost immediately, local residents complained of "discolored, foul-tasting, awful smelling water." Not until fall 2015, however, was it discovered that the corrosive quality of the Flint River's water (19 times more corrosive than that from Lake Huron) leached lead from the more-than-a-century old 500-mile long galvanized iron-pipe distribution system. High levels of lead in the water supply delivered to people's homes – in some cases over six times the recommended threshold by the EPA – produced elevated lead levels in the bloodstreams of young people whom, it is feared, will suffer permanent brain damage and other health problems.

The state-appointed emergency manager repeatedly failed to respond to citizen complaints about the dangers of Flint's water; other city and state officials gamely tried to reassure residents that the water supply was safe, despite the fact that many residents immediately noticed the corrosiveness of the water and even filed a class-action lawsuit to demand action; and, worst of all, the state and city could have averted the crisis altogether by using phosphates to combat the corrosion of its pipes and the leaching of lead into water supplies. Flint had no such program, the state mistakenly claimed the city did have such a program, and – at this moment – though the city has switched its supply back to Lake Huron, much damage has already been done. Who – or what factors – are to blame?

While forensic policy analysis will take years to render conclusive answers, some explanations are readily clear: an emergency manager who was not politically accountable to city residents; the consistent failure of "expert" regulators to respond to what were viewed as costly demands to fix the problems raised by local complainants; and the widespread poverty of city residents (some 40% of the city's 100,000 residents live below the poverty line) all conspired to deny residents the power to affect policy – and to compel officials to use their power on behalf of reform. As one legal scholar has suggested, this idea of a "technical" city, run by administrators with "expertise," is at least partly to blame for the long-standing neglect of Flint's problems. Evidence suggests Flint is not alone. Jackson, Mississippi; Greenville, North Carolina; and Columbia, South Carolina have reported similar problems in the last decade.

Sources: Gardner 2016; Hennessy-Fiske 2016; Highsmith 2016; Pearce 2016; Schragger 2016; Smith 2016

Rhine, Nile, Murray-Darling, Colorado, Mekong, Amazon, and Indus, whose watersheds are shared by more than one nation, state, and province within a country, are subject to varying demands. They also face competing proposals to protect in-stream flow and water quality; control and monitor off-stream withdrawals; and determine where, or if, to build dams.

For international rivers, especially, unequal *power* among riparian states is an important determinant of how water is shared – and how its overall quality is protected. While upstream users often have distinct advantages in controlling river flow, legal precedents (e.g., the Nile basin) may favor larger downstream states due to treaties first imposed by former colonial powers that wielded unquestioned sovereignty over a region (Waterbury 1979; 2002; Hamner & Wolf 1998; Salman & Uprety 2003; Lautze & Giordano 2005; Zeitoun & Warner 2006; Crow & Singh 2009).

With respect to perceived fairness, it is often the case that when any group feels excluded from decision-making; believes the outcome of decisions places them at a disadvantage with respect to water use; perceives they have inequitable access to clean water; or believes that water-dependent resources are being jeopardized, they will likely resist authority. They may mobilize various members of the public through exercising *alternative* sources of power – for example, protest and resistance movements, as in Bolivia, which led to reform of policies that formerly disregarded fundamental rights to water access (Baer 2008; 2015). Complicating issues of perceived fairness, beneficiaries of water politics may not actually live in the very watersheds where the impact of their power is most felt – dividing beneficiary from payer (Hundley 2009).

Two examples illustrate this. First, since 1913, California's Mono Lake, located in the semi-arid Owens Valley, has been the source of a sizeable portion of Los Angeles' water supply – acquired through largely secretive, under-the-table land purchases. While money and political alliances with federal agencies friendly to the city supported these decisions – over time, local residents organized to try and reverse them. A 2013 "Stream Restoration Agreement" concluded between basin officials and the city of Los Angeles required the latter to restore stream flows to historical levels. A series of court decisions brought about by protracted litigation, changes to state regulations, and lengthy negotiations were pivotal in bringing about this change. While partly aided by the authority of science, voter petitions, and fund-raising drives, vocal public protest was also a key (Mono Lake Newsletter 2014; Walton 1993).

Box 1.3 Islamic State, power, and water

Although not a primary means of exercising influence, under conditions of armed conflict, physical power and coercion can be important factors in the politics of water, and in geopolitics more generally. Beginning in the summer of 2014 and continuing through the writing of this book, the so-called Islamic State (ISIS) has adopted the tactic of gaining control of a region's water supplies and then using access to food and water as a means of controlling the populace. Among other instances, ISIS used a version of this tactic in Amerli, Iraq – starving some 12,000 people before the Iraqi army broke its siege. ISIS has also seized control of four dams on the Tigris and Euphrates Rivers to displace communities or deprive them of water. One of these water projects, the Mosul Dam, was seized and threatened with destruction until reclaimed by Kurdish and Iraqi forces. Finally, ISIS has variously held back water – as well as flooded downstream communities – as part of its effort to exercise physical power over water and, most importantly, over territory.

Source: Schultz 2014

A second example is water privatization – a target, worldwide, for many who characterize the transformation of water – particularly drinking water – into a "buyable-sellable" commodity as evidence of the growing concentration of power over water in fewer hands – especially in developing countries. Giant water projects in Ethiopia, South Asia, and elsewhere, as well as growing control over local sources of municipal supply and bottled water manufacturing in India, the Philippines, and other nations exemplify the power of capitalism in furthering inequalities, favoring the interests of international investors and large commercial and industrial interests, and suppressing collective action by those less powerful (Bakker 2010; Lu et al. 2014; Robinson 2013).

Nevertheless, concerted mobilization of disenchanted and disempowered groups in these and other water disputes continues to grow throughout the world (Barlow & Clarke 2002; Barlow 2009; Shiva 2009). A final note – the role of physical power or coercion, while rarely used as a method for "making" decisions – remains important in water politics. This is especially the case in failed states (see box 1.3).

Purpose

Water politics is a purposeful activity. Participants seek tangible objectives such as ensuring an adequate water supply of a quality sufficient for potable use; guaranteeing that lakes and rivers are safe for recreation and support aquatic life; and securing an affordable fresh-water source for meeting food production needs. At a deeper level, however, polities also strive to align water politics to broad, socially constructed principles regarding *how* it should be provided, and by *whom* (Grafton & Hussey 2011).

The concept of "purpose" also captures the importance of goals in policy-making. Water politics participants hold conflicting beliefs about the value of water, its most beneficial uses, and what consti-tutes an appropriate means of acquiring it. These conflicting beliefs manifest themselves in major differences over issues. For example: what objectives should the building of a reservoir achieve? How much should users be charged for water – and how should these charges be levied – e.g., by variation in volumes used? And, do the health and ecological risks of pollution from some economic activity outweigh the societal benefits of using water to generate energy, manufacture a finished good, or produce food?

Contemporary social scientists not uncommonly discount normative issues such as values and goals as determinants of decision-making in favor of more "measureable" factors such as voting, attitude surveys, and the like. In natural resources decisions, however, the importance of goals and purposes has had its persistent voices among urban planners, political scientists, and others. These scholars point to the importance of governmental commitments and the keeping of prom-ises to various groups as determinants of political legitimacy, respect for law, and the assurance of equitable decisions (Anderson 1979; Sproule-Jones 1982; Beatley 1994).

Perhaps most significantly, the purposes influencing water *politics* reflect deeply held beliefs in every society regarding the ultimate objectives of water *policy*. The conviction that water should be used to stimulate regional economic development, for instance, is not easily reconciled with the notion that free-flowing rivers should be left in pristine condition. Purpose in water politics entails strong convictions about the world itself, and what constitutes a "just existence."

This poses complex challenges for those charged with finding grounds for policy compromise (Davis 2001). In polities where demo-cratic accommodation over water policy is not commonly exercised, conflicts over purpose may still arouse discontent – and even cause modification of policy. An example of this is China's efforts to address environmental and economic criticisms of its recent South-to-North water diversion project, which we discuss – efforts somewhat remi-niscent of those taken following criticisms of the building of Three Gorges Dam.

Purpose also helps shape political outcomes by determining who participates in decisions and what motivates them to do so. In most instances, the *purposes* of water politics are based on *cultural values* and *ethical principles*. Culturally shaped traditions, attitudes, and practices toward water have been receiving renewed attention in recent years by those who seek to understand why people embrace certain water policies and stridently oppose others.

In all societies, attitudes toward water and its value are molded by history, custom, primordial traditions, and religious faith. These cultural factors infuse water with widely varying symbolic, as well as practical, meanings that – along with power and process – determine the character of water politics. Some societies exalt water as having spiritual significance because of its life-giving properties and association with fecundity. Others view it as a wholly utilitarian commodity without transcendent meaning (Linton 2010). In both cases, culturally shaped values provide the context that frames political behavior toward water.

In two sub-Saharan African nations – Lesotho and Tanzania – faith-based groups have advocated for water justice for several years. These efforts have strongly galvanized local political activities aimed at: funding community-based provision of clean water in rural areas; fostering sustainable land use practices to protect water quality; and, encouraging off-shore fishing methods that avert over-harvesting. In Lesotho, these efforts are supported by a faith-based organization: the Christian Ecumenical Water Network, and in Tanzania efforts are being led by Muslim Imams using the Quran to encourage conservation (Dickinson 2005; Ecumenical Water Network 2008). In both polities, these objectives have been pursued more effectively, in some instances by these groups rather than by national governments.

"Culture" can also encompass the institutional ethos of an organization that manages water. Generally, urban water utilities – mostly staffed by engineers and other water resource specialists – are pragmatic in their approach to water management and, it has been said, risk-averse, resistant to radical change and conservative in their operational philosophy. From the standpoint of competing purposes, some also contend that this ethos makes water utilities resistant to adopting sweeping, "out-of-the box" innovations such as recycling and reuse or storm-water harvesting to augment local supplies or replenish groundwater basins. They are instead inclined to rely on tried-and-tested approaches with which they are familiar (Kiparsky et al. 2013).

By contrast, *ethics* are founded on normative principles of right or good, and on convictions regarding what one ought to do when confronted with choices about how to act. Disagreement over the equitable price one should pay for water; the ownership of water; the priority to be accorded users during drought; and whether to restore a channelized urban stream to its former pristine self, entail ethical choices regarding the value of water, what constitutes "just" allocation, and whether other species should be accorded rights to water commensurate with those we grant to ourselves.

Ethics is relevant to water politics at all jurisdictional levels. In recent years, international efforts to manage water problems have often prescribed explicitly ethical principles regarding how problems ought to be addressed. UN International Hydrological Program (UNIHP) reports vigorously advocate for water equity, articulating a compelling vision of the need to address injustices suffered by victims of drought, shortages, and contaminated supplies, especially women, the very young, the frail and destitute, and oppressed minorities. UNIHP reports also prescribe protections for, and an end to discrimination against groups denied sufficient water, pointing to vehicles such as the Dublin Principles of 1992 (see box 1.4) as their ethical compass.

Growing concerns with sustainability are linked to an explicit ethical vision regarding the fairness of new water technologies and water-saving measures, as well as the affordability of water. Many scholars suggest that these issues can only be equitably addressed if water politics is popularly accountable and procedurally democratic. Both require reducing inequalities of power stemming from differences in social class, gender, or ethnicity (Swyngedouw 2007; Bakker 2013).

In 2012, the *World Water Development Report* (UN Water 2012), produced by a host of UN agencies with the input of many national agencies, academics, and non-governmental organizations, suggested that the ultimate purposes of water politics should be to protect the quality of water resources, and ensure their sustainable use and development. These purposes can only be achieved – the report insisted – if participation in decision-making is broadly based and representative of the diversity of society's interests. Examples include such issues as the restoration of severely disturbed or polluted water bodies, the fair distribution of water during severe drought, and the economic value placed on water. Embracing diversity and inclusiveness in purpose is an especially critical challenge.

Box 1.4 Can water policy reform be animated by noble purpose?

In 1992, over 150 countries gathered in Dublin, Ireland, at a United Nations conference dedicated to the role of water in sustainable development. While conferees
were acutely aware of the practical obstacles to a globally just water policy, as
intellectual heirs to the 1983 World Conference on Environment and Development
they aspired to articulate ways of ensuring sustainability that encompassed justice
and equity, as well as economic and environmental issues. The conference's final
statement summarizes several lofty, but in the view of conferees, achievable goals
for an equitable global water policy. Among the highlights of the statement are:

- Water development and management should be based on a participatory
  approach, involving water users, planners, and policy-makers at all levels.
- Women play a central role in provision, management, safeguarding of water and
  should be recognized for their contributions.
- Water has an economic value in all its competing uses; and all uses should be
  recognized as having an economic good.

The conference's final recommendation may be its most politically significant:
developed countries: "[must] . . . consider financial requirements for water-related
programs in accordance with these principles . . . internal and external resources
are needed."

Source: Dublin Statement on Water and Sustainable Development 1992

Gender and water as ethical and cultural conundrum

As the Dublin principles suggest, gender equality and inclusiveness
are largely unresolved issues in contemporary efforts to address water
equity. A recent United Nations study on gender and water found that
the "unequal power and access to choices and resources," including
for water, between men and women "are influenced by historical,
religious, economic and cultural realities" (UN Water 2014b). In short,
the process of water decision-making across the globe is gender biased
and grants unequal roles for men and women in managing and using
water. Women also have far less power and influence over water policy
outcomes than men. Moreover, the determinants of these different
roles are shaped by culture as well as by ethical beliefs.

Later, we discuss how these inequalities can be removed. Important
to understand at this juncture is that these inequalities run deep, and
affect factors such as how much time young boys and girls spend collecting household water (in parts of Africa, girls spend over twice as
much time daily fetching water as do boys), to differentials in fetching
among adults (in sub-Saharan Africa, women spend four to five times
longer collecting water). These time differentials affect opportunities

for schooling, gender workloads, and opportunities for pursuing other economic opportunities.

Less well known is the impact of gender inequality on health. Again, as the UN report notes, inadequate access to safe, hygienic, and private sanitation facilities is a source of shame, physical discomfort and insecurity for women, with "Cultural norms frequently making it unacceptable for women to be seen defecating – forcing many women to leave home before dawn or after nightfall to maintain privacy" (UN Water 2014b) – a problem that also makes women more vulnerable than men to urinary tract infections and other risks. Solving these inequalities requires more than changes in the design of water and sanitation infrastructure – as important as such reforms are. They also require changes in law, public attitudes, and access to decisions.

Understanding contemporary water politics – the importance of multiple perspectives

Five general themes are important for understanding contemporary water politics. First, growing demands and the likelihood of climate change is exacerbating the uneven distribution and use of water. Second, threats to water quality diminish its usability and continue to threaten human health and the quality of the environment. Third, demand continues to exceed the availability of freshwater in many places – causing stress and, in some cases, shortages. Fourth, competition over shared waters, in river basins and groundwater basins alike, is growing. This is causing heightened disputes that are becoming more difficult to amicably resolve. Fifth, proposed solutions to water problems, such as desalination, wastewater reuse, and even conservation pose many challenges that revolve around issues such as equity and fairness, public acceptability, means of control, and trust and confidence in institutions.

While our focus on process, power, and purpose encompasses much of the politics surrounding these five issues, we must acknowledge that there are other frameworks and approaches for understanding water politics that it is important to embrace in rigorous investigation of water problems. Aside from gender as a "filter" through which power, process, and purpose may be understood – a topic we introduced above – students of water politics need to be aware that there are other approaches that, while they cannot be exhaustively investigated in this book, clearly intersect with the topics we explore. Some of the most important of these are cultural politics, neoliberal politics, institutional politics, and community-based water management.

Cultural politics considers the ways in which the management of water resource problems is tied to socially constructed notions of nature, how people can and should interact with resources, and the ways in which the systems we develop to manage water afford opportunities for comparative analysis in the same way one might study kinship, food, or land tenure. Cultural politics can help us to understand how various societies, including traditional ones, define water scarcity; how they determine what mechanisms for meeting scarcity (e.g., markets vs. regulation) are most appropriate to its solution; and how to avoid technologically or economically deterministic assumptions about why and how societies choose certain methods of water harvesting, use, allocation, and protection (Peters 1994; Bolding et al. 1995; Gilmartin 1995).

As applied to recent examinations of water politics in parts of sub-Saharan Africa, South Asia, and elsewhere, for example, cultural politics has shed light on process, power, and purpose in ways relevant to our analysis. David Mosse not long ago summarized these findings as recognizing that, among other things "water has long been a medium of state–subject, state–citizen relations. The power and legitimacy of overlords and states are inexorably linked to the provision of water, and the history of irrigation and urban water supply alike shows that much is at stake in the assertion of rights and the allocation of responsibilities in relation to water" (Mosse 2008).

Our discussion of the practice of water supply provision; water rights and water allocation laws; and, how various societies cope with climate variability and water acknowledge many of these cultural issues. Why people accept, or fail to accept, water management practices are often shaped by the influence of cultural politics on process, power, and purpose.

Neoliberal politics stresses the purported advantages of private sector investment, free trade, and globalization of ownership and control of water as means of promoting efficient, affordable, and safe water supplies. Embraced by market enthusiasts, neoliberals favor the growing trend toward privatization of water utilities and the increasing reliance on markets for moving water supplies from wasteful or inefficient practices to high-valued uses – as in parts of the western US and much of southeast Australia.

Neoliberalism has sharp critics who are troubled by the assumption that water is a commodity that should be owned and/or controlled by private parties and who define the value of water in largely economic terms. Their concerns tend to take the form of two interrelated critiques. The first is the contention that, in today's world, a growing population of increasingly dispossessed citizens in the Third World are subject to exploitation at the hands of powerful markets that can exert control over weak governments and hold absolute sway over water services and the prices to be charged for them (Swyngedouw 2005; 2007; Shiva 2009).

Second, they point to compelling evidence that charges for water services are consistently higher in places where water services are corporately controlled. Moreover, these corporate interests hold an economic monopoly over these and other water sources – not only in cities, but also in cases where water rights can be purchased and diverted across entire basins (Samson & Bacchus 2000; Baer 2008). We will examine these arguments when we discuss water supply provision.

Finally, community-based water management is an idea that has recently begun to draw attention in developing societies, and has numerous implications for our framework of process, power, and purpose. This approach contends that in developing countries especially, there are long established, tradition-based, and locally centered laws, rules, and practices for water management. If properly harnessed to modern technologies and methods, these practices could help these societies better manage their water needs. Unfortunately, aid agencies and even some NGOs operating in developing countries tend to overlook these practices when proposing reforms.

Advocates of these approaches suggest that community-based water laws could be adapted to encourage self-help water development and management by citizens – especially poor women and men. These approaches can also help to protect water quality and reduce public health risks from contamination and are locally accessible and trustworthy. Perhaps most importantly, they can match up remedies to water problems with the informal water economies characteristic of many developing countries (Mtsi & Nicol 2003; Van Koppen et al. 2007; da Costa Silva 2011; Petersen et al. 2006). Similar to cultural politics, community-based water management approaches can help us to understand how to meld traditional values and practices to modern needs. Also, they help us understand the resistance that often arises when state-centered or corporate-backed efforts seek to exploit water resources through privatizing supplies, bottling beverages, or imposing large water projects that benefit distant urban populations at the expense of village-based societies.

"Back to the future" – understanding the present through learning from the past

In light of these themes, it may be useful to reflect on the fact that process, power, and purpose have comprised the core elements of water politics since antiquity. Harnessing and managing water resources have been perennial preoccupations of political rulers. In the past, rulers built water supply and irrigation systems through chattel labor or serfdom (an authoritarian process). The tenure and longevity of rulers often depended on how well they managed water – drought or environmental calamity led to "regime change," and power was often centralized. In addition, water policies had two overall purposes: *securing internal stability* and *assuring external security* (avoiding conflicts with neighbors). These objectives led to the formulation of domestic laws governing allocation as well as international treaties permitting the sharing and co-management of river basins (Kamash 2012).

Three broad lessons can be extracted from these experiences relevant for contemporary water politics. First, ancient communities sought reliable, safe, and plentiful supplies through infrastructural, economic, legal, and political strategies (Jansen 2000). Rome was highly regarded for the sophisticated engineering of its elaborate aqueduct system. We now know that these systems were designed not just for water provision, but were equipped with various "branch lines" so as to provide ample supply to rural outlying lands adjacent to these cities. Likewise, in China – citing the Qin dynasty as an example, water provision was a major source of technological innovation. As in other ancient polities, most dynasties were concerned with water allocation and flood control – centralizing management to assure success.

Second, societies early on sought to develop infrastructure to protect the potability and cleanliness of water – as well as to avert threats to the built environment such as flooding. In the ancient Near East, for example, central governments developed and promoted water works to distribute freshwater and dispose of sewage and waste. They also fostered legal innovations to manage water. This was true, for instance, in the Tigris-Euphrates Valley, Assyria, Nile Valley, and Jericho. Later, as large civilizations dominated by Roman-Byzantine hegemony arose, a major preoccupation of urban political elites was assuring adequate water to support growth. An elite group of aristocrats and soldiers exercised state control, and installation and maintenance of water works became important government tasks (Heather 2006; Braemer et al. 2010).

Finally, water management entails multiple decisions regarding distribution, quality, access, and cost – all of which were proven to have differential effects on various groups. Regardless of who makes these decisions, water managers who want their decisions to be seen as legitimate must take the views, opinions, and outlooks of those affected by them into account. In ancient cities, for example, water laws evolved to generally prioritize public, common uses first, followed by private needs. In other words, ancient societies – like their modern counterparts – placed considerable importance upon water equity (Boatright et al. 2004; Coarelli 2007).

In sum, while water management was a major preoccupation of ancient civilizations, as it is in ours, it was also viewed as a means of ensuring public health, sanitation, comfort, and a high quality of life. The building and maintaining of infrastructure was a key responsibility of the state – and *little expense was spared*. In the Middle East, early Europe, and China, the ability to harness water and to divert it great distances not only enabled cities and towns to grow and prosper, but also contributed to the development of agriculture and trade. As in our era, who received water was a source of political contention. We take up this topic beginning in chapter 2.

SUMMARY

- Formal or governmental, as well as informal, non-governmental civil society groups comprise the participants in water politics.
- Authoritative decisions over management and allocation of freshwater are shaped by *governance*; the collaboration of civil society groups and government agencies.
- Water politics embraces *process* – the interplay of participants at different spatial levels; *power* – their authority and influence; and *purpose* – their diverse goals.

RECOMMENDED READING

- Informative books on the value of water as a political issue include: Jamie Linton, *What is Water? The History of a Modern Abstraction* (2010). Also, Joachim Blatter and Helen Ingram, *Reflections on Water* (2001). Both provide good grounding of the various values and attitudes surrounding water use in different cultures and its significance for water politics.
- An overview of contemporary water issues across the globe is found in R. Quentin Grafton and Karen Hussey, *Water Resources Planning and Management* (2001). Also, James Salzman, *Drinking Water: A History*

(2012) is a provocative look at the subtle ways power and authority influence water management.

- A classic, and still somewhat controversial, assessment of the role of power in water politics in antiquity is found in Karl Wittfogel, *Oriental Despotism: A Comparative Study of Total Power* (1957)

WEBSITES

- http://www.unesco.org/new/en/natural-sciences/environment/water/wwap/wwdr/ *UN World Water Development Report*.
- http://www.un.org/waterforlifedecade/gender.shtml Gender and Water.

QUESTIONS FOR DISCUSSION

1. Thinking about your own community, how do power, process, and purpose help to explain decisions regarding water management?

2. What are some barriers to a global system of water decision-making? Can these barriers be overcome?

3. Is the exercise of power always bad in water politics? Can power be joined to aspirations for fairness, equity, and public engagement?

CHAPTER 2

Contested Waters: The Politics of Supply

Overview

When most of us first learned about water in primary school, we probably recall that some two-thirds of the earth's surface is covered by water. However, less than 3 percent of our planet's entire supply is fresh water, and much of this is locked up in ice caps or as soil moisture, while the remainder is found underground in aquifers or on the surface in lakes, rivers, and streams. In short, freshwater comprises a very small portion of the planet's total water supply.

These basic facts do not really tell us how much freshwater is available for use. Nor do they explain how it is managed or allocated. That's because the actual availability of freshwater is shaped by politics. This chapter will discuss how political process, the exercise of power, and competing purposes determine how water is supplied. We explore the politics of water supply in four contexts: water and cities, water and agriculture, control of supplies (private versus public), and water markets. Other supply-related issues (e.g., international disputes) are discussed in later chapters.

In general, all polities seek to provide reliable, safe, and plentiful supplies to citizens through building and maintaining infrastructure to store and treat water, providing economical delivery systems, and instituting laws and regulations regarding rights-to-use. These efforts do not come about by happenstance. Water has to be provided by an investment of financial resources, the application of engineering knowledge and the political will to make decisions.

The process of water supply politics generally involves an inter-play of interests having unequal power and exercised through various forums, depending on the decisional context – e.g., urban supply vs. agricultural irrigation. Over time, water supply has evolved from being a local issue in which decision-making has been dominated by public agencies and regulatory officials to a more contested set of issues involving community groups, private entrepreneurs and investors, and environmental activists, among others.

While various approaches are employed to meet different water needs for agricultural irrigation, domestic and household use, industry and commerce, and other purposes – in general, the politics of supply decision-making tends to be heavily influenced by engineering and economic considerations. In recent decades, moreover, the process of water supply decision-making has had to confront growing demands among various groups and, at times, flat or diminishing sources of revenues. As a result, considerations of equity, fairness, and "rights" to a guaranteed supply of freshwater have become important factors in the process of water supply politics. This is especially true for urban drinking water, but it is also true for agricultural water (Salzman 2012).

Two purposes dominate water supply politics: the desirability of enlarging supply to foster growth, and the aspiration to define an "appropriate" model for ownership or control of supply. In recent years, two phenomena have dominated this latter aspiration. The first is the dramatic growth of privatization – especially of urban water supplies – which has prompted questions regarding political accountability, economic equity, and the willingness of vendors to place public health and other community concerns above profit. A second is a general growth of "market-friendly" policies toward water management and, especially, in redefining water rights in much of the developing world (Bauer 1998; 2005).

Cities and water supply

More than half the world's population lives in cities – some 3.5 billion souls. Putting this in perspective, at its current rate of growth, the world's urban population is increasing by some two people every second. And, in developing countries, this rate is the equivalent of some five million new urban dwellers every month. As a result, demands on water supplies in so-called "megacities" (see below, p. 32) are both enormous and never-ending.

Whether urban supplies are provided by publicly owned utilities or by private vendors, allocation decisions mostly revolve around economic efficiency and reliability. Issues of price and accountability of providers to users have tended to be of secondary importance until recently. Where water is in short supply, this has resulted in rivers and streams being impounded by dams; treatment and reuse facilities being constructed to alleviate shortages; and, rules being adopted to ensure that certain groups and individuals receive adequate supplies regardless of local conditions.

In most of Latin America, for example, sufficient potable water is produced by local utilities to satisfy a wide range of urban residents' needs, and per capita consumption is comparable to that of many developed countries. However, only a small percentage of the urban population consumes most of the water, while the poor consume a relatively miniscule share. In Mexico City, for instance, 3 percent of households receive 60 percent of urban potable supplies, while 50 percent make do with 5 percent. In Guayaquil, Ecuador, 65 percent of urban dwellers receive 3 percent of potable supplies at a price at least 200 times higher than that paid by low-volume consumers connected to urban water networks.

Worsening this inequity, many urban poor are not connected to these networks at all. The limited share of water they consume is often provided by so-called micro-entrepreneurs (water "bootleggers") – small-scale vendors who resell water from the local utility at inflated prices to those lacking indoor plumbing (Swyngedouw 2005; 2007). As in so much else in developing countries, power, sometimes exercised in an ad hoc and extra-legal fashion, determines how water supply is provided.

In general, water conditions in cities, including cities in developing nations, tend to be better than in non-urban areas. According to the United Nations, as of 2010, 96 percent of the world's urban residents had access to improved sources of drinking water (as compared to 81 percent of those living in rural areas). For sanitation facilities, the disparities are even more pronounced: 79 percent of the world's urban dwellers had access to improved sanitation facilities while only 47 percent of rural dwellers did (United Nations 2014c).

Despite these dramatic differences, we must be careful not to confuse "better" with "good." The quality of urban water supply is closely aligned to the revenue base of a city. This, in turn, reflects a city's overall level of prosperity and, often, its size. The significant variance in the economic health of cities results in significant disparities in urban water quality and availability. In California's Central Valley, and in rural British Columbia, for example, small rural communities no more than an hour's drive from major cities such as Vancouver or Fresno may have water quality as bad as, or worse than, cities in some developing countries (Bakker 2009). As we discuss in chapter 3, even in parts of the developed world, water quality can be highly variable.

During protracted drought small city systems may totally exhaust their water supplies. And minority communities – Latino in Central California, for example, and "First Nation" (or indigenous peoples) in British Columbia – often endure virtually permanent health-hazard advisories for their community water systems (Center for Watershed Science 2012). Again, power differentials matter with regard to the *quality* of potable supplies in cities both large and small.

The growth of megacities composed of tens of millions of people poses an especially acute supply challenge in developing countries, where cities already serve as the home for some 80 percent of the planet's urban population. More than two-thirds of the world's urban residents live in cities in Africa, Asia, and Latin America. And, since 1950, the urban populace of these regions has grown five-fold. In Africa and Asia, by 2030 urban populations are expected to double from what they were in 2000 (Satterthwaite 2000). Thus, the political challenges of water provision are enormous.

Typically, political decisions over water supply in third world megacities tend to be made by engineers and planners working for local water utilities, and also by external agencies (e.g., the World Bank) that fund efforts to improve delivery and treatment infrastructure (Bakker 2013). Decision-making power is, thus, concentrated in the hands of an expert few, and long-standing decision-making processes constrain the selection of policy alternatives by favoring wealthier as opposed to disadvantaged local residents.

In post-colonial cities in the developing world, for example, water distribution networks are frequently based on traditional urban planning patterns initially platted to favor delivery to wealthier districts as opposed to poorer ones. Oftentimes, high-quality piped water was made available to the affluent, and polluted surface water was the only option available to the poor (Bakker 2013). A good example is Mumbai, India's economic powerhouse (historically called Bombay under the British Raj).

Despite the fact that Bombay was the leading manufacturing and commercial center of India, and supported a large and diverse population of workers, development of an urban water infrastructure, including proper drainage and sewage service was late in coming and only introduced after the pleas of public hygiene reformers such as Florence Nightingale. Typically, British and other European colonists neglected the introduction of modern sanitary sewers, waste disposal systems, and reliable sources of water supply.

By 1860, after near exhaustion of the city's wells and water tanks, a reservoir system was established northwest of the city, together with a fee-paid distribution system. Coupled with the construction of a drainage system to remove "night soils" and other wastes, the city's public health conditions gradually began to improve. Even so, provision of these services was unequal: Bombay's European quarters received the bulk of the Vihar reservoir system's supply, while natives received irregular deliveries partly because they could not afford to pay the water rates charged by the Raj, and partly because the infrastructure to support their needs was inadequate to the task (Sule 2003; Hunt 2015).

Despite progress in improving water provisioning and sanitation in the world's cities – measured statistically – the virtually constant need to upgrade these services in light of continued population growth constitutes a race against time. Over the next few decades, the world's urban population is expected to increase from some 4 billion to 6.3 billion by 2050 – a higher rate of growth (36 percent) than the overall projected growth of the world's population (26 percent) during this same period (UN Water 2014a).

Growing popular reform movements have taken hold in many countries, often constituting the leading edge of political protests demanding universal access to good quality water and improvement in other vital services. Two political challenges have arisen simultaneously: cities oftentimes cannot raise water rates to cover the costs of the infrastructure improvements these movements demand without stirring general public opposition. This has sometimes resulted in political unrest in the form of demonstrations, refusal to pay for water, and even violent confrontation.

Antagonism toward raising rates has many sources. Two of the most prevalent are the view that water is a basic human right – especially popular in post-revolutionary societies and, thus, should be free or inexpensive (e.g., Mexico – see box 2.1, p. 32), and distrust of water service providers, in part due to a growing trend toward privatization, discussed later in this chapter.

In recent years, protests have arisen in poorer cities throughout the world – and even in many developed countries – over water provision and its cost. In Detroit, Michigan, in 2014 residents organized demonstrations over the fact that virtually half the water utility's revenues in this bankrupt city go to pay interest on bonds sold to private investors. In 2013 in Dublin, Ireland, public protests arose over plans to export water from the Shannon River and to upgrade the city's water infrastructure: an antiquated system taxed by growing demands. Following expedient rationing measures, the city increased the price of water and established a new "semi-state" water corporation that imposed rates on all Irish households so that leaky distribution systems could be repaired, and new sources of water developed (Sheridan 2014; Curran 2015).

Most urban population growth is projected to take place in the poorest of the world's nations – where densely populated slums replete with sub-standard housing already pose enormous challenges in regards to access to safe water and sanitation. A hopeful development is that, between 2000 and 2008, urban areas worldwide experienced a positive trend in both water and sanitation coverage, with access to sanitary toilets increasing by some 20 percent as a result of public investments (UN Water 2014a, 2014c). However, balancing investment in urban water systems against the risk of public protest toward rate hikes to pay for them remains an enormous challenge. Moreover, it is a challenge that is severely testing the political capacity of megacities to make resilient water supply decisions (see box 2.1).

Many of the reports cited earlier pin their hopes for urban water supply on comprehensive urban design and planning strategies that utilize low-impact development techniques to harvest rainwater (thus reducing reliance on distant diversions or transfers of water across basins), conserve precious potable water, bio-filter mildly polluted runoff, and reuse and recycle various grades of wastewater to slake household, landscaping, and commercial needs. In support of these measures, environmentally conscious, well-educated urban residents are joining other UN reports' advocates in campaigns to adopt such measures.

While these approaches are viewed by some as a more resilient means of satisfying growing urban needs, they are not cheap, and they do not work well if hastily imposed. Democratic, bottom-up engagement is necessary for their effective implementation, as we shall see. This is one reason why international efforts to articulate a purpose – and a rationale – for their adoption are becoming so popular.

The International Water Association in its 2013 *Cities of the Future* report suggests adoption of these approaches should be undertaken in order to ensure that cities are both livable and resilient in the face of growing urban populations as discussed earlier. Most significantly, IWA states that these approaches should be adopted through methods that engage various publics, ensure collaborative implementation, promote localized and adaptive solutions that can be disseminated to other urban sectors, and should promote "water literacy" among the urban public. Finally, IWA recommends that "all water is good water" and that future efficiency must "match quality to use" (International Water Association 2013).

The IWA embraces inter-disciplinary methods to solving urban water supply problems. Similar conclusions and recommendations have been drawn by the European Union, UNESCO (whose recent efforts on behalf of water sustainable "cities of the future" promotes interdisciplinary research from a long-term perspective), and the International Water Association (whose "cities of the future" program that connects

Box 2.1 How megacities manage water supply – Mexico City as exemplar

With over 20 million residents, Mexico City has had to implement some of the most ambitious plans to harvest water supplies from outside its immediate region. Most of the Federal district receives its water from the Cutzamala system – one of the world's largest water supply systems. Begun in the 1970s, the $1.3 billion supply system was built in stages, in some instances incorporating earlier projects dating to the 1940s. Delivery to the Valley of Mexico from more than 150 km away is achieved via a system of seven dams and storage reservoirs, six pumping stations, open channels, tunnels, pipelines, aqueducts, and a water purification plant.

The entire system provides almost 20 percent of the Valley of Mexico's total water supply and is not only large, but highly energy intensive, consuming some 1.3 and 1.8 terawatt hours a year, equivalent to 0.6 percent of Mexico's total energy consumption – necessary in order to pump water some 1100 meters from the lowest to the system's highest point. Many communities had to be relocated to make way for this massive infrastructure, and unresolved disputes over proper compensation for losing homes continue to simmer.

Despite the ambitious scale and scope of this project, Mexico City continues to face some of the most severe challenges in potable water provision of any major city. Climate change is very much a motivator for further action, while continued population growth is another. Other options being pursued include efforts to reduce residential water demand, using more reclaimed wastewater for local agriculture and non-potable uses, and employing storm-water capture for groundwater recharge and some community uses. Given the availability of public investment funds and low water tariffs charged in Mexico, the likely effectiveness of these measures is subject to debate.

A National Water Commission report concluded that 40 percent of potable water nationwide was being lost through leaks in urban provision systems, while another 20 percent was "unaccounted water loss" through billing errors and illegal water connections – problems said to be characteristic of Mexico City and other metro areas. While the commission recommended a number of reforms, including a new metropolitan decision-making body supposedly empowered to choose "which sources of water will be used, set timelines and commitments, and monitor all activities carried out under the plan," a continuing challenge in implementation remains artificially low water prices – consumer water rates charged in the Valley of Mexico cover only half of the true costs of service provision. Partly due to low rates, maintaining the Cutzamala system is difficult.

See: Instituto Mexicano de Tecnología del Agua 1987; Downs et al. 2000

water professionals together from over 130 countries on many of these issues and which recently issued the Montreal Declaration on cities of the future) (Howe et al. 2011; UNESCO-IHE 2011).

It remains to be seen how much leverage international standard-setting efforts will have on the politics of water supply in less developed countries. More research is also needed on how well "green" infrastructure performs in different settings, its economic benefits and costs to the environment when compared with traditional water supply systems, and its social acceptability (Palmer et al. 2015). As we discuss later, successful adoption of such innovations requires addressing several public concerns.

Agriculture, politics, and water supply

The provision of water supply for crop irrigation and livestock has long been a powerful stimulus for the construction of water infrastructure. It also has been an arena characterized by contentious decision-making processes, the exercise of unequal power, and debates over divergent purpose. Some contend that water used primarily for agriculture, and provided through large-scale engineered systems, is more directly dependent on hierarchical power than water for urban uses. The hydraulic infrastructure used to store and distribute water for producing food and fiber is usually planned and organized by government, some scholars note, and undertaken at the behest of powerful land-owning interests who work closely with public works agencies to promote construction of large projects (Swyngedouw 2005).

While this claim is generally valid, it overlooks some marked similarities between the politics of urban and rural water supply politics. Agricultural water infrastructure can displace people in rural areas; radically alter productive relations between large water rights holders and poorer farmers or peasants (as has been true for generations in parts of Spain, Portugal, and Latin America, for example); and enrich and improve the lives of some groups at the expense of others. Similar patterns also ring true for cities, as we have seen. Later, when we discuss China's South-to-North Water Transfer system, we will see how forced relocation of residents to accommodate water supply decisions remains a contentious political issue.

Development of water infrastructure can result in a concentration of economic and political power in the hands of a few interests. And, if the water acquired by cities is diverted from (or in many cases shared with) rural areas, as has been true in many parts of the American west, for example, then the result can be tightly controlled provision systems that concentrate decision-making in the hands of a few. The politics of rural and urban water supply can rarely be separated. Spain and the western US afford good examples of this fact.

Spain has been a European leader in development of highly managed water systems. First under the Romans, then under the Moors, and eventually under a consolidated monarchical state that emerged in the late fifteenth century, water works, urban aqueducts, and irrigation systems all came into prominence. Moslem influence was especially significant for water politics in that it established a tradition of locally-managed irrigation regulatory systems such as the Tribunal de las Aguas de Valencia (Valencian Water Court) to allocate scarce water supplies and avert rural and urban conflicts over its distribution (Garrido & Llamas 2009). Irrigation and river navigation were particularly important concerns in a country with large swaths of arid land and the need for cheap, efficient means of communication between regions. In fact, fully one-third of Spain's cultivated cropland was irrigated by the nineteenth century.

In 1902, Spain's Ministry of Development formulated a National Waterworks Plan which was notable for its inventorying of existing national infrastructure and projected demands, especially for irrigation, and for its more than coincidental sharing of aims with the US Bureau of Reclamation – also established in 1902. Throughout the early decades of the twentieth century, this plan served as the basis for water transfers from northern to southern Spain (e.g., the Ebro River) as well as efforts to develop river basin management authorities to develop and allocate supplies for several watersheds.

The country's most far-reaching efforts to manage water, however, came about with the end of its Civil War in 1939. Between 1950 and 2000, some 20 dams per year were constructed and surface water acreage doubled. Spain now ranks fourth in the world in the number of impoundments per capita (Garrido & Llamas 2009).

The overall purpose of this centrally-directed water resource development, heralded by the Franco regime as a means of promoting rapid economic development, was to provide cheap water for irrigated agriculture, hydropower for cities and industrial manufacturing, and flood control and navigation to promote social resilience and improvement of internal communications. The political legacy of this system has been a series of policies that guaranteed state provision of inexpensive water for hundreds of thousands of farmers, many of whom also receive subsidized homes and farm implements; strict, centrally-imposed rationing during time of drought; and the dominance of civil and agricultural engineers in urban as well as rural allocation and overall water decision-making.

Following membership in the European Union in 1985, Spain's water policies moved toward closer harmony with those of more established democracies in the region. Many water management decisions have now been relinquished to "autonomous communities" (i.e., sub-national regions), and water marketing is being more widely employed to promote efficient use. However, the continued promise of cheap water supplies, reliance on large-scale public works, and – ironically – political devolution of authority to regions and markets have imposed considerable strain on the country, particularly in light of protracted drought in recent years.

Murcia is a case in point. Farmers in this arid region in the country's southeast have been planting water-thirsty crops such as tomatoes and lettuce, while some land has been transformed into golf courses and resorts that consume billions of gallons of water daily. While it's rumored that overexploitation has been spurred by bribing local officials, what is certain is that farmers and others have been buying and selling water on a growing black market for years, and that the powerful "National Irrigators Congress" has the support of the country's agriculture minister to revive plans for further diversion of water from Spain's north, including from the Ebro basin (Edgecumbe 2013). In short, while Spain's political system has evolved in a more democratic direction, the legacy of previous decisions formulated during the Franco era still impose their imprint on policy – a phenomenon political scientists call *path dependency*.

A similar path dependency can be seen in the United States. Throughout much of the nineteenth century, as European settlers migrated in sizeable numbers to the west, a fervent belief arose regarding the benefits of cooperative efforts to irrigate land, divert water to growing cities, and "equalize" the benefits of water resources development to growing numbers of immigrants. While these attitudes took root in a more populist way than in Spain, their legacy continues to animate political debate – and policy – over water supply in the region (Feldman 2016). Thanks to figures such as Benjamin Cummings Truman, Charles Howard Shinn, and most notably, William Ellsworth Smythe, widespread public support for national government investments in water projects received an enormous boost in the west (Smythe 1900; Starr 1990).

Smythe was especially evangelical regarding water supply development's purposes. Irrigation, he felt, was a means to develop a self-reliant, virtuous society of yeoman farmers. It would not only lead to economic betterment, but would further the cause of democracy in rural areas and in the cities that provided services to them.

Aside from organizing "irrigation congresses" that had enormous influence on policy, advocates linked the economic advantages of water resources development to deeper moral and religious arguments. "Reclaiming" arid, but potentially fertile, land would produce a thriving middle class, a healthful rural lifestyle, and a new civilization that would unleash the talents and abilities of the common man. It would also generate unprecedented economic opportunities through flood control, power generation, and industrialization benefitting the entire nation, not just the west.

Irrigation enthusiasts helped pass laws and other policies favoring those who first claimed rights to water use in an area (see chapter 6). This led to establishment of water markets, permitting the sale or lease of water to higher-valued purposes, so long as these uses were deemed beneficial to growing needs for food production and urban water supply. It also led to control of water provision by a tightly knit network of local users, federal agencies, and legislative boosters (Gleick 2003; MacDonnell & Fort 2008).

The enthusiasm of these groups partly led to creation of the Bureau of Reclamation in 1902 – an agency whose official purpose was utilitarian. Its enabling act stated that the west was an under-watered wasteland: an ideal place for irrigation to create a productive agricultural paradise through using "surplus fees from sales of land (to) be set aside for a '*reclamation fund*' for the development of water resources." Only the federal government possessed the money, engineering skills, and bureaucratic means to establish a comprehensive plan for watering the region (National Reclamation Act of 1902; see also Clayton 2009; Jones & Wills 2009).

Westerners did not act alone in promoting these purposes, or in undertaking these processes. Outside private interests (e.g., land investors, settlers from the east, immigrants from overseas) and public interests (e.g., competing federal agencies with different missions) that sought to justify their existence and missions all influenced decisions (Nugent 2001). While advocates sought support from outside the west for their plans to harness water supplies by damming rivers, federal funds were aggressively sought for locally guided purposes. As one observer stated, westerners sought "to get the purse strings without the purse" (Hundley 2009).

Thus, in the name of democratic inclusiveness, centralized, federally directed processes were undertaken with the strong support of local interests to harness water. The legacy of this system persists today in what is commonly termed distributive politics – the use of taxes and direct benefit transfers on behalf of identifiable localities and groups – similar to what took place in Spain. While distributive politics usually originates in the desire to be politically accountable to powerful interests and voter blocs, its outcomes affect social equity by allocating certain benefits to some regions but not others (Golden & Min 2013).

Key to the durability of such policies is that their outcomes are viewed as widely beneficial to many. In the case of the US and Spain, distributive water policies promoting rural development have been seen as nationally valuable, and based on comparable purposes. Similar patterns of water politics persist in other countries.

Public vs. private ownership – process, power, and purpose

There are two general ways in which water supply is allocated: public and private provision. In public systems water is "owned" by governmental entities: typically, legally chartered special districts which supply water to customers through tax revenues and/or charges directly levied upon users. These entities receive their water from other public or private suppliers (e.g., government agencies that operate dams and reservoirs, or farmers, ranchers, or industries willing to sell unused water to which they have a claim).

Privately owned providers are stockholder-owned, for-profit enterprises that provide water supply and treat wastewater. These enterprises levy a fee upon consumers calibrated to cover the marginal costs of providing water services (i.e., provision and treatment), *plus* provide an additional return-on-investment. Most local governments have long relied on some type of private investor or public-corporate partnership to furnish water (Bakker 2010; Morgan 2012). Privatization is viewed by many as an effort to transform water from a public good, access to which is regarded as a basic human right, into a marketable commodity that can be bought, sold, and leased to earn a profit for those who provide it.

Comparing public and private models of water provision is easier if we examine archetypes of each and how they operate. For the public or more precisely, "public utility" model, the US is a good example since public water utilities, which typically originated as a type of special government district, are the most common means of providing water services. Historically, the antecedents of US water utility districts are traceable to the late nineteenth and early twentieth centuries. At that time, farmers in the western US banded together to form irrigation districts, a type of farm-cooperative organization, in order to secure reliable water supplies with governmental assistance.

The vagaries of climate and water supply – coupled with the potential for water rights conflicts in rural areas – compelled the development of organizational alternatives that could provide the means to jointly control and share scarce water. The success of this innovation in rural communities convinced a number of growing municipalities in other parts of the US to form special independent districts to regionalize water services and, thus, more efficiently address the growing public health problems of region-wide water contamination and water-borne disease which could not effectively be solved by communities acting alone.

Sometimes lost in debates over privatization is the fact that, in many US cities, water supply was initially managed as a private enterprise. It was only later – in light of concerns over public health and the spread of infectious illnesses noted above – that cities moved from private to public entities to more safely manage their water supply systems.

Initially, joint-stock or other investor-owned enterprises harvested groundwater, built surface water storage reservoirs, installed miles of pipelines, and connected households and businesses for a fee. In the nineteenth century, for instance, this privatization model operated in numerous cities – east and west. New York, Philadelphia, Los Angeles and, beginning in the early twentieth century, Las Vegas, were among the places where these enterprises operated: sometimes netting huge revenue returns through operating on high profit margins and virtually monopolistic control of local water sources (Fogelson 1993; Moehring & Green 2005).

Since that time, the public water district – for both irrigation and urban provision – has become the most popular way of providing public water supplies in the US. Despite the historical dominance of this model, in recent years, a number of water utilities and the communities that rely upon them have turned – or *re-turned* – to privatization as a means of reducing costs associated with rapid growth which has strained efforts to repair and/or update water infrastructure and acquire additional supplies.

In the US, public water utilities are generally supported by taxes and fees levied on water and wastewater treatment customers. They may also sell development bonds to raise larger amounts of capital for major construction projects – meaning that they may be indebted to private investors. Typically, public utilities employ a three-part operating strategy when planning for additional water supply: they assess future needs, explore supply as well as demand-management alternatives for meeting these needs, and they then estimate the costs for each alternative followed by developing plans to appropriate funds for adopting the preferred alternative(s).

Needs assessment generally involves projecting both population growth and growth in water demand due to the various demands of different economic activities. Population growth alone is never an exact gauge of water demand because type of water use determines, to a large extent, the volumes of water – as well as the degree of water quality – that will ultimately be required to meet future needs. For example, some types of manufacturing may use large amounts of water, but do not necessarily require water that is of potable (i.e., drinkable) quality. Thus, a community that anticipates, for instance, certain types of industrial expansion (e.g., petroleum refining), but only very limited residential growth, may still have to plan for massive amounts of new water supplies. To use the example of oil refining, it takes approximately 77,000 gallons of water to refine 100 barrels of oil.

Generally, regional assessments adhere to a consistent methodology. Historical water usage data is supplemented by information on system deficiencies, population growth and other demand-related projections. To accommodate the uncertainties inherent in such projections, 50-year time horizons employing various growth "scenarios" are often utilized to compare alternative sets of needs and to facilitate long-term planning. Finally, a wide range of alternatives is embraced in these assessments. Most include some analysis of, for instance, new pipelines or distribution network connections to existing water sources, new or altered impoundments, ways to supplement surface water supplies with available groundwater (or recharging available groundwater with surface flows), water harvesting (e.g., storing of storm-water runoff in special off-stream space), and – increasingly – measures to better conserve water. Usually, suites of options are adopted, and economic and environmental assessments are undertaken for each alternative to permit comparison of their benefits and costs.

One of the best archetypes of the private water provider is France where private, for-profit companies operate municipal water services and provide local distribution, wastewater treatment, and water sales and marketing services. Three corporations are predominant in the French water market: Veolia (formerly Vivendi Environnement, which controls 56 percent of France's waterworks), Ondeo Suez (with a 29 percent share), and Bouygues-La Saur (13 percent of water supplies). The remaining 2 percent of the country's public water supplies are municipally owned and operated.

The French experience is particularly important because the large companies that provide municipal water also have an economic reach that extends well *beyond* France – in particular, to former French colonies in the developing world and elsewhere. For example, Suez has 118 million customers in over 130 countries, while Veolia serves

> ## Box 2.2   I love Paris . . . when its water is publicly owned
>
> In 2008, Paris's then Socialist mayor Bertrand Delanoe ended contracts for the city's water supply with the two private firms that had controlled its water distribution systems since 1985 – Veolia on the right bank of the city and Suez on the left. Publicly owned Eau de Paris, which took over from 2010, has since become a model for other French cities and metropolises beyond. The result has been a decline in profits of these companies, forcing them to search for other sources of revenue (e.g., waste management), and recognition in France and elsewhere that "remunicipalization" is an option for cities to earn their own profits from water while lowering prices.
>
> Since 2008, Rouen, Saint Malo, Brest and Nice have returned to public water management, and Bordeaux, Rennes and Montpellier will follow suit by 2018.
>
> In 2011, public operators' share of drinking water management in France rose to 39 percent from just under 30 percent in 2004, and their share of water purification to 58 percent from 45 percent. This is a major turnabout given that private companies have had a dominant role in France for more than a century, and in other parts of Europe (including England, Wales, Spain, Italy, and Denmark.
>
> Since the Parisian decision, attempts to privatize have met with resistance throughout Europe – especially in Italy and Greece – and support for public ownership appears to be growing as a result of the European Citizens' Initiative, a 2012 addition to the EU treaties aimed at boosting direct democracy. As a result of stalled efforts to further privatize water in Europe, and with only about 10 percent of the US water market open to private utilities, Veolia and Suez have turned to emerging markets in China, India, Latin America, and the Middle East. In the latter, there is growing questioning of the costs and benefits of private ownership. Ironically, the decline of privatization opportunities in France might be exacerbating the potential for new conflicts elsewhere – as one Veolia official stated: "Whenever I visited a prospect around the world, and it must be the same for our peer (Suez), they would ask me why they would do business with me if even the French capital has no confidence in the French water firms."
>
> *Source:* De Clercq 2014

124 million customers in over 100 nations. Conflicts have been engendered between for-profit companies and communities in developing nations. They also have begun to generate political conflict in France – where it all began (see box 2.2).

How is power exercised in private systems? Critics argue that private providers are less responsive to public demands for equity, safety, and cost in four respects. First, organizations such as the International Union for the Conservation of Nature (IUCN) believe privatization is transforming water into a commodity that provides material gain for profit-making enterprises, but fails to regard access to freshwater as either a human need or basic human right. IUCN and others charge that many of the international organizations that serve as global forums for discussion – and potentially for setting global standards regarding both water quality and quantity – are more preoccupied with the interests of private vendors than with those of citizens for access to clean water.

Second, critics charge that public participation in decisions regarding pricing, service, and access is limited under privatization because corporations make decisions, not elected officials. Because corporate boards advised by business managers, and not publically accountable elected officials, set policies, the process of decision-making is exclusive and elitist – rather than inclusive and democratic. They often point to two factors when making this argument: first, in countries like the US where only 14 percent of municipal water supplies are privately owned, water is more expensive; and, second, privatization discourages water conservation and encourages water consumption to maximize profit and finance new infrastructure (Shiva 2009).

Third, water providers' operations are said to be less transparent than is the case with public providers. Once control over local supplies are relinquished to private companies, these enterprises shield their operations from public scrutiny because they consider their products and services to be proprietary interests that must be protected from potential competitors. The well-documented and widely reported experience of Bolivia with privatization in the past two decades is a good example of this criticism. It is also a case that looms large in the annals of economic globalization of water rights (see box 2.3).

A final disadvantage of privatization claimed by its opponents is that it severely exploits the poor – particularly in developing countries. In reality, water exploitation of the poor is a complex issue, for which the underlying culprits may not be privatization per se, but poverty, political inequality, and a lack of accord with fundamental human rights. Studies on the differential impacts of water pricing and location on different groups confirms this. One survey of municipal water utilities in low-income countries conducted for the United Nations found that 89 percent of these utilities had no cost recovery measures in place, 9 percent had partial cost recovery of operation and maintenance costs, and only 3 percent made any effort to recoup the costs of capital outlays. In general, utilities do not recover their capital costs, no matter what they charge.

Moreover, as Carl Bauer's numerous investigations of water management in Chile have shown, for example, where unfettered free-market approaches are adopted for water provision, and when

Box 2.3   Bolivia and privatization – an enduring conflict

Bolivia's privatization effort in the early 1990s remains a hallmark of the abuses latent in private control of urban water supplies. While proponents of privatization claim that the high rates charged by corporate water providers were necessary in order to improve water infrastructure, expand service areas, and compensate for the legacy of corruption that squandered available economic resources that could have been used to upgrade water supply and treatment in the past, they also charge that a pre-existing "anti-privatization sentiment" over which they had no control contributed to public protests.

Charges were imposed upon water taken from private wells – under the pretext that private vendors were given, by formal agreement and in the cause of greater efficiency, absolute and total control over an entire community's water supplies. After martial law was imposed in response to protests, Bechtel eventually abandoned its Bolivian water operations. Following similar unrest in La Paz toward the operations of a French-owned company, Aguas de Illimani S.A. (a subsidiary of Suez) abandoned its Bolivian operations.

This case affords an interesting example of two forms of private sector monopolization. The first and most obvious form of monopoly was horizontal integration: in effect, the private companies that controlled water rights operated as exclusive trusts in the communities in which they were licensed to operate – holding exclusive control over all supplies of water. Less obvious but equally important was that they were vertically integrated enterprises that controlled virtually all aspects of water provision: from collection, storage, distribution, treatment, marketing, and retail sales. Moreover, because their employees were corporate, not public sector workers, they could not as readily be held to account for their actions by disgruntled citizens and civil society groups by, for example, being voted out of office.

Since 2005, following the election of a reformist president, Evo Morales, a Ministry of Water was formed and given responsibility to oversee public supply through equal, universal access to water. While the country's constitution now guarantees a right to water and bans privatization of supplies, citizen participation and democratic decision-making remain largely unfulfilled due to a continued lack of accountability of officials to citizens for water provision.

Source: Baer 2008; 2015

these approaches are enshrined in law in the form of privatized water rights, the result is the transformation of water into a commodity. This commodification of water rights impedes public sector intervention to alleviate conflicts over water rights, prevents priority being accorded socially beneficial uses, and because of its stress on "laissez faire" processes of decision-making, obviates emphasis on water quality or protection of environmental resources. In Chile – especially under the notorious military dictatorship in the 1970s and 1980s of

Augusto Pinochet – the inability of private, market-based rights to adjudicate conflicts between irrigated farms and hydroelectric power interests led to stagnation of agricultural development (Bauer 1998; 2005).

This neoliberal model of water management, when adopted in developing countries, leads to different water sources being controlled by so many different institutions that "(a)cquiring water is a complex and time-consuming task, and it requires intimate knowledge of the political ecology of the city's water: where it flows at different times of year and how cost and quality vary across time and space." Thus, for residents of most large cities in the Global South, water is neither 'public' nor 'private': it has aspects of a public good, and of a commodity (Bakker 2013).

Where private ownership leads to abuse, the reason is often weak human rights traditions worsened by the dominance of private property rights and the "cultural framing" of water as a commodity. Property interests in water, in private and public ownership systems, should be viewed as subject to a set of constraints designed to ensure that water is managed on behalf of a broader public interest. These constraints include ensuring safety and security, prioritizing conservation, appropriately investing in infrastructure to meet future needs, assuring equity in allocation, being committed to community-level planning, and ensuring sustainability. Everyone, including the general public, must share in these duties (Arnold 2005).

Finally, what about affordability and water charges? A general "yardstick" of affordability used by many international agencies is that charges should not exceed 3 percent (in some cases up to 5 percent) of net household income. In practice, surveys show that in developing countries households connected to urban public systems pay on average 1 percent of incomes on water bills, including the cost of sewerage (which may be double the charges for water). However, this average is not a very reliable indicator given the wide variability among income levels in developing countries.

Generally speaking, the poor tend to pay a higher share of their household income for water. In developing countries this is complicated by the widespread use of informal and small-scale private water distributors charging full market prices. As we have seen, in such cases the poorest households can pay 3–11 percent of income on water. As this inequitable economic burden on the poor has become more widespread, pressure on governments and service providers has increased to ensure delivery of a minimal supply of potable water to all households at a reasonable price.

Achieving this objective would require tariff rates based on a household's ability to pay and provision of subsidies to cover the excess cost of service delivery for those who can least afford to pay. In short, whether or not absolute charges are small as a proportion of income, when a family earns very little money, even a small percentage of that income for an essential service like water is burdensome.

Marketing – water as tradeable commodity

In many countries, there are growing pressures to buy and sell water in order to move it from lower-valued to more "beneficial" uses. Perhaps the best examples of this are seen in the US and Australia. Having fewer than 24 million people in an area the size of the US, but being uniformly semi-arid (with the exception of some coastal zones), Australia has long faced the challenge of providing a stable water supply to thirsty cities and profitable farms. Since the 1980s, New South Wales, Victoria, and South Australia have embarked on extensive systems of water markets which effectively buy and sell water on formal "water exchanges" that then permit water to be transferred from water-rich regions to areas in greater need. The peculiarities of Australian water law make water marketing especially appropriate.

Each state and territorial government has a water register that records water access entitlements – essentially, permitted rights to using one's designated allocation, which specifies the amount of water the water rights holder controls, and the designated purpose for which it is ordinarily used. This allows water to be traded on the national stock exchange, much as would other commodities.

When marketing began in Australia, water rights were directly connected, or bundled, to land title or property rights, as in the US. In 2004, however, amidst the Millennium Drought – the most severe in the country's history, a National Water Initiative "unbundled" land titles and water rights, including ownership details and transactions, in order to more easily facilitate the buying and selling of water throughout the country – and beyond the borders of a given state (the so-called National Water Market) (Australian Government – National Water Market 2015).

The most significant claim made for the efficacy of this emerging national market is that since the late 1990s, large increases (well over 100 percent) in allocation and entitlement trading have occurred, especially in the country's Murray-Darling Basin, the nation's agricultural heartland. Selling water for higher-valued uses has increased the nation's gross domestic product by $220 million

Box 2.4 Water marketing in Australia

Australia has a series of nationally coordinated water markets with an exchange in Canberra, the capital. Water can be moved virtually anywhere, and participants in the exchange can trade actual water currently available, or even buy and sell "water futures." Among the many participants involved are farmers, irrigation system operators, water utilities, environmental groups, the federal government – and many "intermediaries" who facilitate, and profit from, trades – including brokers, banks, and other lenders.

One of the legacies of the country's recent Millennium Drought (approximately 1996–2010) was the need to regulate the amount of water farmers could take for irrigation. In some instances, the government revoked water withdrawal permits, particularly in the agriculturally rich and important Murray-Darling basin. Once the drought subsided, farmers with withdrawal permits, which prescribed the volumes they were entitled to withdraw, continued their irrigation practices.

In late 2012, in an effort to slow the use of agricultural irrigation withdrawals and, most importantly, to protect in-stream flows for fish and waterfowl, parliament, led by the then Labor Party government, came up with a novel idea – a "reverse market." The government would determine how much water farmers and others can withdraw from streams in the Murray-Darling River basin while still protecting in-stream values. The government would then pay farmers and others the difference in order to purchase water rights to restore the rivers, In effect, through a special fund of A$1.7 billion farmers are paid to leave water in-stream.

Source: Vasek & Wilson 2012

and, most significantly, afforded a high degree of flexibility in water management – reflected in recent moves to use markets to enhance the protection of environmental resources (see box 2.4).

In the US, water marketing occurs mostly in Western states where appropriation law makes possible the transfer of large volumes of water from rural areas with declining agricultural activity to cities, as well as from agriculture to "in-stream protection" needs. In a number of states including Oregon, Washington, California, Montana, Texas, and Nevada, environmental organizations with long-standing traditions of purchasing or leasing land from private landowners for conservation easements and habitat protection areas collaborate with farmers, ranchers, and others to protect in-stream flows. This is done by buying up water rights in order to protect fish and wildlife, establishing market exchanges, and urging legal reforms to prohibit transfers that negatively impact fisheries and wildlife (Kenney et al. 2000).

One of the best examples of the use of markets to protect in-stream flows, and thus the well-being of threatened or endangered species, is the case of conservation easement purchases in Northern California. At nearly a mile above sea level, Mills Creek is the highest salmon spawning area in North America. The creek is also a long-standing source of irrigation water for farms. The Nature Conservancy, an organization which has long employed the purchase of conservation easements to protect endangered species, has purchased available water rights to the creek by developing an innovative "banking and accounting system."

In effect, farmers can use water that is dedicated to fish when the farmers most need it for irrigation, while during critical migration periods farmers leave more water in the creek – thereby amending their surface appropriation rights by leasing them to the Conservancy. The revenue raised in exchange for this temporary lease of water is sometimes used for the replacement of inefficient and costly delivery system infrastructure with more efficient groundwater wells (The Nature Conservancy 2015).

In general, water marketing requires a large infrastructure for moving water. It also requires a water rights system that allows buying and selling of water, as the Australia example illustrates. In the US, water rights and property rights are tightly co-mingled, particularly in western states that practice appropriation rights ("first in time, first in right") systems (see chapter 6). Appropriation rights makes the buying and selling of water easier than does riparian law – (found mostly in states lying east of the 100th meridian), because, in the former, those who possess water rights as a result of their control of property overlying an aquifer or adjacent to a stream are allocated a specified quantity of water. This right inheres in the timing of their claim to the property they control: the more senior the rights holder, the more water one is entitled to. By contrast, rights to water under riparian law systems are not usually quantifiable.

However, the relative ease with which markets can be developed in the western US has not meant that markets are introduced without political controversy. Disputes have arisen in two distinct contexts. First, water markets have generally sought to move water from agriculture to urban and municipal uses. This has resulted in the physical diversion of water from rural to urban areas and, oftentimes, from one watershed to another. Such transfers generate concerns regarding the potential impacts to an exporting region's economy and way of life, including adverse environmental impacts to fisheries and wildlife, and the danger of "bidding wars" that might drive the cost of water to levels that could leave poorer communities vulnerable to price gouging (Tarlock 1997; Keenan et al. 1999; Samson & Bacchus 2000).

Second, because water markets facilitate the movement of water from one region – and set of uses – to another, they place a high value on economically efficient solutions to supply and demand problems and may, as a consequence, not wholly embrace environmental and social impacts. In Southern California, recent water marketing controversies involving the Salton Sea and Imperial Irrigation District exemplify this type of controversy.

Imperial Irrigation District farmers whose lands are adjacent to the Salton Sea determined that they could make more money leasing their water rights than by growing crops. A 2003 "Quantification Settlement Agreement" – negotiated through the auspices of the US Department of the Interior – facilitated the leasing of water rights by requiring Imperial Irrigation district farmers to fallow a portion of their land and adopt more efficient irrigation techniques – ostensibly to both save water and protect the region's fragile ecology (the increasingly desiccated Salton Sea is an important habitat for endangered and threatened migratory bird species).

Since the city of San Diego needs the water, and is limited in how much more water it can obtain from the Colorado River, the arrangement appeared to be a good match for all parties involved. Some local environmental groups, however, worried about harm to the Salton Sea through diminished runoff that would normally replenish the Sea through irrigation return flows, challenged the legality of the trade in state court. In 2014, the trade was declared legal under California's "public trust doctrine" which mandates that the state must protect "the people's common heritage of streams, lakes, marshlands, and tidelands" (Ingram & Oggins 1992). Finding no appreciable harm, the court allowed the trade to continue.

This controversy is not over. The invocation of the public trust doctrine is a reaction, as some note, to the aspiration to preserve and protect "nonmaterial values that are poorly reflected under the prior appropriation doctrine in general, and in water market decisions in particular" (Ingram & Oggins 1992). Other urban areas also buy water from Imperial Irrigation District, and continued concerns over impacts on the restoration of the Salton Sea mean that environmental issues will influence prospects for future trades. Such issues prompt further questions about the politics of markets: for example, do they actually move water from lower- to higher-valued uses, or merely lead to a monopolization of water rights by those with the deepest pockets?

In sum, water marketing can benefit the environment as well as the economic interests of water rights holders. Experience suggests that laws and regulations must be adopted that explicitly protect equity and environmental quality in basins-of-origin (e.g., mandating return flows, protecting in-stream values, incorporating expiration dates for trades, and the like); impose clearly defined and transferrable water rights and access to price, supply, and demand information; incorporate public review; and feature explicit environmental protection measures such as water banks for trades across state lines and requirements that a portion of the water remain associated with its previous uses. While marketing may encourage water efficiencies through inducing switching to low water demand crops or more efficient water-delivery methods, other measures need to be taken in conjunction with markets to assure that such efficiencies are adopted.

Conclusion – water supply equity

Whether water supply is controlled and managed by public or private entities, or provided for cities or agricultural regions, considerations of fairness in its management hinges most of all on public access to decision-making; the accountability of decision-makers to users; and the proper exercise of stewardship. We offer three observations regarding the roles of process, power, and purpose in water supply politics.

First, when there are clear, transparent, and appropriate roles for public and private entities that work in water, with strong public oversight of both, then there is also likely to be greater access to decisions regarding water use and management – and greater likelihood of fair outcomes from those decisions. The key issue regarding access is not whether the "owner" of water is a public or private entity but whether these entities permit broad and diverse access to decision-making processes. This appears to be a compelling lesson, especially in the experiences of mega-cities and their efforts to equitably meet growing water demands. This observation is also true, as we saw, with respect to water markets – those decision-makers who make the effort to address the needs of the majority of stakeholders – as well as the needs of the environment – are more likely to be viewed as fair. And it is further true for rural and agricultural water supply decision-making, where in many societies, decisions have historically been made by tightly-knit networks of users and their political "patrons" as in Spain.

Second, regardless of whether water infrastructure and water itself are controlled by public or private entities, accountability can only occur when strong, vital, and energetic local communities and civil society groups oversee their operations. In general, we find these pre-conditions to be more commonly found in developed societies than in less developed ones. Public agencies can be as unresponsive or even as oblivious to larger questions of public good as private corporations who seek to acquire control over water solely to earn a profit – again this is a lesson we saw in our discussion of urban water supply controversies in a number of cities, even in Paris.

Likewise, as we saw in our discussion of water marketing, private ownership and control may facilitate opportunities for efficient and, thus, socially beneficial management and allocation of water from lower to higher value uses. The failure to continue to be viewed as responsive – as has happened in France, for example, can lead to a reversal of political outcomes: a rejection of private ownership in favor of a "return" to public ownership.

And third, commitment to stewardship must be measured by the values and aspirations held by those charged with managing water supply – not their roles. Private interests can be as far-sighted as public entities in valuing stewardship and in putting this principle into practice – assuming that conditions facilitating access and accountability discussed above are firmly in place. Conversely, while private enterprises and interests can be strongly resistant to principles of stewardship, experience would suggest that public entities – especially government agencies that favor massive dam-building or reclamation projects – have often performed no better.

Public water managers in nineteenth-century Bombay were far less committed to water stewardship than twenty-first-century private water markets in Victoria, Australia have proven to be. And large public works agencies in the US and Spain often pursued irrigation developments with a fervor that was strongly biased in favor of agricultural and urban growth at the expense of protection of in-stream values.

Likewise in many developing nations, host governments that invite private investment in schemes to rapidly develop new supplies of potable water are becoming greater culprits than the private corporations they contract to manage urban water supply systems. Politicians concerned with re-election may impede implementation of progressive pricing policies that shift the burden of paying for new water systems from the poor to the middle classes, or to businesses, out of fear of losing votes in the next election (Lu et al. 2014).

Some forms of private ownership and control may lead to greater efficiencies and economies-of-scale in water management. They may also encourage conservation and – from the standpoint of governance – lead to more equitable means of amassing the capital necessary for improving, maintaining, and expanding domestic – particularly urban – water supply and treatment systems. These are crucial needs, as we have seen.

SUMMARY

- Supply decisions are dominated by economic and engineering demands to build public works. Increasingly, disempowered groups demand a voice in decisions.
- "Mega-cities" have a profound impact on supply, generating conflict between providers and users over who should pay to build and maintain water supplies.
- Agricultural users hold sway over supply decisions in rural areas, working with agencies that control the infrastructure. Markets increasingly influence allocation.

RECOMMENDED READING

- Good analyses of privatization issues in water supply are: Erik Swyngedouw, "Dispossessing H$_2$O: The Contested Terrain of Water Privatization," *Capitalism, Nature, Socialism* (March 2005), which provides a good overview – and critique – of water privatization which places the issue of control squarely within the domain of politics and social equity. Vandana Shiva, *Water Wars: Privatization, Pollution, and Profit* (2009) is another critical, important account of the impacts of privatization on the developing world. Also, Madeline Baer, "The Global Water Crisis, Privatization, and the Bolivian Water War," pp. 195–224, in *Water, Place, and Equity* (2008) and "Water Wars to Water Rights," *Journal of Human Rights* 14 (2015), offer detailed accounts of privatization in Bolivia and its consequences.
- William E. Smythe, *The Conquest of Arid America* (1900) is a classic tract that discusses the ideological fervor of irrigation boosters in the American west.

WEBSITES

- http://www.un.org/waterforlifedecade/water_cities.shtml United Nations Department of Economic and Social Affairs, 2014.
- http://www.iwahq.org/3p/themes/cities-of-the-future.html International Water Association, 2013, Montreal Declaration on Cities of the Future.
- http://geo-mexico.com/?p=9034 Water challenges facing Mexico City.

QUESTIONS FOR DISCUSSION

1. Are international efforts to establish standards for sustainable practices a useful means of meeting the water supply challenges of mega-cities? Why or why not?

2. What makes the supply of water for rural needs politically unique? How is the purpose animating agricultural water supply different from that of cities?

3. Is privatization of water supply a more efficient, fair, and practical way of providing water? Why or why not?

4. Can water markets protect water supplies for the environment while moving water to high-value uses? What protections are needed to assure their fairness?

CHAPTER 3

Clean, Green, and Costly: Water Quality

Introduction – pollution politics

There are few environmental issues more fiercely debated than water quality. Water pollution affects public health, the environment, and the economic well-being of entire nations. Since pollution has many sources, and its abatement is complex and fraught with tradeoffs, the politics of water quality is among the most complicated of environmental problems to manage.

Over the past 40 years, considerable progress has been made in improving the quality of freshwater used for human consumption, eradicating many of the sources of environmental degradation from pollution, and treating wastewater through methods both basic as well as technologically advanced. Nonetheless, as several studies point out, poor water quality remains one of the most serious problems facing the planet.

Water that is contaminated with inorganic compounds and untreated sewage degrades the function of aquatic ecosystems, poses acute risks to people – especially the very young and very old – and complicates efforts to lift people out of poverty. Water pollution is an especially serious challenge in developing countries, and cost-effective alternatives for treating human wastes are urgently needed. Over 80 percent of "used" or disposed water worldwide is not collected or treated, even though improved sanitation and safer drinking water could reduce diarrheal diseases by nearly 90 percent, for example (WHO 2008; Corcoran et al. 2010).

In recent years, public education efforts tied to improving hygiene and environmental protection have become a high priority in many developing countries. However, the need for more stringent regulation and management of industries and other enterprises producing toxic substances is both great, and largely unmet, because many governments place a high regard on rapid economic development, at virtually any environmental cost. So-called "clean technologies" – methods that emphasize natural means of treating wastes, together with processes that reduce non-point or "runoff" sources of pollution (especially nutrients) – have become an important set of options receiving greater attention by decision-makers (World Resources Institute 2005). Their adoption is still largely limited to highly developed nations, however.

In developed and developing countries alike, adopting particular pollution abatement options entails hard choices regarding land and water management and public expenditure. Fortunately, while the health of ecosystems has "historically been a concern of the richer, more developed countries and their environmental movements" (UN Water 2012), growing appreciation of the benefits of environmental goods and services has propelled the issue of clean water onto the policy agendas of virtually every country.

Experts often distinguish between *macro* (large scale, sector-level) and *micro* (personal, individual-level) causes of water pollution. Discharges of sewage, as well as treated and untreated wastes, which stem from activities that release toxic chemicals, bacteria, viruses, and parasites, are typically considered *macro* sources. These sources can also release chemical substances not typically thought to be toxic, but which can harm the environment of streams, rivers, lakes, bays, estuaries, and coastal zones.

In addition to gross pollutants, water quality can be affected by activities that degrade the capacity of water bodies to sustain plant and animal life, such as nitrogen and phosphorus, ubiquitous substances generated from fertilizer runoff from farms and lawns, as well as human and animal wastes and even from wastewater treatment systems. These pollutants have become among the most serious degraders of water quality.

Human activities can also introduce so-called "contaminants of emerging concern" into our waterways. These contaminants are generally found in personal care products, drugs, and other consumer items. These *micro* sources of pollution cumulatively affect human health and the environment. They are also far more difficult to manage than conventional pollutants because they are nearly impossible to regulate. What we do about all these problems depends on how seriously we view their consequences. It also depends on the political influence of those impacted by them.

An overview of water quality politics – past as prologue

In general, water pollution has been managed through two broad strategies. First, polities achieving some degree of technological sophistication have funded public works designed to eliminate human, animal, and industrial wastes from cities, and to detach or "disconnect" them from human contact. Second, these public works and their overseers have been vested with the mission of primarily protecting human health. Protection of the environment has historically been a secondary consideration.

These strategies underwent little overall change until the mid-twentieth century when developed countries began to realize that while oil, detergents, paint thinners, and other residues from industrial manufacturing deposited in streams may not necessarily directly harm humans – assuming that drinking water is actually treated – discharges of these substances kill fish and plant life, and lead to other gross nuisances (see box 3.1).

Connected to both of these strategies has been a third approach: to assure that the water humans consume is not contaminated with the waste products they generate, rivers have often been regarded as sewers. Thus, separately constructed aqueducts and supply systems were built to transport water from pristine springs and rivers many miles distant from cities. It was not until the nineteenth century, with the advent of what came to be known as the "sewered city," that treating wastes in order to minimize the spread of water-borne disease became common practice. Not until the twentieth century, moreover, did societies begin to see the advantages in treating, purifying, and later intercepting pollution from waterways so as to protect non-human life and environmental quality.

Growth in this awareness was also accompanied by an overall change in public attitudes toward water pollution that had long-term political significance; what some have called the emergence of a "hydro-social contract," the belief that a community's values dictate a kind of tacit agreement among the public, government, and business regarding how water should be managed. This contract is ultimately expressed through engineered infrastructure, laws and regulations, and governance institutions (Lundqvist et al. 2001).

Ancient Rome exemplifies all three approaches. The provision of clean water became of prime political importance as the city grew as the commercial hub and political capital of an expanding empire. The city's first aqueduct was built in the fourth century BC and was quickly followed by several more. At the height of its power (second century AD) Rome was fed by eleven aqueducts that could provide upwards of one million cubic meters per day to the city, or approximately one thousand liters of clean water per person per day (Connolly & Dodge 1998; Coarelli 2007).

Box 3.1   How can a river catch fire? In Cleveland – it happened more than once

In June 1969, the Cuyahoga River, which runs through the center of Cleveland and drains into Lake Erie, caught fire – a dramatic event that graphically illuminated the legacy of decades of oil and industrial wastes upon the city's foremost water-way. Ironically, while it "badly tarnished a city's reputation," the fire initially drew little attention from the public or the media. Moreover, it was not even the first time the river had burned: not only had it caught fire several times beginning in the early twentieth century, but a more serious fire in November 1952 completely engulfed a ship.

What the 1969 fire did achieve was to serve as a sort of punctuation mark on decades of water pollution which, throughout most of the city's history, was viewed by its residents as "a necessary consequence of the industry that had brought prosperity to the city." This attitude only really began to change in the 1960s as the American environmental movement began to grow. Ironically, in 1968, Cleveland residents overwhelmingly approved a $100 million bond initiative to fund the Cuyahoga's cleanup, and by the time of the fire de-industrialization led to the closure, or reduction in manufacturing, of many of the steel mills and other factories responsible for the pollution.

As one observer noted, the 1969 fire "was not really the terrifying climax of decades of pollution, but rather the last gasp of an industrial river whose role was beginning to change." Cleveland's first African American mayor, Carl Stokes – elected in 1967 – joined with his brother, US Representative Louis Stokes, to urge greater federal involvement in pollution control. Their advocacy played a key role in congressional passage of the Clean Water Act of 1972 – the foundational legislation for America's water pollution control system. Thus, in its own peculiar way, the burning Cuyahoga was important for changing attitudes toward urban rivers not only in Cleveland but also throughout the nation. Given the Clean Water Act's symbolic impact, it would not be mistaken to credit it with global importance as well.

After 1969, the river's quality not only improved, but the Cuyahoga came to symbolize evolving urban views of rivers as community amenities that could be capitalized upon as sources of recreation, real estate investment, and even entertainment.

Source: Rotman 2015

As reported to us by contemporaries, including Sextus Frontinus, the city's curator of aqueducts during the reigns of the emperors Flavius and Trajan, water supply and sanitation were important public functions with numerous political ramifications. Constructed at great expense, local officials were obliged to maintain and repair them. Special magistrates were appointed to oversee these activities under Emperor Augustus (Purcell 1994).

Rome was also an innovator in water and hygiene. Public baths and lavatories were state-provided for the benefit of the general populace.

By the early fifth century AD, the city had 11 imperial baths (*thermae*) that could accommodate hundreds of people at a time. Fed by aqueducts and reservoirs, they were important gathering places and considerable effort was expended to make them attractive. Other Roman cities soon followed suit and such facilities were built throughout the empire.

From public fountains, water was supplied to baths and also directed to public latrines. These, in turn, drained through engineered structures such as the "Cloaca Maxima" (an early combined storm and sanitary sewer system) and thence to the Tiber (Boatright et al. 2004). A common error made by modern interpreters of these engineered systems, however, is that the Romans were primarily interested, as are we, in hygiene and removal of dirty debris. It appears that drainage and sewer systems were designed, instead, to remove standing water, not to sanitize water supplies (Koloski-Ostrow 2015). In effect, the model established by Rome, with some variation, became the standard for urban water quality maintenance for some time thereafter.

With the advent of two major eras in water development – termed by some scholars the water supply and sewered city eras (Brown et al. 2009) – a phenomenon that occurred first in London, then spread throughout Europe, North America, and Australia by the early 1800s – human and animal waste disposal became a higher priority public concern and, thus, a more rigorously engineered enterprise. Foul standing water generated noxious odors, while outdoor disposal oftentimes led to outbreaks of cholera, typhoid, yellow fever and other infectious diseases as waste collected in street gutters, cesspools, and streams. This eventually led to public outcry for innovation in developing sanitary sewer systems to shuttle waste (and wastewater) out of cities such as London, Paris, and New York through sanitary and combined sewer systems that discharged waste to local water bodies (Koeppel 2000).

These innovations also led to major changes in water politics, including efforts to promote public as well as private investment in the design and development of reticulated sewer systems and improvements to waste transport (Brown et al. 2009). These, in turn, hastened increased public oversight of sewage systems and consolidation of water services, in some cases transforming ownership of supply from private, investor-owned enterprises to public ones (see box 3.2).

The provision of these services, like those for urban water supply, was strongly linked to changes in the "hydro-social contract." A widespread conviction grew that, once the capacity to design systems able to provide water safely, economically, and reliably is made available

Box 3.2   Cities, water, and public health – New York City

New York City first acquired its water supply through the efforts of private investors and only later developed a public-controlled system. From 1624, when the city was founded, till the eighteenth century, domestic water supplies were obtainable from sources in the immediate vicinity. Initially, these consisted of shallow, privately owned wells. Under Dutch rule, sanitation and water quality were decidedly poor: accumulations of human and animal waste were common, contaminated runoff into holding ponds was frequent and there was no concerted effort to regulate harmful activities impinging on locally adjacent well users. New York's initial efforts to develop a water supply system were largely animated by two concerns: accommodating population growth and averting communicable disease.

Under English rule (after 1664), improvements were marginal. Foul, standing water was common, and outbreaks of epidemics stemming from poor water quality, including yellow fever and cholera, were not unknown. In 1677 the first general public-use well was dug near the fort at Bowling Green, while the first city reservoir was constructed on the east side of Broadway between Pearl and White Streets in 1776: about the time the city's population grew to over 20,000. Initially, water pumped from wells near the Collect Pond, east of the reservoir, was distributed through hollow logs laid along main thoroughfares in Manhattan.

As the city grew, pollution of wells became a serious problem, as did periodic drought. These problems led to concerted efforts to supplement local supplies through cisterns and springs in upper Manhattan (a less developed area). Following the outbreak of a yellow fever epidemic in 1798, New York sought a safer, more secure, and disease-free water supply. In 1800 the Manhattan Company (forerunner of Chase Manhattan Bank) sank a well at Reade and Centre Streets, pumped water into a reservoir on Chambers Street and distributed it through wooden mains to a portion of the community – the city's first quasi-public water utility.

Led, ironically, by two New York statesmen who soon became mortal enemies – Aaron Burr and Alexander Hamilton – the city's Common Council was persuaded to obtain state legislative endorsement of the Manhattan Company's charter. Burr and Hamilton had different motives in advocating the charter and the company: the former sought financial profit through transforming the "surplus" revenues of the firm to his own design, while the latter was swayed by the desire to unburden city residents of a tax-supported public system.

In 1905, a Board of Water Supply established by the state Legislature cooperated with the city in developing the Catskill region as an additional water source – with the former planning and constructing facilities to impound Esopus Creek, and to deliver the water to the city via the Ashokan Reservoir and Catskill Aqueduct – a project completed in 1915 and given over to the city's Department of Water Supply, Gas and Electricity for operation.

Sources: Koeppel 2000; Glaeser 2011; New York City 2011

for the benefit of the privileged few and those with high social status, it then should be made available to all, as a virtual public right, and through public expense (Brown et al. 2009).

Pollution politics – national variants of process, power, and purpose

At the center of most water quality disputes are local governing authorities, utilities, farmers, landowners, industries, and urban residents. Consequently, the most vigorous contests over regulation and control, management of pollutants, defining of risks, and avoidance of hazards occurs at the local level. Over time, we have seen this trend extend to developing countries. As we will see, growing concerns over how local pollution sources affect entire catchments, and contaminate estuaries and coastal zones, have led to an increase in national and transnational efforts to regulate and manage risks – and to engage in national and transnational *processes* for pollution control, such as the Rhine Commission.

Water quality issues today are primarily local in origin. As a consequence the process for water pollution politics also tends to be locally centered – as in the past. While every country has a national set of water quality protection standards, as a practical matter local authorities are responsible for their enforcement and implementation. National and state governments intercede when local efforts fall short. Their intercession amplifies the hydro-social contract by extending the range of players and appropriate values that guide pollution policy, including voices of aggrieved groups.

An important distinction in the process of water pollution politics is between single point-of-origin discharges (e.g., water treatment plant, factory, concentrated animal feeding operations), and runoff from paved and unpaved surfaces, farms, eroded and denuded lands, air pollution deposited on surface waters, and storm water. Non-point runoff is more ubiquitous; affects many more protagonists; and over time has expanded the process of water pollution politics to encompass intractable and difficult to resolve issues (e.g., land use, agricultural production, and urban design). This has led to transformation of the process of pollution abatement to affect many more political levels and jurisdictions as regards control and management (Hoornbeek 2011).

Beginning in the 1960s, industrialized nations began aggressive regulatory efforts to reduce pollution and improve the health of water bodies. After 1970, the US and other developed countries lowered point source discharges over 90 percent by imposing: discharge per-mits upon factories, wastewater treatment plants, and other point source facilities. Over time, initially in Europe, economic incentives – effluent fees, taxes, and other measures – were adopted to supplement regulations in order to induce facilities to reduce pollution even further. While significant improvements in water quality have been achieved, water pollution has proven to be a stubbornly resistant prob-lem everywhere, despite differences in decision-making processes.

Comparing water pollution politics

The efforts of four polities to manage pollution – the US, France, Russia, and China – are instructive as to the challenges faced by water pollution abatement efforts. These polities range from those that have traditionally had a high regard for various forms of public engage-ment in environmental practices to those where such engagement has been, until recently, almost non-existent.

In the US, the Clean Water Act prescribes that water quality stand-ards must: establish water quality goals for a specific water body, and serve as a basis for prescribed treatment controls and strategies that go beyond mere "technology-based levels of treatment." The latter means that avenues and approaches that avert pollution, as well as treat it (i.e., anti-degradation approaches) should be embraced in order to forestall harm. In short, legal purpose is broadly defined.

As in other highly industrialized polities, the process that led to water pollution regulation in the US was lengthy and complex. Common law practices intended to protect downstream users from harm were found to be consistently wanting by the late nineteenth century, leading to an 1899 Rivers and Harbors Act that was largely a ban on "nuisance" dumping of solid wastes into the country's water-ways. Specifically mandated federal goals and regulatory limits on discharges did not come about until after World War II with passage of the Federal Water Pollution Control Act, followed by the establish-ment of explicit quality standards in 1965.

By the late 1960s, the laxity of existing standards, slow pace of pollu-tion cleanup, concerns over drinking water quality, and public outrage over gross pollution contributing to the growth of a publically backed environmental movement (see box 3.1, p. 55) led to the current Clean Water Act. The basis for this Act was the 1972 Federal Water Pollution Control Act and its mandate to "restore and maintain the chemical, physical, and biological integrity of the nation's waters" and the out-lawing of the discharge of any toxic or non-toxic pollutant without a permit, as well as compelling adoption of best available technologies for pollution abatement (Copeland 1999; Bruninga 2002).

While successful in reducing point source discharges and in encouraging a wave of wastewater plant construction, by the 1980s it became clear that more effort was needed to restore water quality by directly addressing the effects of non-point pollution. A series of citizen lawsuits forced the EPA to rigorously enforce Section 303(d) of the Clean Water Act by requiring states to establish standards for remediation for all streams failing to meet prescribed quality standards. The framework by which these objectives is to be achieved is called the "total maximum daily load" or TMDL, and it allows certain "loads" (i.e., amounts) of various pollutants to be allocated among polluters, so that appropriate control actions can be taken and water quality standards for a segment of a stream or other water body achieved. The TMDL provides an estimate of pollutant loadings from all sources within a water body, predicts the resulting pollutant concentrations, and then allows regulators to "parcel out" allowable loads – providing the basis for establishing or modifying controls on pollutant sources.

Politically, the TMDL process is intended to encompass the impacts of all activities upon a water body, whether generated by point, non-point, or background sources (e.g., atmospheric deposition of contaminants from combustion). The TMDL concept has successfully been applied to waste-load allocations for point source discharges in low flow situations where non-point sources are not a concern. However, the EPA's goal is that TMDLs also consider the effect of all activities or processes that cause water quality-limited conditions for a water body (see table 3.1).

These activities could include thermal changes, flow changes, sedimentation, or other impacts on the aquatic environment. Thus, actions to reduce non-point source pollution are both welcome and encouraged (US EPA 2012), and high levels of public engagement and stakeholder participation are encouraged. As regards the latter, an important development in US pollution policy is the growth of economic innovations that permit adopting various "offsets" or trading schemes to reduce pollution. Overall, while progress has been discernible, continuing challenges remain, including the capacity of states to enforce TMDLs (states remain principally responsible for water pollution policy enforcement), the persistence of runoff pollution, and new sources of contamination.

In contrast to the US, France – a "unitary" political system with a heritage of strong central government and politically weaker and less

Table 3.1 Examples of best management practices for water pollution abatement

Agriculture	Silviculture
Animal waste management	Ground cover maintenance
Conservation tillage	Limiting disturbed areas
Contour farming	Log removal techniques
Contour strip cropping	Pesticide/herbicide management
Cover crops	Proper handling of haul roads
Crop rotation	Removal of debris
Fertilizer management	Riparian zone management
Integrated pest management	Road and skid trial management
Livestock exclusion	*Mining*
Range and pasture management	Block-cut or haul-back
Sod-based rotations	Underdrains
Terraces	Water diversion
Construction	*Multicategory*
Disturbed area limits	Buffer strips
Non-vegetative soil stabilization	Detention/sedimentation basins
Runoff detention/retention	Devices to encourage infiltration
Surface roughening	Grassed waterway
Urban	Interception/diversion
Flood storage	Material ground cover
Porous pavements	Sediment traps
Runoff detention/retention	Streamside management zones
Street cleaning	Vegetative stabilization/mulching

Source: US EPA 2012

politically independent regions – manages its surface waters through a national-level regulatory regime. This system delegates authority to six river basin agencies, corresponding to the major drainage basins within France. Each basin agency is charged with assisting municipalities and industries in meeting national water quality standards. These basins also oversee the distribution and management of river systems and the allocation of wholesale water supply.

Because they are primarily concerned with the prevention of water pollution and the provision of water supply, these basin authorities employ several methods of pollution abatement, including economic incentives such as loans, grants, and fines as a form of standards enforcement (Ministère de l'Amenagement du Territoire et de l'Environnement 1999). Central to the process of establishing, enforcing, and implementing these incentives is a multi-faceted process of public participation, consultation between central ministry "inspectors" and locally elected officials, and conjoint national-basin-local determination regarding fines and other penalties.

In general, basin agencies set pollution charges based on the volumes of water drawn or degraded in order to reduce the ultimate costs of pollution control to the nation. Charges are paid by all water users in a basin and are levied by a complex formula based on the mass of pollutants discharged, estimated costs for decomposition, and actual water used (i.e., withdrawn). In effect, any activity that uses water generates some form of pollution – point or non-point – and is thus subject to charges to cover cleanup costs. These charges, intended to induce preventative action, are supposed to alleviate the need for the ministry to have to resort to more formal penalties.

Revenues collected by basin agencies belong to that basin to spend on pollution abatement and water supply projects in conformance with multiyear plans for meeting water resource objectives (UN World Water Assessment Programme 2003). These plans are developed with the assistance of *comités de bassin* (basin committees) – advisory boards made up of water users and local government representatives, and assisted by environmental NGOs. A 1992 Water Act began a steady process of local devolution of water quality policy in France, whereby a "Master Water Development and Management Plan" is to be developed by each watershed.

Basin agencies work with local governments in drafting plans for management and development of water resources. Thus, these agencies share authority with private companies, government departments, and environmental organizations in undertaking river basin planning, and those individual watersheds facing significant water quality problems must develop special mitigation plans (Newson 1997).

France appears to suffer from many of the same water quality challenges faced by other developed nations. Drinking water quality is generally very good. In some rural areas with large agricultural activity, however, pesticides and nitrates from fertilizer and livestock manure have been found, especially in the farming regions surrounding Paris, where as much as 20 percent of the rural population may be exposed to contaminated drinking water – a total of some 1.5 million people. In addition, selenium contamination has been detected in areas of groundwater overuse, further underscoring the gap in water

quality between urban and rural areas – a gap that appears to be growing, according to one consumer organization study (Melvin 2014).

One criticism of the French system is that water management plans
are generally driven by water quality interests and concerns instead
of "ecosystem protection" goals. The latter tend to be more decentralized in nature and place an emphasis not only on human water
consumption concerns but also on the preservation of endangered
and threatened species (Buller 1996). If true, this places France firmly
within the long-established pattern of many polities where pollution
abatement has been viewed as primarily directed at protecting human
health, and only secondarily the environment.

Russia may best be characterized as a transitional society in which
upward pressure from various publics and NGOs have compelled
changes in environmental quality and in encouraging more openness
in bureaucratic rule-making. Given its authoritarian past, and slow
and uneven transition to democracy, Russia exemplifies the impacts
of past policy as a barrier to policy change. One legacy of the Soviet
period is the large number of major water projects that have significantly altered river systems as well as water quality. For example, due
to a chain of hydroelectric dams, it now takes 18 months for water to
flow from Rybinsk to Volgograd on the Volga, and fish parasites are
not vigorously prevented from migrating while fish passageways are
blocked.

Many major reservoirs in Russia are used for both municipal supply
and industrial consumption, and "both treated and untreated water
is often released with little concern for downstream use" (Henry
& Douhovnikoff 2008: 443). In addition, approximately half the
country's population consumes drinking water that fails to meet some
health or environmental standards due to the presence – in quantities deemed harmful to human health – of chlorinated hydrocarbons,
chloroform, heavy metals, and other contaminants. Among the major
issues are continued discharges of untreated, raw sewage, particularly
in the Baltic and Caspian Seas; drinking water quality that falls far
below required standards; and a lack of adequate funding and infrastructure for abating point or non-point pollutant and contaminant
sources (OECD 1999).

Drinking water quality problems are ubiquitous in large urban
areas, villages and rural areas alike. In recent years, pollution problems have shifted from industrial discharge and agricultural runoff to
municipal wastewater discharge – accounting for some two-thirds of
water pollutants as of mid-decade. Lack of funds for municipal water
treatment (estimates are that over $200 billion is needed to raise

potable water quality) has exacerbated these problems and prompted efforts to seek international assistance. Thus far, loans and other forms of international assistance from such entities as the European Bank for Reconstruction and Development (EBRD) and the World Bank for various projects has tended to be concentrated in regions where water pollution contributes to the degradation of regional seas shared by several nations (Smith 2006).

Process-wise, a robust NGO sector in Russia has arisen in response to water problems, with many preservation-activist groups forming in communities along the country's great waterways. One of the largest and best known of these is "Help the River" – an NGO patterned closely after the US and European "River-keeper" volunteer citizen networks. Help the River operates an extensive water quality monitoring network, and volunteer training system, along the River Volga and its tributaries. "Help the River" has been instrumental in setting up a series of small, portable water quality testing labs on the Volga and its major tributaries. It has also identified sources of toxic discharges from industrial plants, working with plant operators to reduce these adverse discharges and clean up effluent spills. Simultaneously, it has organized local citizen demonstrations and protests against recalcitrant polluters.

While successfully partnering with local government officials to cooperatively address river cleanup issues, like NGOs in other countries, Russian environmental groups have been less effective in compelling the enforcement of existing laws. In fact, under President Putin, a number of environmentally threatening activities that were prohibited are now allowed under the federal "Water code," including home-building and storage of wastes near waterways, and the decrease of water protection zones for inland seas from 2 km to 0.5 km. Moreover, government spending for water quality protection – particularly expenditure on protecting drinking water quality – is down 90 percent from 1980 levels.

Finally, China offers an intriguing example of a "built from scratch" effort to develop a pollution control system in a polity where virtually none existed prior to the 1990s. By the later part of that decade, it became apparent to Chinese government authorities that national water quality standards were so weak – and the number of industrial manufacturing and other emitters so high, and growing – that many water bodies were failing to meet modest pollution limits. Water pollution accidents were not only frequent but also officially underestimated by environmental regulatory bodies.

A 2005 Songhua River benzene spill brought considerable domestic pressure and international embarrassment to the nation and prompted adoption of a national Water Pollution Prevention and Control Law – passed by the People's Congress in February 2008. The law was a modification of a 1996 statute that, at the time, raised the bar for the country's expectations with respect to protecting water quality.

A major feature of the 1996 Act was an effort to establish a set of total emission requirements aimed at bringing an entire water body within national quality standards – conceptually similar to the US TMDL approach. These requirements mandated that emitters lower their discharges to ensure that overall standards could be met within water bodies (Li & Liu 2009). Three additional innovations were introduced in this law. First, the 1996 Act specified that in order to prevent water pollution, it is necessary to first formulate unified water quality plans on the basis of river basins, and not on administrative regions. Second, the law instituted a system for controlling total discharges of major pollutants into water bodies where pollutant discharge has conformed to standards, but water quality still does not meet national standards (i.e., in US parlance, a water body that is "impaired"). And third, the Act required that urban sewage be centrally treated and local governments construct central treatment facilities (Ministry of Environmental Protection 2007).

While notable in aspiration, however, the law was weak in achievement. In 2008, the basic framework of the law was strengthened as a result of severe water pollution across China, and a series of water pollution accidents that impeded economic and social development in various regions. The newer Water Pollution Protection Control Act introduced four major reforms. First, governments at or above the county level are to incorporate water protection considerations in national economic and social development planning; to prevent and treat water pollution; and to be responsible for the quality of the water in their respective administrative domains. Second, it also requires evaluation of local officials' efforts in fulfilling the law's objectives in their performance reviews; i.e., provincial governments must sign a responsibility pledge with the State Council to commit to fulfilling the environmental protection target set up in the 11th Five-Year Plan, which includes reducing chemical oxygen demand by 10 percent in the period 2006–10.

Third, the 2008 law for the first time also places public participation requirements on governments charged with regulating, maintaining, and alleviating water pollution. Information about national water quality must be released to the public in a consistent, unified format.

Meeting this objective requires transparent explanation of: how water samples are obtained and analyzed, and the applicable standards for evaluating water quality that were used. The national Ministry of Environmental Protection is singularly responsible for releasing information about national water quality to "avoid confusion and ensure that the public is provided with accurate and reliable information on water quality."

Finally, stiffer fines are now levied against violators, and drinking water "source protection zones" (which ban potentially water-contaminating activities) are being established nation-wide. Proposals for even tougher standards – e.g., daily compounded fines for violating water quality standards (administrative penalties comparable to those levied under the US Clean Water Act), and permitting public interest intervener groups to sue the state – did not make it into the law (Li & Liu 2009). The government is simply not ready to embark on such boldly democratic steps to ensure the protection of water quality – at least not at this point in time.

Comparative lessons: power, inequality, and pollution

As these vignettes reveal, power and influence over water quality tends to reside in a wide range of entities: from industries and utilities on the one hand, to environmental and community-based NGOs on the other – and within government-invested agencies. As in water supply, this power is *not* held equally. In general, the degree to which power over water quality issues is broadly rather than narrowly shared tends to be associated with a polity's level of development of representative institutions, and the strength of its civil society sector.

These four cases also affirm that the more advanced a nation's economy and political-regulatory system – and thus, the stronger its environmental (as well as consumer) groups, the more power over water quality concerns environmental protection advocates have. Civil society groups tend to have greater authority in establishing pollution regulations; are more vocal in their advocacy of stream protection and of public health; and are more directly involved in monitoring the quality of water bodies and overseeing those formally charged with their protection in democratic, than in non-democratic or authoritarian systems.

Conversely, in developing societies, where large economic sectors that promote growth at virtually any cost exercise more influence over environmental decision-making, pollution politics tends to be controlled by industries and agri-business groups. In developing societies too, the civil society sector tends to be weaker than in more advanced societies. This is reflected by the relative weakness of environmental groups in participating in pollution politics. Pollution controls tend to be less advanced in technical sophistication, and insufficiently operationalized due to resource constraints. Moreover, water quality standards are often poorly enforced due to development pressures. An important caveat is that similar relationships can be discerned at sub-national levels and in more developed polities. Thus, for example, economically disadvantaged regions within advanced industrial states and provinces (e.g., California's Central Valley) may experience high levels of water contamination, and poorly organized and funded NGOs that consequently exercise weak influence on water quality decisions (Santa Cruz Declaration 2014).

While examples of sub-standard water quality practices tend to be widespread and variable, particularly in rapidly developing countries such as China and to some extent Russia – three generalizations regarding effective governance of pollution can be offered. First, water quality suffers when there is low investment in environmental controls, little proactive effort at preventing sources of widespread contamination, neglect of national monitoring and observation systems, and – obviously – poor investment in treatment systems. While this problem is widely recognized, competing national priorities make rapid progress in improving water quality difficult throughout the world (UN Water 2012).

Second, population growth and economic development are increasing environmental pressure on land and water by shifting diets from predominantly starch-based to meat and dairy products. These require more water – worsening non-point water pollution. This is especially a challenge in countries such as China. Producing 1 kg rice, for example, requires about 3,500 L water, 1 kg beef some 15,000 L, while a cup of coffee uses about 140 L. Dietary shifts have also posed a significant impact on water consumption over the past 30 years, a trend likely to continue well into the middle of the twenty-first century. This will place additional pressure on water quality by diminishing stream-flow (FAO 2006; Hoekstra & Chapagain 2008). Similarly, efforts to industrialize are already increasing pressures on point source pollution. Thus, the problem of water quality is not merely one of neglect of investments or political will, but partly a problem of matching investments in water quality to the progress made in achieving economic growth. Russia and China both exemplify this challenge.

Third, despite progress made in addressing flagrant causes of pollution – in developed as in developing countries alike – the challenge

posed by "legacy" practices (i.e., inappropriate but widespread pollution management approaches) remains another challenge. While
Russia is clearly an example of this, as we have shown, another, more
fitting example occurred in Hungary.

In October 2010 a tailings dam collapse adjacent to an aluminum
smelting facility contaminated a large segment of the Marcal River
basin with arsenic and mercury. Ten people were killed while farms
and villages throughout the region were severely impacted. Described
as the greatest environmental disaster ever to occur in this region, an
unusually candid report prepared in 2011 by Hungarian university
faculty and Greenpeace, and supported by parliament, concluded the
accident was the result of "negligence, to ignoring signs, severe omis-
sions and issues of liability" (The Kolantar Report 2011).

These problems stemmed from the systemic failure to aggressively
adopt EU environmental protection guidelines designed to ensure that
companies acquire adequate liability insurance in cases of accidental
releases of mine tailings, vigilant monitoring of site conditions that
could lead to dam failures, and regular inspections. Moreover, these
conditions are the legacy of a Soviet-style central planning system that
disregarded – or at least severely discounted – environmental quality,
public health, and safety, and exalted industrial output (The Kolantar
Report 2011).

The politics of innovation – "thinking outside the pipe"

In recent years, water quality experts have engaged in a robust debate
regarding the best *means* to alleviate pollution. Some contend that
water quality should *mostly* be protected through repair, restoration,
and mitigation undertaken by means of stringent legal requirements. Others advocate economic inducements that utilize flexible
"pollutant trading" or offset-based schemes, often in combination
with some form of what has come to be termed low-impact development, in order to gradually improve the quality of impaired waters. In
both instances, what are at stake are frontal challenges to the hydro-
social contract discussed earlier in this chapter. In effect, does society
expect pollution mitigation to be mandated solely by top-down regulatory authority, or incentivized through economic benefits to improve
water quality?

The underlying logic of trading is a credit-based system where a
polluter earns credit by measurably reducing the amount of a pollutant in discharged effluent. This credit can then be traded with
other dischargers, or applied towards another pollutant by the same

discharger. Trading schemes can range from multi-party trading markets to more holistic, multi-objective approaches having as their goals reduction of total pollutants at lower cost to society coupled with the generation of other social benefits (e.g., improved in-stream flow).

There are some 50 trading programs worldwide: mostly in the US, with others in Australia, New Zealand, and Canada. Local stakeholder input must be embraced in trading scheme design and in determining the value placed on various benefits. Inclusion of the public and polluters in decision-making is also required to ensure trust and confidence, and to bargain and negotiate objectives and foster workable compromises. In general, the structure of a pollution trade to protect water quality must conform to prescribed legal criteria that define how pollution is to be managed, and goals that should be achieved. This is only one of the formidable political challenges involved in making trades work, as the following examples illustrate (Selman et al. 2009; Cochran & Logue 2010).

Pollutant trading: a tale of two watersheds

Like many US states, North Carolina has found it difficult to meet the EPA's TMDL standards for two major pollutant sources: nitrogen and phosphorus. In the 1980s, runoff from farms as well as permitted point source discharges from water treatment plants in cities led to low dissolved O_2, fish kills, and the loss of riparian vegetation in the Tar-Pamlico River basin – a watershed that drains into one of the most robust estuarine fisheries on the Atlantic seaboard. In 1992 the state sought EPA permission to adopt an innovation – a "nutrient trading framework" – that would trade like-for-like (i.e., nitrogen for nitrogen, phosphorus for phosphorus) between point and non-point source contributors. Point source polluters – for the most part, sewage treatment plants – are grouped together in an association and are empowered to trade credits among themselves. However, once their nutrient loading "cap" is exceeded, the association must offset further discharges by making payments to the state's agricultural cost share program. This program secures nutrient reductions from non-point sources in the Tar-Pamlico Basin. The "best management practices" funded by the program include water control structures to treat cropland by detaining contaminated water (allowing nutrient removal), and averting nitrogen and phosphorus runoff, while also planting nutrient feed crops (row crops that "eat" nitrates).

The economic benefit provided by the program is that cities do not have to upgrade municipal water treatment facilities, a highly expensive proposition and a significant burden on consumers' water bills as well as local taxes. In theory, at least, it should cost less to invest in non-point reductions and, if they work over time, such an approach should yield more benefits to water quality (Powers 1999; Jacobson et al. 1994).

The program's overall performance record is mixed, to say the least. By 2011, nitrogen concentrations in the basin had fallen some 30 percent, while phosphorus concentrations have declined nearly 45 percent. And, some 90 percent of farmers participate in the program. Moreover, the ecological health of the Albemarle-Pamlico Estuary has shown signs of gradual improvement with declines in fish kills and declines in nutrient inputs. Despite these measureable improvements, by the state's own admission "water quality standards have *not* been (fully) met," and further measures may be needed, including controls on aquaculture (fish ponds), and reductions of atmospheric dispersion of nitrates from power plants and other sources (North Carolina Dept. of Environment and Natural Resources 2014).

Moreover, it remains unclear how much influence the trading scheme itself has had on these outcomes, especially since public engagement has been fairly low. Despite this mixed record, the program represents one of the few efforts in North America to apply market forces to pollution abatement through a basin-wide approach to managing both point and non-point pollution that especially targets the most serious non-point problems (Koontz et al. 2004).

An alternative to the "like-for-like" approach is a pollution-offset program being pursued in Australia. The Jacksons Creek Pilot Project in Victoria is exploring a trade-off among dissimilar pollutants with different environmental impacts. The goal of this experiment is to develop a means to measure *net positive environmental benefits* from an offset scheme.

Jacksons Creek is a rural sub-catchment of the Maribyrnong River, northwest of Melbourne, Australia's second largest and fastest-growing city (fig. 3.1). The area currently supports low density residential and agricultural land uses; however, Melbourne's expanding urban growth boundary has placed significant population growth and development pressures on the catchment. Regional planners project population in the largest community in the watershed, Sunbury, to double from about 37,000 to over 73,000 residents between 2014 and 2036. Melbourne's regional transportation corridors extend into the watershed, spurring additional residential and commercial development and underscoring the need to better anticipate the water quality impacts of future growth.

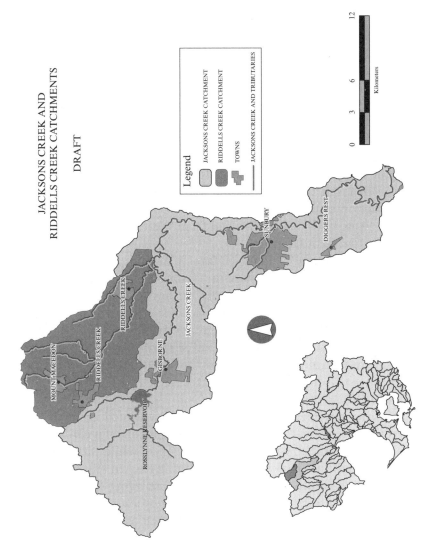

JACKSONS CREEK AND
RIDDELLS CREEK CATCHMENTS

DRAFT

Legend

JACKSONS CREEK CATCHMENT

RIDDELLS CREEK CATCHMENT

TOWNS

JACKSONS CREEK AND TRIBUTARIES

MOUNT MACEDON

RIDDELLS CREEK

RIDDELLS CREEK

JACKSONS CREEK

GISBORNE

ROSSLYNNE RESERVOIR

SUNBURY

DIGGERS REST

0   3   6   12
Kilometers

Figure 3.1 *Jacksons Creek catchment*

During Australia's Millennium Drought (1996–2010), severe low flow conditions affected the entire region. Jacksons Creek – and its major reservoir – became nearly depleted. Low flow conditions were so serious that the ecological health of the Creek was severely threatened, and for a brief period during the drought, the local water provider, Western Water, sought to use discharged treated effluent to increase the flow in Jacksons Creek, figuring that somewhat degraded water is better than no water at all for the continued maintenance of a water body's in-stream flow. Regulatory issues made these efforts contentious, however, and thwarted their implementation.

With the end of the drought, a return to more normal rainfall and more stable flows in Jacksons Creek, another alternative to protect water quality was opportunely afforded. A subsidiary benefit of the drought was increased reliance on recycled wastewater – especially for end-uses where potable-grade drinking water was not needed (e.g., growing of some row crops, or industrial and power plant cooling). When the drought ended, demands for using recycled wastewater fell to a fraction of what it had been in the region. There was now a surplus of treated effluent discharged from Western Water's recycled wastewater treatment facilities.

This treated effluent is high in total nitrogen and phosphorus and considered not compliant with Victoria's environmental protection policies. As in the US, wastewater agencies are required to progressively reduce nutrient concentrations in effluent discharged to waterways over time. What if the availability of recycled water, coupled with lower demand for its use, allowed its discharge into streams to enhance in-stream flow – an important environmental objective during drought (Victorian Water Industry Association 2007; Western Water 2010; 2013)?

Victoria allows wastewater agencies with exceptional needs to take cost-effective steps toward full regulatory compliance if it can achieve other environmental objectives. In this instance, while nitrogen and phosphorus might not be reduced, discharging treated effluent might lessen the risk from other pollution sources including synthetic steroids from urban runoff and nutrients from livestock. Moreover, other environmental benefits might be produced, such as a stream healthy enough to support the beloved platypus.

Before Western Water could adopt this scheme, however, protagonists agree that engagement by ecologists and community stakeholders – as well as water agencies – will need to occur. If successful, further adoption of the offset scheme would allow discharge of effluent to waterways, allowing environmental benefits to be counted as a beneficial use of recycled water, and Western Water could achieve the goal of 100 percent beneficial reuse of effluent. While Western Water and other water providers view this as a money-saving approach, Victoria EPA would also like to determine if an offset approach offers greater flexibility for meeting environmental objectives that can be applied in other watersheds. The scheme – if it is advanced – may still be years in the offing (Feldman et al. 2015).

Unlike the North Carolina case, the Victoria situation has not yet been implemented. A life-cycle analysis comparing offsets and other options will probably have to be undertaken by performing a detailed ecological assessment of the watershed, and the net impact of potential management measures. A stakeholder participation process to engage the community and assess concerns has already begun.

The politics of unconventional pollutants

As recently as a decade ago, few people had ever heard the phrases "contaminants of concern," "emerging contaminants," or "persistent organic pollutants." Today these different, but largely synonymous, pollutants – which have as their common source the use and disposal of personal care, household, or other consumer products – are among the most troublesome sources of pollution worldwide. They include a wide range of toxic chemicals that can be transported long distances, persist for long periods in the environment, and accumulate in one or more species and are then distributed to others through the food chain.

These contaminants are so ubiquitous as to practically beggar the imagination. They include many common prescription as well as over-the-counter drugs and cosmetics ranging from nutraceuticals (vitamins) to pain-relievers, antibiotics, and even veterinary drugs, as well as fragrances, antimicrobials, surfactants, and fluorescent whitening agents. Some newer classes of chemical compounds such as nano-materials and genetically modified food items, as well as pesticides, polycyclic aromatic hydrocarbons (PAHs), polychlorinated biphenyls (PCBs), and dioxins are also included as contaminants of concern because, and surprisingly, they are often found in ordinary household products ranging from furniture to lawn and garden products and fire extinguishers. What makes them "emerging" is not their newness, but the fact of their recent recognition as posing risks to health and the environment (Glassmeyer 2007; US EPA 2015).

Of particular concern is that they can enter the environment after we (or domesticated animals) use them; sewage and waste treatment systems are generally not equipped to remove them without sophisticated and expensive modifications; and the risks they pose to human health and the natural environment are not fully understood. While the concentrations of these substances in public water supplies are generally low (when they can be detected at all), they may disrupt aquatic endocrine systems and increase bacterial resistance to antibiotics in even small doses.

Moreover, the number of such chemicals is growing annually, and not all of them have been tested for toxicity. World-wide, countries have begun to work together on a four-pronged strategy to address this problem: long-term *monitoring* of their accumulation in water supplies; introduction of advanced treatment technology to remove contamination caused by pharmaceuticals and personal care products (PPCPs) (granulated carbon, UV light); dedicated public outreach programs to encourage their appropriate disposal (e.g., disposing in land-filled trash, not in drains); and community "take back" programs for their safe disposal. Despite bans on the manufacture of some contaminants of concern (e.g., PCBs), others remain difficult to manage or regulate as a result of industry resistance.

International agreements such as the Stockholm Convention provide a register, and a means for countries to coordinate efforts to cooperate in reducing threats from persistent organic pollutants. Dioxins and furans are tightly regulated in Europe and North America (declines of over 80 percent have been achieved). However, the more ubiquitous of these substances, such as "microbeads" – typically found in many personal care products (see box 3.3) remain largely impervious to compelling action, despite a variety of bans proposed by many nations, and several US states.

While proposed bans have recently been supported by several multinational corporations (e.g., Unilever, Johnson & Johnson, and Procter and Gamble – which have promised to discontinue their manufacture), and over 60 NGOs representing 32 countries, various US state bans define micro-beads in ways that allow legal loopholes for products that degrade slightly after disposal, and provide no timeline or definition for what is deemed fully biodegradable (Rochman & Kross 2015).

Conclusion: a "green" solution to pollution?

The politics of water pollution has largely revolved around finding engineered solutions to the problems of waste disposal and treatment, minimizing threats to water quality through regulating discharges, and – primarily – protecting human health through various methods

Box 3.3   What are "micro-beads" and why should we worry about them?

Commonly found in soaps, bodywashes, toothpaste, lip gloss and nail polish, microbeads are tiny plastic particles usually smaller than two millimeters in diameter. While their composition varies, they often contain polyethylene (PE) or polypropylene (PP), polyethylene terephthalate (PET), polymethlyl methacrylate (PMMA) or nylon – in short, plastic.

Because most wastewater treatment systems do not filter out microbeads, they are becoming widely found in bays, gulfs and seas, and inland waterways worldwide – and that's not all: fish species we harvest for food have been known to eat micro-plastic particles at an alarming rate and the toxins absorbed in those plastics transfer to the fish tissue.

Plastic microbeads absorb persistent organic pollutants (long-lasting toxic chemicals like pesticides, flame retardants, motor oil and more) and other industrial chemicals that move up the food chain when the toxic-coated beads are consumed by fish and other marine organisms.

In the US, the FDA requires that if a product contains microbeads, the company has to list the ingredients. Not all countries require this, however. Several US states, Canada, Australia, and many EU nations are considering bans on products that contain plastic microbeads. Many of these bans on microbeads do not go far enough – much proposed legislation contains loopholes allowing microbeads to be replaced with other kinds of plastics, and no formal ban can remove the micro-beads already found in our waterways.

Perhaps this issue exemplifies what some call a "wicked problem." Companies want to keep the plastic in their products because: it is cheap and easy to source; smoother than natural alternatives like apricot shells, jojoba beans, and pumice; and thus, a better exfoliant for daily use. Unfortunately, it also generates divergent risks to people and the environment, and poses tradeoffs between providing solutions to certain social problems at the expense of creating another.

Sources: Rittel & Weber 1973; Barnes et al. 2009

of abating contaminants in drinking water. In recent years, another paradigm has emerged: one predicated upon a combination of more integrated approaches to land-use planning and water management (primarily to better manage non-point pollution) coupled with employment of various innovations – both centralized and decentralized – to diversify local water supplies.

Variously called Low Impact Design (LID) in the US, Integrated Urban Water Management (IUWM) in the UK, Water Sensitive Urban Design (WSUD) in Australia, or more generally "integrated water resource management" or IWRM (Wong & Brown 2009), these approaches share the objective of bridging the artificial divide between water supply and quality. Predicated on the idea that the effects of pollutant runoff, especially that caused by storm water, can be most effectively addressed as close to the source of the problem as possible, these approaches require a renegotiation of the hydro-social contract to hasten acceptance of new ways of conceiving of water quality management in cities.

This new paradigm has begun to take hold in many urban areas around the world. Localized remedies such as storm-water harvesting via rainwater tanks connected to roofs so as to provide water for domestic and neighborhood use; rain gardens; bio-filters and bio-swales and lagoons, as well as other "natural pollutant attenuation" approaches are being used to pre-treat pollutants, encourage groundwater basin replenishment, and reduce runoff into creeks, streams, and estuaries (Burns et al. 2014).

LID strategies rely conceptually on using the environment itself as a sort of "natural capital" – a means of offering a kind of green infrastructure to improve the efficient use of water as more sustainable and affordable alternatives to traditional water development schemes – what we often term "gray infrastructure." Politically, this approach offers many challenges. We discuss several of these in detail later.

As for water quality, implementation of management strategies for integrated water management requires overcoming two major institutional impediments. The first of these is zoning and urban design rules that dictate streetscape concerns related to so-called "best management practices." These include location, size, and aesthetic "fit" with neighborhood-based codes, dwelling proximity, and responsibility for upkeep. They also include the need to determine how to share and allocate costs among various beneficiaries (Berke et al. 2003; Naidoo et al. 2006; Huitema et al. 2009).

A second institutional obstacle is inter-jurisdictional: the administrative systems that affect the use, development and management of water and the delivery of supplies at a quality suitable for designated end-uses. Because the impacts of these innovations often straddle many jurisdictions and affect a large number of diverse stakeholders, processes that facilitate consultation with various groups across these jurisdictions is necessary.

In California, for example, where special planning "sub-regions" for LID measures have been established, incentives provided by state-level funding for adoption of LID innovations has helped forge collaborative arrangements among large water utilities and other distributors. However, these collaborative arrangements are highly variable and it is not yet certain that levels of trust among non-governmental partners will be sufficiently high to encourage a high quality of conjoint planning (Hughes & Pincetl 2014). Experience has shown that concerns over fairness in implementation of LID approaches are bound to arise, especially in communities with lower-income and other under-represented groups who have legitimate concerns that their health and well-being are adequately protected.

As appealing as integrated water resource management or IWRM is, however, it is not without significant political challenges. Among these are defining the boundaries or spatial scope of an effort to establish its principles. If defined as "the watershed," what defines its boundaries, and who defines them? Assuming these arrangements span various jurisdictions, what sorts of collaborative arrangements must be established to render decisions having wide consensus? And, given the impacts upon, and implications for IWRM decisions upon water infrastructure, certain types of land uses, and project financing, will communities be willing to relinquish political control over these factors to some non-local entity (Young 2002; Blomquist & Schlager 2005)?

An intelligent path forward is to engage the community, planners, developers, water agency officials, and others to explore the following issues – with special regard for their significance in the context of an uncertain, climate-change constrained future. First, storm-water-harvesting systems must not only be built, they must be satisfactorily maintained; and their product water has to be used for potable substitution, such as for flushing toilets. Widespread adoption may be hampered by concerns held by some water professionals and segments of the public regarding using treated urban runoff as a substitute for freshwater supply. Studies suggest that acceptability is generally contingent on perception of the safety of product water use, trust and confidence in managers responsible for its oversight, assurance that responsible organizations are well trained, and incorporate stakeholders in decisions (Podolosky 2012).

While these factors are important, other issues also affect the inclination to adopt – or not adopt – LID approaches. These projects may dramatically affect land values by requiring large and sometimes highly coveted areas of land for development of LID facilities. Negatively, they may also impede various utility or other operations along waterways. On the other hand, if done with wide input from a variety of stakeholders, they can be implemented in ways that generate numerous employment, real estate, and construction benefits.

As cities throughout the world face an uncertain, climate-change constrained future, an issue we discuss in chapter 5, inducements to adopt LID measures for both water supply and quality may become more attractive. If so, their adoption will require significant changes in processes of decision-making for the protection of water quality – and water supply.

SUMMARY

- Efforts to mitigate water pollution are mostly tackled as local efforts to protect human health; only later encompassing environmental impacts in larger regions.
- An important issue is the availability of innovations that serve many objectives: supply as well as quality, for example.
- The objectives of water quality policy have changed over time – from providing clean, safe water for people, to also social equity and environmental amenities.

RECOMMENDED READING

- A global synopsis of water quality problems, particularly in developing countries, is found in: WHO (World Health Organization), *Safer Water, Better Health: Costs, Benefits and Sustainability of Interventions to Protect and Promote Health* (2008).
- A comprehensive analysis of current US water pollution programs is J. A. Hoornbeek, *Water Pollution Policies and the American States – Runaway Bureaucracies or Congressional Control?* (2011).
- Perspectives on various strategies for managing water pollution are offered in R. R. Brown, N. Keath, & T. H. F. Wong, "Urban Water Management in Cities: Historical, Current, and Future Regimes," *Water Science & Technology* (2009). The article discusses how urban water quality management has evolved through several historical phases reflecting changes in science, public attitudes, and institutions. Also, D. L. Feldman, A. Sengupta, L. Stuvick, E. Stein, V. Pettigrove, & M. Arora, "Governance Issues in Developing and Implementing Offsets for Water Management Benefits: Can Preliminary Evaluation Guide Implementation Effectiveness?" *WIRES Water*, 2015, discusses how economic incentives can be supplemented by other techniques to improve water quality.

WEBSITES

- http://water.epa.gov/lawsregs/lawsguidance/cwa/tmdl/dec3.cfm The TMDL Process (March 2012 update).

- http://www.wilsoncenter.org/publication/quest-for-clean-water-chinas-newly-amended-water-pollution-control-law covers water pollution policy in several countries, including recent policy in China.

QUESTIONS FOR DISCUSSION

1. What are the obstacles to protecting water quality in developing countries? How can they most effectively be overcome?

2. Why are some water quality problems more complex than others? What makes "emerging contaminants" a particularly complex political problem?

3. How do low-impact developments and other "integrated water management approaches" seek to integrate water quality and water supply management?

CHAPTER 4

The Water–Energy–Food Nexus

Complicated links between food, energy, and water

All food sources depend on water for processing and manufacturing, as well as for growing crops. Similarly, most forms of energy require water for cooling and locomotion (e.g., steam generation in nuclear and fossil fuel plants). While it is easy to conjure up figures on how much water is *used* to produce food and energy, as various *World Water Development Reports* note, for example, it is much more difficult to ascertain how much water is actually *needed* for these activities. This is because of growing demands for food and energy, and debate over how our reliance on water could be reduced if we were less profligate in how we use water. Moreover, as for other water uses, "these uncertainties are compounded by the impact of climate change on available water resources" (UN Water 2012: 2).

These and other uncertainties surrounding connections between water, energy, and food – and their political ramifications – are the focus of this chapter. Solar voltaic and wind generation are notable in being sources of electrical energy that do *not* directly rely on water to generate power. However, they are not entirely disconnected from water, or from water politics. The manufacture of solar panels has been linked to contamination of rivers and streams in China, Taiwan, Malaysia, and the Philippines. Transforming metallurgical grade quartz – the material from which most solar voltaic panels are comprised – generates large amounts of silicon tetrachloride. While recyclable, it is expensive to reuse, leading some manufacturers to discharge the by-product into streams, releasing hydrochloric acid that pollutes waterways, acidifies soils, and releases harmful fumes.

Another dangerous chemical, hydrofluoric acid, used to clean photovoltaic wafers, has been known to kill fish and livestock in rivers adjacent to solar panel manufacturing facilities. One such incident occurred in 2011 in Zhejiang province, China (Mulvaney 2014). In many countries, weak regulation and powerful economic pressures deter effective action to avert such accidents and disposal methods.

Because wind power does not require water for cooling or for generating electricity, it avoids water withdrawals and consumptive uses (i.e., water not returned to its original source). However, this also means that water not used for power generation becomes more readily available for other uses, posing other challenges. In Western Europe, for instance, the EU Commission is considering the impacts of energy policy on absolute and "per kilowatt hour water use" in preparing proposals for a 2030 climate and energy framework to assure electricity system security and resilience. This issue may become divisive in the future as hard choices regarding energy facility siting and looming water shortages become more imperative (European Wind Energy Association 2014). For example, should anticipated deficits in water that might be available for power generation spur more wind or solar power development – or, conversely, will failure to develop these sources lead to greater water use for energy?

Similar issues have arisen within the US. A Department of Energy study concluded that communities in water-stressed regions could meet growing energy needs without increasing demands on scarce water resources by greater reliance on wind and solar power. This would also provide "targeted energy production" to serve critical local water system needs such as irrigation and municipal systems – a connection to the food and water. Estimated water savings in the interior west from wind power developments – measured as water withdrawals averted, and water not consumed – are, for a 1,200 MW plant, 3.15 billion gallons and 1.89 billion gallons, respectively, while for a 4,000 MW plant, these savings rise to 10.51 billion gallons and 6.31 billion gallons (US Department of Energy/Energy Efficiency and Renewable Energy 2008; American Wind Energy Association 2015).

Globally, the overall use of water for the production of various forms of energy is projected to decline over time due to greater reliance on renewables and higher rates of energy conservation (see table 4.1). This is a trend that has important implications for water and energy use, as we shall see.

Trends in the "food–water" nexus are more complex because of changing patterns in global agriculture. Cultivating crops for "biofuels," for example, has grown steadily in recent years – a development that fosters an unusually problematical link between water, energy, and food, as we shall also see. Moreover, national variations in available arable lands pose special problems in some countries such as China.

Table 4.1 Water withdrawal by sector by region (a) Population, energy consumption and water consumption for energy, 2005–2050; (b) as (a) but with improved energy efficiency

(a)

World	2005	2020	2035	2050
Population (million)	6290	7842.3	8601.1	9439.0
Energy consumption (EJ)	328.7	400.4	464.9	518.8
Energy consumption (GJ/capita)	52.3	51.1	54.1	55
Water for energy (billion m³/year)	1815.6	1986.4	2087.8	2020.1
Water for energy (m³/capita)	288.6	253.3	242.7	214.0

Source: Adapted from WEC (2010, table 1, p. 50, various data sources).

(b)

World	2005	2020	2035	2050
Population (million)	6290	7842.3	8601.1	9439.0
Energy consumption (EJ)	328.7	364.7	386.4	435.0
Energy consumption (GJ/capita)	52.3	46.5	44.9	46.1
Water for energy (billion m³/year)	1815.6	1868.5	1830.5	1763.6
Water for energy (m³/capita)	288.6	238.3	212.8	186.8

Source: Adapted from WEC (2010, table 2, p. 51, various data sources).

The construction of Three Gorges Dam on the Yangtze River, discussed earlier, was not only an expensive energy project (costing an estimated US$30 billion, and a source of dislocation for hundreds of thousands of people, but it also destroyed valuable arable lands – China has only 7 percent of the world's total land available for farming (Wong 2015). Together with policies that encourage profligate water use through underpricing of water and inefficient irrigation practices, none of this bodes well for the country's efforts to rationalize food production (Wong 2015).

Some contend that food and energy interests exert a disproportionate influence on the process by which decisions to manage water for food and energy are made. In the US, for example, historians who have studied the development of major reclamation and power projects in the American west, for instance, have been drawn to this conclusion (Worster 1985; Pitzer 1994). Others maintain that the water–energy–food "nexus" is an excellent example of the so-called distributive model of politics – whereby politicians target public policy outcomes to voters or other key political support groups by providing tangible benefits to constituencies living in specific regions. While blatant, or at least very strong, favoritism is shown in targeting these policies, cultivation of support is often made *after* these projects have been implemented – a means of strengthening reciprocally-beneficial political networks – a phenomenon that has been observed in India as well as the US (Golden & Min 2013).

To better understand the links between these three policy areas, we need to recognize that while water, food, and energy are directly connected by engineered infrastructure, they are also directly connected by politics. Decisions to control and allocate water in order to promote agricultural productivity and facilitate abundant energy supplies have been consciously made in both highly industrialized countries and developing nations.

Since the early twentieth century, increases in food productivity and the advent of an "age of plenty" has been widely recognized as having been made possible through massive energy-intensification in agriculture, various biotechnology innovations, and engineering applications in irrigation, and through other technological advances. All of these were brought about by political decisions to harness rivers through building large dams and other infrastructure.

Likewise, reliance on fossil – and later nuclear – fuels as well as long-standing reliance on various forms of both high- and low-flow hydropower, resulted from conscious decisions to utilize water for energy. In both instances, the intended motives were to increase regional productivity and prosperity, as well as the quality of life for residents of various watersheds (Entekhabi 2013).

Another inter-connection that is becoming widely recognized in discussions of the water–energy–food nexus is the impact of greenhouse gases, generated by fossil fuel emissions, on food production and water availability. While global change induced by carbon emissions has direct impacts on weather, climate, and water, greenhouse gases also degrade soil conditions which, studies show, may be mitigated – or repaired – by integrated nutrient and pest management as well as more efficient management of water and energy use on farms.

In recent years, students of water politics have affirmed the overall challenge posed by the water–energy–food nexus as one of resource security – ensuring that food production practices, energy generation, and water uses are integrated in ways that ensure no one of these sectors becomes unsustainable in the face of growing demands. In short, acknowledging that activities in any one of these sectors generate negative externalities that affect the sustainability of the others (Stockholm Environment Institute 2011). The 2011 Bonn Conference – whose preparatory foundation was laid by the Stockholm Environment

Institute (SEI) – helped illuminate the political challenges clearly, and in a manner that remains influential in policy circles.

In Bonn, participants discussed how productivity and the availability of water, energy and land vary enormously between regions and production systems, as well as how potential to increase resource efficiency by addressing tradeoffs between, say intensive agriculture – which may have high water productivity on one hand, but low energy productivity on the other, by "addressing externalities across sectors" (Stockholm Environment Institute 2011). For example, according to the SEI, nexus thinking:

> would address the energy intensity of desalination (also termed 'bottled electricity'), or water demands in renewable energy production (e.g. biofuels and some hydropower schemes) or water demands of afforestation for carbon storage. Also, action to avoid land degradation saves water and energy, for example by increasing soil water storage and groundwater recharge, as well as reducing the use of energy intensive fertilizer (Stockholm Environment Institute 2011: 5).

One means of achieving integrated management on a large scale is by grouping together intake systems for water and energy distribution in agricultural regions (Lal 2004; Jiménez-Bello et al. 2010). The political changes needed to achieve this goal are formidable, however – as we shall discuss. Let's examine these connections – starting with water and energy.

Nexus I: The Politics of water and energy – power, process, purpose

We now explore four critical aspects of the politics of the water–energy nexus. These are: (1) the quest for economic development through expansion of energy supplies – especially electrification; (2) balancing the need for environmental protection against energy production; (3) integrated resource management for water and power (i.e., better synchronizing demands for each, as well as their interconnections); and (4) using water for oil and gas extraction (i.e., hydraulic fracturing for fossil energy extraction, also known as "fracking").

The harnessing of rivers to generate electricity and promote other economic benefits has been widely practiced in many countries – and in many different eras – especially during the Great Depression of the 1930s and, later, the post-World War II period. Despite long-standing connections between energy and water management in large-scale river basin management plans, however, connections have often been described mechanistically – under the assumption that operational decisions are largely engineering problems, and only secondarily as questions requiring an understanding of politics. Despite this, numerous political hurdles have had to be overcome to develop such schemes (Hooper 2005).

A few river basin management schemes have explicitly acknowledged the political connections between water and electricity for regional development. The Niger Basin Authority, Tennessee Valley Authority, Damodar Valley Corporation (India), and Snowy Hydro (Australia), for instance, are all comprehensive schemes that were established to promote economic development. This comprehensive mission is not only articulated in their charters, but these agencies have often encouraged, with various degrees of success, integrated planning for water, electricity, and other resources (Hooper 2005).

Australia's Snowy Mountains Scheme illustrates the complex politics involved in integrating these three sectors into a single plan. When designs for harnessing the Snowy River, which rises in the Australia Alps, were originally proposed in the late 1940s, two competing plans were initially forged by the states of New South Wales and Victoria, respectively, making policy compromise difficult.

The former proposed that the Snowy River be diverted into the Murrumbidgee River for irrigation and agriculture – and placed little emphasis on hydroelectricity generation. By contrast, the latter wanted a larger generation of power, and diversion of the Snowy River into the Murray River system. A third state, South Australia, weighed in with other concerns: that either of these plans, if adopted, might reduce downstream flows on the Murray River, the principal water source for agriculture in the region and for the city of Adelaide (Bergmann 1999; Australian Bureau of Statistics 2012).

Federal intervention was required to reconcile these divergent aspirations, and to authorize, fund, and build a coherent project. However, at this time, the Australian central government (the "commonwealth") exercised limited authority in forcing a solution without agreement by the states. Thus, special legislation was required to establish a broad-based national plan for harnessing the Snowy River system, and to empower its operation. Following the issuance of findings by a special committee formed in 1947 to examine not only the use of the Snowy River, but diversion of several neighboring and connected streams including the Murray and Murrumbidgee, a comprehensive management scheme was proposed and agreed to by ministers from Victoria, New South Wales, and the federation in 1948.

Finally, in 1949, parliament passed the Snowy Mountains Hydro-electric Power Act establishing the Snowy Mountains Hydro-electric Authority with responsibility for the investigation, design, and construction of the scheme. The final plan, implemented following state approval in the early 1960s, was considered "a milestone towards full national development" as a result of its commitment to the dual purposes of meeting the need for increased generating capacity after World War II and in diverting the Snowy River inland to Australia's dry western region (Australian Bureau of Statistics 2012). Ultimate approval and implementation was the result in no small measure of the fact that the project served multiple purposes and, thus, placated many interests.

Forging closer political connections between the energy and water sectors has become the focus of regional organizations devoted to addressing the economic development needs of poorer countries. In 2013, a water dialogue convened by the Southern Africa Global Water Partnership urged "breaking down silos towards integrated planning and implementation of development imperatives" by addressing food, energy, and water links within watersheds. It urged that government agencies and civil society groups able to speak for all three of these sectors (water, energy, *and* food) come together within place-based, regional management entities – a lofty goal.

It also called for examining case studies of collaboration that result in closer integration of energy and water planning; foster strong private–public partnerships; incorporate climate change considerations in managing these inter-connected sectors; and strengthen the capacity of river basin authorities to use price mechanisms and legal authority for coordinating these sectors. The aim of such case studies is to draw lessons regarding how to foster socially equitable outcomes through incorporating civil society groups in decisions – thus ensuring that such schemes actually operate as a "nexus" (Global Water Partnership 2013).

Balancing environmental protection goals against the production of energy is a more recent development in the water–energy nexus. One of the best examples is the Colorado River basin in the southwestern US. Disagreement between environmental interests that have sought to protect the vast un-dammed canyons and tributary streams still remaining, as well as the basin's endangered species on one hand, and economic interests concerned with water storage and power generation on the other, have been recurrent issues in this basin. The operation of Glen Canyon Dam and Lake Powell has been at the forefront of this debate.

In 2009 a US District Court ruled that the "flow regime" for Glen Canyon Dam was damaging habitat needed by the endangered hump-back chub in the Grand Canyon. This decision required the US Fish and Wildlife Service to reconsider how the dam's operations affect chub habitat. However, because the suit – partly brought by the Grand Canyon Trust – noted that water releases for power, timed in ways that did the most damage to downstream ecology, it also implicated the dam's operator, the US Bureau of Reclamation. As an attorney for the plaintiff stated, "It is time for Reclamation to act responsibly when it comes to protecting one of this nation's great natural treasures" (Pitzer 2009: 1).

Meeting this objective and balancing these twin issues of water for electricity supply on one hand, and endangered species protection on the other, has been a difficult challenge. In the 1990s, the Interior Department instituted the *Glen Canyon Dam Adaptive Management Program* in collaboration with affected states and tribal nations in the basin. In May 2012, as a result of the court's decision, the Bureau introduced two long-term research and experimental programs to ensure high-flow releases, protect native fish, and improve the Grand Canyon by better conserving downstream sediment (a key to habitat restoration) as well as controlling non-native fish predation.

While some native flora at the canyon base has recovered, on the whole, these measures are all *adaptive* steps that require continuous monitoring, assessment, tweaking, and – most of all – long-term commitment to program maintenance to ensure they work as they were intended, especially in light of long-term climate changes. Such persistent program commitment, however, may be beyond the capacity of current governance affecting the region. Will changes in federal government administrations result in re-alignments of the priorities for this program? Could the operational regime for Glen Canyon be revised in a direction that more strongly favors power generation over ecological protection (Office of the Secretary 2012; US Bureau of Reclamation 2014)?

Recent studies have examined whether water and electricity – from various generating sources – can be conjointly governed in an integrated fashion. This is an especially difficult challenge because these resources are typically regulated by different agencies of government and provided by different utilities. In the US, while nearly 40 percent of freshwater withdrawals nationwide are used for thermoelectric power plants, variation by state is huge.

California, a recognized leader in coordinated planning at the intersection of these resources, uses less than 1 percent of its freshwater withdrawals for thermoelectric power generation. This is largely achieved through policies that require power plant developers to consider dry cooling – using air, rather than water, to cool steam used in generators. Its statewide renewable portfolio standard requires that 33 percent of its electricity be powered by renewable energy sources by 2020, and between 1996 and 2004, 22 percent of all new electrical generating capacity in the state uses reclaimed wastewater, while over half of newly-planned electric capacity as of 2015 is slated to use reclaimed water (US Department of Energy 2014; US Government Accountability Office 2015). All of these measures save water as well as energy.

While many studies concur that: "when we manage one of these resources we are really managing both," and that more serious attention should be paid to how effectively this conjoint management occurs (US Department of Energy 2006), integrated management is very difficult to achieve. One hurdle is identifying the impacts different electrical power plants have on water resources and, conversely, the vulnerabilities of specific types of electricity generating systems to changes in water availability. While a number of investigations have attempted to determine the water use impacts on electricity generation – and the impacts of transporting, heating, and treating water on electricity use, ranges of estimates vary widely.

In the American west, for example, such estimates do not include estimates of energy consumption – especially, the costs of pumping water over mountains. Moreover, the federal government does not compile information on energy use by water projects except for hydropower projects that explicitly *produce* electricity (Macknick et al. 2011; Fort & Nelson 2012; Water in the West 2013).

In addition, there are regulatory challenges in changing electricity generation options in order to conserve water. Some states and communities impose restrictions on using reclaimed water, particularly municipal wastewater, in order to lessen the impact of electricity generation on water supplies and wastewater treatment. Cost, performance, and physical limitation factors also may impede widespread adoption of wastewater reuse as a means of saving water and energy (Electric Power Research Institute 2003).

"Fracking" as microcosm of energy–water nexus politics

Hydraulic fracturing or "fracking" is the process of injecting water and chemicals at high pressure into shale rock formations to fracture rocks and extract gas and oil. A water-intensive process, it often employs toxic chemicals, the composition of which is proprietary and thus frequently not disclosed. It is also a proven and effective means of extracting these fuels. In 2001, some 2 percent of US gas and oil were produced through hydraulic fracturing. Today, due to its more widespread practice, some 35 percent of US gas and oil reserves are being tapped through this approach. The US is currently the world "leader" in this practice, with China not far behind.

Worldwide, public officials are beginning to focus on the potential contamination of surface and groundwater from hydraulic fracturing chemicals – and with the salts, heavy metals, and radionuclides this process may release. In the US, Congress requested that the EPA conduct a study to better understand the impacts of hydraulic fracturing on drinking water resources – which concluded that no visible harm has been generated. At the state level, there is an evolving patchwork of policy responses to ensure operators and regulators effectively manage potential water supply and quality issues arising from hydraulic fracturing. Some states (e.g., New York) have enacted drilling moratoria in certain resource basins and watersheds in an effort to protect water quality.

While fracking is often publically contentious, the importance accorded energy development tends to drive policy. China, with some 36 trillion m^3 of shale oil reserves, is the world's leader in potential yields from fracking. The government wants to produce some 6.5 billion m^3 of shale gas annually. Of 13 provinces selected as priority areas, seven currently suffer from acute water shortages – and, while water for extracting gas will compete with water demands for food production, industrial uses, and public supply, there have been no plans to relent on fracking – as we will discuss (Yang et al. 2013; Biello 2014).

Fracking has also become widespread in Europe (the UK and Poland, especially – see box 4.1, p. 91), Asia, and Australia. France and Bulgaria are, notably, the only European nations that explicitly prohibit the practice of fracking – largely due to fears of the risks to local water supplies and their quality. The highest risks of fracking to water quality emanate from improper storage and handling of fluids at the well site; spills and improper lining of pits; injection of wastewater into disposal wells (which can trigger earthquakes); and the potential for groundwater contamination from chemicals.

Despite growing reliance on hydraulic fracturing as a means of unleashing millions of cubic feet of methane and billions of barrels of petroleum, there is little consensus on how to manage its risks. One recent analysis of legislative needs for regulation of fracking in California, for instance, noted that while known risks to water quality stem primarily from the causes listed above, a paucity of peer reviewed studies on the actual risks to water quality, as well as a lack of other credible and unbiased information, impedes sound policy-making (Kiparsky and Hein 2013).

Lack of credible information not only leads to a lack of public confidence but – by the energy industry's own admission – apprehensions have not been effectively alleviated. In many places, public clamor for regulations to sharply curtail fracking through public notice and review, as well as proposals for outright bans, have been introduced. Polarized views regarding benefits and risks, resistance by energy producers to transparency, low levels of public trust, and lack of credible, unbiased information are at the center of current debates over fracking and its impacts (Kiparsky & Hein 2013).

Those who take a *precautionary* approach to the politics of environmental risk (e.g., the European Union) tend to also take a very stringent approach to the governance of fracking. In 2012 the EU adopted a risk-based framework to provide a "clear, predictable and coherent approach to regulating unconventional fossil fuels" (AEA Technology 2012). A prime concern is that, because fracking is water-intensive, and some water used in the process is unrecoverable, adverse impacts to aquatic habitats and ecosystems, as well as to regional water supplies for public use, may result.

For some EU members, these issues have become politically contentious. France represents one of the more extreme models of protectiveness and has adopted an anti-fracking stance. The country sits upon one of the largest deposits of shale gas in all of Europe, much of which lies beneath the city of Paris. Despite pressure by a number of energy giants who claim they have the expertise to safely extract the gas, and who appeal to France's need to decrease its reliance on imported gas from such sources as Russia (Chu 2014), the government has formally banned the use of chemically-treated water injected under high-pressure for deep-bore drilling. President Hollande has stated a commitment to keeping this ban in effect indefinitely because of concerns over protecting the country's pristine rural character, natural beauty, and integrity of its groundwater – a resource already affected by serious contamination.

However, economic pressures (France, like other EU members, imports much of its natural gas from Russia) are leading to a push within the country's economic ministry, and by other EU partners to at least undertake an assessment of the potential gas reserves extractable through fracking, and to commit itself to using as many home-grown reserves as possible to counter dependence on Russia. Moreover, if the

Box 4.1 Fracking as local dispute – energy and water in Poland

What if directly under your country lay the third largest supply of recoverable shale gas in all of Europe; the supply was sufficient for 35–65 years; and your only other source of gas in the vicinity was one of two politically volatile neighbors? Welcome to Poland.

For over a year, Chevron sought to develop a shale drilling site in the country's southeast but was eventually deterred by vocal protests organized by residents of a village of fewer than 100 residents who formed an environmental group to oppose its efforts. Green Zurawlow – named after the village – blockaded the proposed site, plastered the village with banners, placards, and posters, and inspired groups in other European countries to organize comparable "anti-fracking" campaigns.

A 2012 study by the Polish Geological Institute estimated recoverable shale gas volumes under the country at between 346 and 768 billion m^3. With the country bordering Ukraine, and heavily reliant on gas from Russia, the attraction of secure domestically-produced supplies had a lot of initial appeal. As former prime minister Donald Tusk stated in 2011, "After years of dependence on our neighbour (Russia), today we can say that my generation will see the day when we will be independent in the area of natural gas and we will be setting terms," adding that well-conducted exploration, "would not pose a danger to the environment."

What happened? Test wells have not performed as expected or suffered regulatory delays, and foreign investors have pulled out. In addition, falling oil prices, continued supplies of cheap coal and EU pressure to increase cost-competitive renewable power generation have all fueled opposition. And environmental impacts from test bores have fueled conflict. Local roads were damaged from seismic tests, and some villagers claim their water wells became polluted from these tests. There have also been reports that water tainted by shale salts may have entered the Radunia River which supplies water to Gdansk, the birthplace of Poland's Solidarity movement.

Chevron's public outreach campaign has also backfired. While the company has donated to several charities in the region, and offered gifts to residents' children, it has also been accused of bribing local officials and vocal dissidents.

Finally, while the debate has become a classic "jobs" vs. "environment" contest – the latter has been more compelling. Although the region suffers from high unemployment, the former mayor of Zurawlow, a supporter of Chevron, lost re-election to an opponent who favors geothermal energy. And, in November 2015, the French water company, Veolia, was ordered to stop processing shale effluent in a nearby water purification center because of permitting infractions.

Source: Neslen 2015

UK does manage to drive gas prices down through exporting shale gas, France may have no other recourse but to embrace such a policy as well.

In the US, leadership in the politics of anti-fracking has come mostly from environmental groups. The Natural Resources Defense Council has proposed putting critical watersheds off limits. It has also suggested requiring adoption of strong well siting, casing, and cementing and other drilling best practices, and it endorses the right of communities to restrict fracking through zoning ordinances.

In contrast, China, home of the world's largest shale gas reserves, has a number of regions that already suffer from severe water stress (<2000 m^3 available per person), and has little regulation to deter harmful depletion of water reserves also needed for the agricultural, industrial, and domestic sectors. Geological conditions make it likely that fracking fluids returned to surface waters will introduce heavy metals, acids, pesticides, and other hazardous materials to soils and aquatic environments – worsening water pollution risks in these regions. Moreover, with few groundwater quality protections, and few robust protections for water supply or regulations to sufficiently protect water from contamination (see chapter 3), these concerns are likely to increase as mining and extraction efforts accelerate (Yang et al. 2013; Biello 2014).

As with other energy–water nexus issues, an important question is whether fracking is any more environmentally harmful than, say, reliance on the burning of coal or the use of nuclear energy. As in these cases, debates over fracking tend to be disputes over competing purposes: preservation of pristine water supplies versus economic exploitation of fossil energy. Likewise, as in other water–energy nexus debates, power over decisions is concentrated in the hands of select groups – environmental and energy interests and their respectively supportive governmental ministries. Process is even more complicated, with international markets and the desire to be competitive and independent of other countries being important political factors affecting fracking prospects and determining which risks – economic or environmental – are most important to decisions.

Nexus II: water–energy–food

Connections between water use, energy consumption, and food production – as well as appreciation for "sub-connections" among them (e.g., high energy demands to move water; relationships between water shortages from drought, food productivity, and food prices) have long been recognized. Despite this, no single, clearly articulated purpose has guided the politics of the water–energy–food nexus.

One compelling narrative is emerging in the politics of this nexus: given changes in climate and a growing population, (and, thus, growing demands for energy, food, and water), a conservation-animated purpose *should* guide this nexus. Such a conservation-animated purpose would seek to balance the world's growing appetites for both food and energy while using water more sustainably. Can this purpose be achieved?

Production of ethanol and biodiesel fuels, especially for transportation, has increased some 100-fold since 1975: approaching 120,000 liters annually since 2010 (Shrank & Fahramand 2011). Moreover, overall energy demands are expected to grow by some 60 percent over present needs by 2030 in developing countries. As a result, greater demands for biofuels, produced by converting biomass such as trees, grasses, left-over agricultural residue from crop harvesting, and algae, are likely to arise. These demands, and the way they drive the use/re-use of these products, will impose dramatic impacts on local economies in three principal ways.

First, diversion of cropland from food to energy-crop production, coupled with efforts to restrict imports of food to *encourage* more domestic farming and greater food security, will likely cause food prices to rise. While agriculture accounts for some 70 percent of total global water withdrawals, in less developed regions where energy-crop production is growing the fastest (figure 4.1), it accounts in some

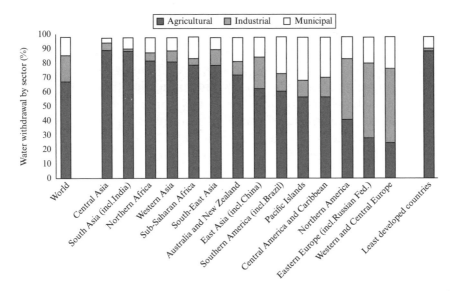

Figure 4.1 *Water withdrawal by sector by region (2005)*

Source: FAO AQUASTAT(http://www.fao.org/hr/water/aquastat/main/index.stm,accessed in 2011)

cases for over 90 percent of use. Thus, demands for water are also likely to increase its price.

Ethiopia is a good example of this challenge. Committed to investing at least 10 percent of its national budget to improvements in agriculture, the country greatly requires foreign investment to improve infrastructure, water and land productivity, and personal incomes. While rehabilitating marginal lands and growing rain-fed crops could increase benefits to the water, energy, and food sectors, the focus of national investment is currently high-input agriculture, including biofuel production that can generate short-term increases in revenues (Stockholm Environment Institute 2011).

Second, population growth in less developed nations will escalate demands to produce more food, increasing pressures to consign more land to cultivating crops. At present, increased costs and environmental impacts from various "inputs" into crop production such as fertilizers and pesticides, which farmers are compelled to apply to their lands to ensure high yields and ample profits, are becoming acute in many developing countries, while rapid conversion of virgin forests, meadows, and grasslands into cultivated farms and grazing land will further degrade freshwater quality and, in downstream communities, contaminate drinking water supplies.

Third, as food prices rise, the cost of water used for production of *both* food and biofuel crops, and to treat new sources of water supply contamination resulting from this higher production, will *also* increase. The added costs of energy for pumping groundwater to irrigate these crops, and the impacts on water supplies of energy demands, pose another little recognized but important connection (UN Water 2012). These impacts will continue to be mostly borne by the poorest and least powerful members of society: those living in rural areas are forced to produce *more* food, fiber, and biofuels to sustain their livelihoods, and to pay more for clean, potable water.

Another important factor in the water–energy–food nexus is the process of decision-making. As is the case for water supply and quality, the politics of energy and food are policy-making realms dominated chiefly by regional interests – including landowners in agriculturally rich but water-poor regions, and industries seeking sources of cheap, plentiful energy. In the US, for example, irrigation remains the dominant category of water use in western states, despite urban population growth. Consumptive water demands for agriculture have long been a primary impetus for construction of large-scale, centralized provision systems.

Water devoted to agricultural uses in the American west comprises some 80 percent of total western supplies. While modest shifts of agricultural water to municipal and industrial uses could meet growing urban demands, the losses that would be sustained by food production are thought by many to be a serious tradeoff that would dramatically affect local economies (US Bureau of Reclamation 2012).

As in the water-energy portion of the water–energy–food nexus, the last decade has witnessed a growing effort to identify ways to encourage better integration of these sectors. One impetus for this integration is to ensure that food production – especially food equity – is better embraced in decision-making. One potential tool is integrated assessment, an emerging approach to understanding the ecology of urban areas. An advocate for this approach has been the UN's Global Water Partnership (GWP). GWP has sought a less fragmented means of managing water, land, energy, and related resources in order to maximize social welfare more equitably, ensure food security, and permit adaptation to a changing climate.

GWP and others pin their hopes on a process they refer to as strong "inter-sectoral dialogue." Advocates of this approach start from the premise that the water–energy–food nexus is obviously shaped by a wide range of forces including domestic markets, global trade agreements, agricultural subsidy policies (at the national level, especially), energy prices, and even poverty reduction/economic development policies and programs. All of these have profound impacts on local interactions between the food, water, and energy sectors. Thus, keeping all these factors in close alignment is difficult, if not utterly impossible, except at the local scale where stakeholders can work together to apply integrative approaches that fit the contours of food production – and food needs – in a given region (Moriarty et al. 2007; WWAP 2009).

For the water sector, they urge greater emphasis on integrated water resources management, particularly at publically accessible local scales, to achieve higher levels of food production with less water and less energy. Some scholars prefer the phrase "integrated crop water management" to suggest ways this can be practically achieved. They point to the need to understand the vegetation dynamics of different regions. They also noted that water management options traditionally vary from country to country.

While water harvesting by collecting excess rain run-off in cisterns is common in the Sahel region in Africa, it is not widely used in semi-arid regions in Asia or North America. Moreover, while the yield increase potential of crop water management is especially large in water-scarce regions such as in China, Australia, the western US, Mexico, and South Africa, recent studies suggest that governance factors are absolutely essential for making these methods work. For example, if upstream farmers reroute otherwise wasted water to increase irrigation and production, less water returns to downstream users affecting the latter's production – suggesting that "a lot of local government regulation and incentives such as-micro credit schemes are needed to put crop water management into large-scale practice" (Jägermeyr et al. 2016).

Can these three sectors be politically aligned? Can laws and fiscal measures that influence water management, service delivery, and levels of demand become truly integrated? And, can they be spatially linked in order to promote equity?

Two case studies from India illustrate the steps that might be taken to make the water–energy–food nexus a truly connective network through political reform (see box 4.2). Keys to reform are three-fold: modifying traditional subsidies of both water and power; directly involving food producers in monitoring, establishing rules, and implementing conservation practices for water and electricity; and demonstrating real economic gains through these practices that benefit entire communities.

In sum, the water–energy–food nexus has nurtured a powerful, technocratic dominated decision-making network that is information-intensive and increasingly hierarchical (Entekhabi 2013). Power tends to be concentrated in the hands of technically-trained people employed by private and public entities. Control of this network – as well as its benefits for food and energy production through harnessing water more efficiently – are characterized by disparities among rich and poor nations.

Global food and energy production tends to favor wealthier nations that control information and dominate technology innovation. Water-rich countries are also able to control flows of "virtual" water in the form of food exports (McLaughlin 2013). To the extent reforms are achievable, they not only help bring about alternative routes to local prosperity in developing countries, but they also reduce the concentration of power over these essential resources in the hands of technocratic elites, thereby broadly distributing greater authority to non-elite groups.

Conclusion – the future nexus and its political challenges

The current water–energy–food policy landscape is complex and fragmented. Water and energy policies have been developed independently of each other, and in many cases there are strong regional and

Box 4.2 Groundwater governance and the water–energy–food nexus in India

The states of Andhra Pradesh and Gujarat have undertaken groundwater reform programs in an effort to avert overdraft, maintain food security, and conserve energy. The Netherlands-funded "Andhra Pradesh Farmer Managed Groundwater Systems (APFAMGS) Project" was implemented by the UN's Food and Agricultural Organization in the late 1990s. Instituted in over 630 villages in seven drought-prone districts, the program's goal was to forestall groundwater depletion in a large, extensive shallow aquifer system.

A participatory hydrological monitoring program was established to provide farmers with the knowledge, data and skills to understand the hydrology of groundwater, while a series of local groundwater management committees in each aquifer or hydrological unit estimate the total groundwater available in a district, and prescribe appropriate cropping systems to match. The committee disseminate information to the entire farming community and also encourage water saving and harvesting projects, promote low investment organic agriculture, and help establish rules to ensure inter-annual sustainability of groundwater resources. Results have been positive: there has been a substantial reduction in groundwater use through crop diversification and irrigation water-saving techniques and greater profitability despite less water use.

In Gujarat, the traditional provision of free groundwater and subsidized electricity to pump it contributed to severe groundwater overdraft, near bankruptcy of the State Electricity Board, and poor power supply to farmers and rural residents. Efforts to rationalize pricing were met with local resistance, politicians lost their jobs, external funds for modernizing the system were withdrawn, and pressures on local aquifers continued – all, that is, until an alternative innovation was introduced: the Jyotigram Scheme embraced continued power subsidies but provided them contingent on a more rationalized basis. Villages are given 24-hour, three-phase power supply for domestic use and in schools, hospitals and village industries, all at metered rates. Farmers operating groundwater tube-wells continue to receive free electricity, but for 8 rather than 24 hours a day, and they receive it on a pre-announced schedule designed to meet peak demands.

The separation of agricultural energy from other uses and the promise of quality supply gained political support for the plan. The Jyotigram Scheme has dramatically improved the quality of village life, spurred nonfarm economic enterprises, and halved the power subsidy to agriculture. While groundwater is still free, the scheme has indirectly raised the price of groundwater supply from tube-well owners in the informal market by 30–50 percent, thus providing a signal of scarcity, and reducing groundwater overdraft. Jyotigram is now a flagship program of the Government of Madhya Pradesh, Karnataka and Andhra Pradesh.

Sources: Shah and Verma 2008; IWMI 2011; Govardhan Das and Burke 2013

national differences in policy frameworks and objectives. Given the importance of water in energy production and the increasing uncertainty of available water supply for energy, there is a growing need for a more coherent approach in managing relationships between these sectors. While observers frequently speak about the need for regional institutions able to integrate sectors (Stockholm Environment Institute 2011), existing institutions that have the confidence of nation-states – including some river basin compacts and commissions – may be in the best position to address this goal, but only if they can be strengthened through consent of their member states.

For food and water, the political nexus is perhaps even more problematical. The production of food and fiber, and of biofuels, affects water supply and quality in incredibly complex ways. More crop cultivation adds more nitrogen into the earth's metabolism exacerbating greenhouse gas production, algal blooms, and eutrophication in lakes, rivers, and estuaries. While the latter problem could be averted by policies that encouraged the use of feedstocks with lower nutrient inputs, biofuel production will still put pressures on surface and groundwater supplies in already over-taxed and vulnerable crop-growing regions.

Changes in agricultural subsidy policies might affect this nexus in favorable ways by, for example, a variable subsidy for ethanol production depending on its profitability; greater encouragement of cellulose biofuel production as opposed to corn ethanol; and, as noted earlier, pollution abatement practices which encourage overall nutrient reduction in farming (NRC 2008). The challenges in making such changes will be huge given the entrenched power of some agricultural and biofuels interests, however, and the resistance toward changing long-standing tax and subsidy policies. This is another example of the "path dependency" issue discussed earlier.

The energy–water nexus faces a comparable set of political challenges that, like the food–water nexus, are largely technical in origin, but strongly dependent on politics in order to be reformed. For example, the ability to "match" energy availability and water demands might lead to more efficient ways of using both resources. However, unlike the electricity sector, the water utility industry is dependent on the availability of its sources and is unable to "generate" water on demand. Moreover, most efforts to, for instance, "ration" water in times of drought or shortage depend on the voluntary willingness of consumers to cut back. Unlike electricity use, consumers cannot be compelled to adjust their use of water on demand.

By the same token, advanced automation and better weather forecasting processes can help conserve water and energy (e.g., foreknowledge of extreme weather events such as "El Nino"). These innovations could better guide and inform siting and adaptation decisions for new power plants or water supply sources. Achieving such integration, however, requires inter-agency coordination and data sharing which, up to now, have rarely proven to be easy – even in climate-savvy places such as California, for instance – due to inconsistent funding, weak staff support within agencies, and lack of guidance regarding how to fairly divide costs among agency partners (Feldman 2015).

Recent research has concluded that a number of ventures could be useful in reforming the energy–water (or water–energy) nexus, especially in highly developed economies. These include the assistance of third party "certification" programs to evaluate efficiency performance. Examples are programs such as those offered by the US Environmental Protection Agency's (EPA) Energy Star, Water Sense, or the US Green Building Program's Leadership in Energy and Environmental Design (LEED) initiative. Innovations that depict the impacts of different energy and water uses: from precision water-energy reports on handheld devices in the home, to utility-level tools permitting better demand forecasting are also important innovations. Who will pay for them remains an open question, however.

There are creative ways to fund such innovations – cap and trade funds or surcharges on utility bills, for example. However, any new source of funding is likely to generate controversy, and assigning benefits and costs to participants engaged in efficiency programs will require upfront agreements in order to assure that electricity and water providers undertake follow-on assessments of joint efficiency programs and share information on costs relative to benefits. There are models for rebate programs to encourage water conservation and end-use efficiency – such as those for low-flow appliances, installation of more efficient landscape irrigation systems, and even installation and replacement of lawns with drought-tolerant landscaping, as we will later discuss. Finally, many electric utilities have a good record of providing rebates for energy-efficient appliances. Clearly, opportunities are available.

Effective policy frameworks must be able to project policy scenarios that incorporate future variables such as climate change. They also should encompass changes to energy technologies so as to accommodate their possible impacts on water availability (US Department of Energy 2014). These options assume, of course, that policy-makers share consensus over the problem of climate change. As we discuss in chapter 5, such consensus on that issue is far from certain.

SUMMARY

- Globally, the production of food and energy constitute the largest uses of water and are closely intertwined. Their interconnections strongly influence the exercise of power and the processes of decision-making for water.
- Energy–water nexus issues revolve around development through electrification; protecting water quality while producing energy; achieving integrated management of water and power; and employing hydraulic techniques for oil and gas extraction.
- An important narrative in the "food" aspect of this nexus is how climate change, population growth, and food and energy demand are creating new challenges for managing all three resource sectors in a more integrated fashion.

RECOMMENDED READING

- A good overview of the water–energy nexus is featured in US Department of Energy, *The Water–Energy Nexus: Challenges and Opportunities* (2014) – a thorough review of technological, economic, social, and regulatory challenges facing the integration of these sectors. More regionally-focused, Denise Fort and Barry Nelson, *Pipe Dreams: Water Supply Pipeline Projects in the West* (2012), provides an excellent discussion of the water–energy nexus on the western US and the political implications of further efforts at inter-basin water diversion. Also, see the National Research Council's *Water Implications of Biofuels Production in the United States* (2008). This report considers the ramifications of biofuels on water supply and quality, and the prospects and opportunities for policy reform.

WEBSITES

- http://www.scientificamerican.com/article/can-fracking-clean-China. "Can Fracking Clean China's Air and Slow Climate Change?" *Scientific American*, January 27, 2014.
- http://www.water-energy-food.org/en/news/view__1892/food-energy-water-nexus-an-integrated-approach-to-understanding-chinas-resource-challenges.html
- www.unwater.org/documents.html UN Water 2012.

QUESTIONS FOR DISCUSSION

1. How does the development of biofuels complicate the water–energy–food nexus?

2. Why are debates over the environmental and other risks to water from "fracking" so contentious?

3. What types of economic incentives can help to conserve water use for energy production and food production? What barriers must be overcome?

CHAPTER 5

Drought, Flood, and Everything In-Between

Water as extreme hazard

Flood and drought are natural events that are often made worse by human action. How is this so? Flooding is a periodic and entirely normal event that may occur whenever rainfall, snowmelt, "super" tides or other phenomena conspire to force streams to overflow their banks, or sea levels to rise above normal heights. This happens when too much precipitation falls within a brief period over a landmass, rapid snow melt causes too much water to flow, or tropical storms sweep waves of water onto the shore.

We worsen these natural conditions by paving over porous surfaces, and then exposing them to hazardous chemicals from lawns, gardens, and even parking lots – thus assuring that runoff will be greater in volume, and more degraded in quality. We also worsen flooding when we alter streams and shorelines through dredging, channelizing, stream straightening and shoreline and stream-bank development – placing more people at risk. Some contend that when we construct protective measures to alleviate flood damage, we also encourage more building within floodplains, exposing more people and property to risk – and generating an illusion of security.

Droughts, like floods, are also normal events. Severe, long-lasting droughts have been historically traced in reconstructions of past climates – especially in regions such as the American west (Diaz & Wahl 2015). While scientists continue to debate whether recent droughts are temporary, or represent the emergence of a "new normal" caused by climate change, there seems to be strong circumstantial evidence that long-term changes in climate are leading to warmer temperatures, less precipitation in many regions, more winter rainfall as opposed to snow, earlier snowmelt, and decreases in spring and summer stream flows.

Again, the consequences of drought can be worsened by human action. Overuse and poor management of scarce water resources, together with measures that encourage, rather than suppress, over-use of water – especially for end uses not especially appropriate to the climatic conditions of certain regions – can contribute to stress, and worsen impacts on water-dependent local economies. In the future, if more intense droughts do occur, they are likely to generate more intense heat waves and wildfires, placing additional burdens on water supplies. Potentially adverse impacts range from soaring demands for energy for cooling (at precisely those times when water for power generation is likely to be in short supply) to the need to relocate residents from wildfire-prone areas adjacent to cities (Aghakouchak et al. 2015).

In short, decisions over how to cope with drought and flood are infused with politics. Flood and drought policies tend to be formulated by public works and water management agencies in collaboration with private interests that seek to control and harness rivers and waterways, store surface water for extended time periods, and – once flooding or drought occurs – provide bountiful relief and recovery-driven efforts for the losses communities suffer from these events.

The desire to avoid or abate floods has been a significant driver of demands by various interests for river channelization, dam-building, flood-proofing, floodplain management, and, of course, for flood recovery efforts on the part of those enduring loss. Likewise, compensating for the effects of drought has been a powerful motivator for harnessing rivers, over-drafting groundwater basins, rationing or reallocating water supplies, and – more recently – for schemes to conserve, re-use, and more efficiently manage water. As in other areas of water policy, drought and flood politics also intersect with other policy domains, including the politics of migration, urban planning and the built environment, and environmental justice.

Finally, flood and drought politics take place in a domain best characterized as natural hazards management. This is a domain where the ability to improve flood and drought forecasting, and to precisely predict threats to human life and property, are increasingly being pursued in order to dissuade people from putting themselves in harm's way. In recent years, an important question has been raised with respect to hazards management: are there strategies that can influence people's perception of the risks from extreme events and help them better adapt? We also examine this issue.

Flooding and drought – political process

Decisions on how to manage, prepare for, or reduce threats from drought and flood are made by a ubiquitous category of officials called "water managers." Because water serves a number of functions – from municipal supply to agriculture and energy production – the term covers a wide variety of officials, each of whom shares "decision space" with other managers at various levels of policy-making. This is significant for the process of flood and drought politics for three reasons.

First, officials have divergent interests and political roles. This makes coordinated responses – and the setting of priorities – difficult. The municipal water official charged with imposing lawn watering restrictions during drought may share authority for drought management with, say, a national agency official charged with operating a storage reservoir, members of the legislature who must make choices regarding funding for recovery efforts for an endangered species, and regional (state/provincial) officials who purchase water to comply with regional water compacts.

While sharing decision space, when it comes to both drought and flood, these officials may have little time in which to make critical decisions; operate under pressure from political, legal, economic, and other forces; and have divergent interests. For example, because farming on floodplains is profitable, efforts to avert flood damage through building levees or other projects may compel some officials to forge alliances with groups that want to enhance water supply, as opposed to, say, those favoring the protection of ecological resources (Ray et al. 2007).

Second, weather extremes can lead to disasters: the one (drought), a slow onset crisis; the other (floods) occurring more rapidly. Water managers are acutely sensitive to the salience of crisis, and the relative costs of action versus inaction. They often have to weigh the financial and administrative consequences that arise from efforts to cope with flood or drought, while simultaneously worrying about more routine matters such as finding water and supplying it to customers.

Although the former may be more catastrophic in their consequences, the latter are ongoing imperatives that make long-term planning for climate extremes a political challenge. There is only so much time officials have to spend on all the problems they potentially confront (Cash et al. 2003). Moreover, because the responsibilities, rewards, and resources for hazard reduction are borne by numerous officials who are motivated by different goals, it is often difficult to reach a political consensus before a disaster regarding how to coordinate responses (National Academy of Sciences 2014).

Third, water managers are bound by institutional constraints that affect how they respond to weather extremes. These constraints also influence the resources, authority, and incentives at their disposal when they do respond. A manager given authority for fortifying a region against flooding or drought, but having few resources at her disposal – and few regulatory or institutional incentives to respond – may perceive these threats to be lower in priority than more routine tasks (O'Connor et al. 2005). Moreover, because many water managers work for mission-oriented agencies that often require them to operate within narrow procedures of decision-making – sometimes referred to as "heuristics" – they often tend to become conservative and risk averse during crises, especially when they have incomplete or uncertain information regarding the magnitude of a hazard.

Water managers are more likely to trust familiar information, and to discount information from outside as opposed to internal sources. The former is more compatible with their organizations' missions (Kahneman et al. 1982; Knopman 2006; Vandersypen et al. 2007). These process factors arise in both highly-developed as well as developing countries alike, and can be seen in responses to flood and drought.

Varying power, evolving process, divergent purpose – flood

As a type of natural disaster, flooding does not impact everyone equally. Moreover, flood hazards can be partially attributed to human negligence, arrogance, or hubris. Earlier, we cited the case of the Hungarian tailings dam collapse of 2010 that inundated a large area along the Marcal River. In addition to causing serious water and soil contamination, it was also an example of human-made flooding, killing nearly a score of people and inflicting considerable damage to property – all because of Hungary's failure to adopt EU environmental protection guidelines designed to protect the public from such hazards (The Kolantar Report 2011).

Another example is the Indus River basin floods in Pakistan in 2010, where wealthy landowners in southern Sindh province dynamited dikes to protect their flood-threatened properties. Levee systems were breached at locations adjacent to poorer villagers where farmers grew wheat, rice, and cotton. The latter were powerless to oppose their wealthy neighbors' armed militias. Breeching the levees not only worsened the disaster, but also ensured that its impacts fell most heavily on those least able to recover (Rodriguez 2010).

Between such extremes, the roles of power and purpose in flood politics inhabit a more problematic domain, particularly as regards flood abatement. In the US, for example, a common response to flood hazard is fortification. Post-Hurricane Katrina, New Orleans is often cited as the "poster child" for the politics of flood fortification, at almost any cost, to restore at-risk neighborhoods and to compensate poor communities for long-term and disproportionate burden sharing (Morse 2008). A better example, however, is Sacramento, California, one of the nation's highest catastrophic flood-risk zones.

After years of pursuing fortified levees, upstream impoundments and other measures endorsed by agricultural, real estate, and residential interests, changes in federal flood abatement policy have led to political changes in state and local strategies. Since 2005, led by the Sacramento Flood Control Agency (SAFCA), the region has adopted a combination of fortification measures and non-structural approaches designed to shift the burden of abatement costs on those building on flood plains. Changes in floodplain land-use policies are also being gradually modified to encourage risk-averse behaviors to lessen property losses (see box 5.1).

This case study reflects a larger change in flood policy and a subtle shift in power. An oft-cited refrain of flood plain politics is that society-as-a-whole consistently bears the burdens and costs of flood

---

Box 5.1   The Sacramento Solution – many measures, gradual risk reduction

A number of expert sources consider the Sacramento region the most flood-prone city in the nation. A 2011 *New York Times* article quoted experts as stating that "an earthquake or violent Pacific superstorm could destroy the city's levees and spur a mega-flood that could wreak untold damage on California's capital region."

Although long dependent on expensive structural measures to avert serious flooding, since 2005, the region has adopted several measures at a cost of $4.1 billion. These include a combination of structural fortifications and more adaptive measures:

- Fortify existing levees on American River – adding anti-seepage "cutoffs."
- Enlarge Folsom Dam (but NOT building new dams) – 2008.
- Offer preferred risk flood insurance to residents of American and Sacramento River floodplains.
- SAFCA adopted a Development Impact Fee program to offset effects of future floodplain development projects.
- Residents in the so-called "200 year floodplain" voted to assess themselves special tax to finance local share of improvements.
- In 2007, the state adopted land use and environmental enhancement policies for the region (e.g., more wetlands restoration) to offset flooding.

While these steps are adaptive and more flexible than remedies adopted in the past, as even the US Army Corps of Engineers concedes, the Sacramento area remains "among the most at-risk regions in America for catastrophic flooding."

risks accepted by – and sometimes foolishly and voluntarily adopted by – those who choose to reside in flood-prone regions. Reality is more complicated, however. For some, residing in a flood-prone region is a choice knowingly taken because the amenities of living near water are perceived as outweighing the risks. For others, however, one resides and works where land is most readily available and affordable.

After more than a generation of debate, the US Congress in 2012 adopted a significant policy change in the federal flood insurance program initiated in 1968. This reform reflects a subtle shift in power toward groups concerned with the cost of subsidies to re-build and the desire to embrace the real risks of floods in community decision-making. The Biggert-Waters Flood Insurance Reform Act extends the US National Flood Insurance Program (NFIP) while requiring significant program reform in order to make it more financially stable, while ensuring that flood insurance rates more accurately reflect the real risk of flooding.

Over time, the costs and consequences of flooding have continued to increase, making the NFIP fiscally unsustainable. Biggert-Waters adjusts premium rates to better reflect the true cost of flooding; a greater proportion of insurance holders will no longer pay subsidized rates. Those with subsidized policies for non-primary residences, businesses, or severe and repetitive property losses will lose subsidies, and, subsidies will no longer be offered for policies covering newly purchased properties, lapsed policies, or new policies covering properties for the first time.

Rate changes will have the greatest effect on properties located in Special Flood Hazard Areas (SFHA) constructed before a community adopted its first Flood Insurance Rate Map (FIRM) (Guston 2001; Biggert-Waters Act 2012). In short, these changes in flood insurance policy represent a subtle shift in power away from flood insurance beneficiaries and towards advocates of fiscal conservatism. Whether these reforms produce a better risk management framework will take time to assess.

With respect to power, process, and purpose in flood politics, there has been growing appreciation of the importance of flood hazard information in averting harm and changing peoples' attitudes and behavior toward flood risk. An important discovery in recent years is that risk information must be delivered through multiple media, traditional and electronic, to ensure that all types of vulnerable populations are reached. While younger populations are more reachable through Internet sources, older communities still receive flood risk information, both for preparedness and for hazard alleviation, through more traditional sources of media.

While social media can connect various informal information sources to diverse groups, older populations continue to be less receptive to receiving flood risk information from social media sources, suggesting the continued existence of a "digital divide" (Cretikos et al. 2008; Bird et al. 2012; Feldman et al. 2016). Related to this is the persistence of what students of risk communication term "risk information deficit" – the lack of confidence in risk communicators by the lay public, especially by older less information-"savvy" recipients – a phenomenon that has been observed in coastal communities vulnerable to flooding in Australia and California, for instance.

Social media may "democratize" access to risk information making it more readily available to various members of the public. However, trust and confidence in those responsible for managing flood hazards will continue to vary depending on overall trust and confidence in government, and in the opinions of experts of various sorts.

Information, trust, power, and purpose – drought

At the other climate extreme, the management of drought offers profound lessons in the exercise of power in water politics. An important aspect of power inequalities in the case of weather extremes generally – and drought in particular – is the availability of information on its probability and consequence for people from diverse backgrounds. Access to, and usefulness of such information for under-represented groups is often characterized by an "asymmetry of knowledge," which varies greatly from country to country, and even different regions in the same country.

In northeast Brazil, scientists, local farmers, and a variety of community groups now work together to prioritize water protection policies and programs; institute participatory management councils and user groups to negotiate water allocation agreements; and institute new and novel management methods. This was not always the case. In the 1990s, an interdisciplinary group in the state water management agency in Ceara, COGERH, was established to foster collaboration between social and natural scientists working for the state water agency on one hand, and local farmers on the other.

Traditionally, there was little trust or mutual regard between these two groups. Thus, the goal of this effort was to develop a series of participatory management councils in the Lower Jaguaribe-Banabuiú River and to negotiate water allocation agreements that effectively account for changing weather conditions. Staff scientists (*técnicos*) currently work with farmers to disseminate knowledge about drought and storage reservoir operations so that the latter can enhance their ability to respond to drought and flooding.

The exchange of information that is taking place through these efforts is serving to build trust and confidence between local stakeholders and central government officials. It has also resulted in a greater willingness among basin residents, including farmers, within the basin to share the risks of weather extremes, avoid over-depletion of local supplies, and locally monitor water conditions (Lemos & de Oliveira 2004; 2005).

One of the ongoing challenges in weather forecasting for extreme events that makes this "information asymmetry" common is the lack of adequate incorporation of users' needs into information networks through empowering people to be able to use weather information. This requires providing adequate training and outreach, reward and development opportunities, and most of all – by soliciting from users input regarding what kinds of information are most useful for effective flood and drought preparedness or recovery. In effect, this entails more than merely sharing power; it is predicated on viewing climate and weather information as having a broader *purpose* – as a tool of education, enlightenment, and, ultimately, citizen empowerment.

In many parts of the world, the politics of drought (as well as flooding) are becoming more democratic, bottom-up, and collaborative, largely as a result of two complementary changes in the alignment of power regarding climate and weather information. The first is growing apprehension over climate change, which is opening up opportunities for under-represented groups with knowledge and insight over its effects upon local water use to influence decisions. The second change is growing pressure by under-represented groups for greater equity, fairness, and representation in flood and drought decision-making. This is beginning to compel a more inclusive view of information, especially, in larger cities.

Confidence in drought information, and thus trust in government-prescribed solutions and remedies, also reflects larger issues regarding trust in political institutions, especially when persistent drought strikes an area not usually subject to it. Taiwan affords a recent case. Generally receiving some 98 inches of rain a year, Taiwan is so plentifully supplied with water that utilities charge extremely economical rates, and water use is traditionally profligate – with per capita usage higher than that in Western Europe or the US.

A lengthy drought beginning in 2013 depleted many of the nation's reservoirs, leading to restrictions on the use of tap water supplies to five days a week in towns in northern Taiwan, including some suburbs of Taipei. The drought also led to severe rationing along the west coast and compelled greater use of recycled water in factories. The country's 94 reservoirs are currently at an average 50 percent of capacity and the central government is considering a number of vigorous, and potentially controversial, remedies for relief. These include massive dredging of silted-up reservoirs and imposing higher water rates to provide capital reserve for repairing and replacing the country's notoriously leaky urban water infrastructure.

Plans to deliver water – household by household, if necessary – to the elderly and disabled are also being implemented. Rates charged by the government-run Taiwan Water Corporation are scheduled to increase by some 10–30 percent in 2016 with the highest tiers to be applied to the island nation's biggest water users.

Despite this flurry of political activity, there has been a remarkable absence of complaint, virtually no public "panic," and a largely positive behavioral response to the need to conserve. All of this appears to reflect the nation's political culture, and the electorate's largely trustful attitude toward the state. Few have complained about taps being turned off, and many citizens are voluntarily finding ways to save water and to use it more efficiently in the household and workplace.

According to one regional official whose district has been especially hard hit: "(p)eople know the government has prepared, so they're not panicked," and the government has widespread support for re-examining water management practices ranging from reservoir management to urban water distribution networks (Jennings 2015: A5). In effect, citizens view drought politics in Taiwan as a means of showing patriotic loyalty to the system. Measures being pursued to adapt to the drought are largely viewed as socially equitable, and compliance with them is seen as reinforcing political stability and economic continuity.

Climate change and water politics

Climate change is one of the most contentious environmental issues of our time. Although scientific consensus over climate change is strong, it is still viewed with skepticism in some quarters. In a number of countries – not just the US – some critics contend that certain groups are using the issue as a pretext for remaking economic and, especially, industrial policy. They also contend that these groups are using climate change as an excuse to tighten environmental standards with respect to water use.

The impacts of global climate change on water are enormous. As far back as the 1980s, climate scientists' models indicated that changes in patterns and amounts of precipitation would be an important consequence of climate change (Waggoner 1990). Growing demands for water, as we have discussed – even without the added burden of climate change – are placing enormous stress on water resources. These demands come from increasing population and expansion of human activity into semi-arid regions across the planet such as the American Southwest, Spain, North Africa, and the Middle East. Demands are also growing in other drought-prone regions such as the Southeast US. Moreover, we now know that previous climate changes have had dramatic impacts on past civilizations (see box 5.2).

Climate change may already be affecting the variability of precipitation worldwide. Floods that previously had a probability of 1-in-100 years are now more frequent in some areas. Snowpack – the dominant source of fresh water for the West – is lower in volume and, on average, melts earlier in the spring. This will continue to adversely impact a variety of decision-makers from farmers (who will have to plan their irrigation schedules accordingly) to water utility planners (who will have to plan ahead for potential decreases of supply in summer months, especially).

Worsening climatic conditions will have dramatic impacts especially in poorer, less developed countries, and will generate severe pressures for adaptation. Policy-makers and private sector leaders, regardless of their personal opinions about climate science, will require help

---

Box 5.2   Climate change, water politics, and the ancient Near East

The importance of scarcity for water politics cannot be over-emphasized. Recent research on the Assyrian Empire, for instance, claims that this mighty domain, powered by an overwhelming military machine, likely collapsed some 2,700 years ago as the result of a combination of overpopulation and protracted drought. Climate change alone did not prompt the empire's fall. Nor was its collapse caused by the fact that the empire's cities, including its capital Nineveh – which grew to great size through abundant, rain-supported harvests – began to suffer food shortages.

What likely happened is that under the reign of King Sennacherib, the strain of overpopulation and poor weather caused a "no harvest" period beginning in 657 BC. Within five years of this no harvest period – as chronicled by a court astrologer – the country was racked by a series of civil wars followed by a joint attack by Babylonian and Median forces that destroyed Nineveh in 612 BC. Interestingly, the authors of this study draw parallels to contemporary Iraq and Syria, asserting that current conditions in this region bear a striking resemblance to the past.

Source: Kiderra 2014

translating and applying climate knowledge to water decisions (Guston 2001). A willingness of decision-makers to act will require more than crisis. We know from our discussion of drought and flooding that the inclination to take action varies by familiarity and level of information. Officials most likely to use climate information are likely to have experienced weather-related problems in the recent past. Previous negative experience with weather extremes tends to heighten feelings of vulnerability. In short, these twin issues – translating climate information and a willingness to use it – pose serious political challenges regarding the politics of climate change and water.

The politics of water and climate are anchored by three factors. These are: a producer-driven *process* of decision-making which defines the problem in ways that are tractable to other scientists, but not always to lay audiences; *power* over information traditionally concentrated in a handful of expert participants; and a divergent perception of *purpose* held by protagonists.

The political process for climate change and water begins with the science of climate – who defines the problem; with whom do they communicate; and what influence do they have on decisions? The notion that scientific discovery and findings simply "flows" from scientists toward decision-makers who need it is a misconception of the science communication process. Climate forecasting for water is the result of a process of two-way communication between scientists and political decision-makers at all levels (Jacobs et al. 2005).

Historically, the provision of climate and hydrologic forecast products has been a producer- rather than a user-driven process. As a consequence, the development of products such as forecasts and predictive tools and models has been largely skill-based rather than a response to some explicit demand from water managers for a certain type of information. Collaboration among resource managers (i.e., information "consumers") and forecast producers can occur, and can generate a process of "mutual learning," whereby people with different disciplinary backgrounds and experiences can learn how to share information adroitly in response to specific resource management problems.

One factor that makes information sharing difficult is that scientists – and we include climatologists, hydrologists, civil and environmental engineers, or social scientists – often have difficulty communicating with one another, much less with decision-makers. This is due to differences in language, problems and foci investigated, and various disciplinary-bound issues (Sivakumar 2011).

Exacerbating these knowledge–power differentials between producers and consumers is the fact that participants in the climate–water policy-making process occupy different roles, as we discussed earlier in this chapter. Some are in the position of having a "wide angle" vantage point through which making decisions over water through application of science is possible. This may be true, for instance – at top levels of agencies charged with formulating fisheries restoration programs or watershed management policies, for example. However, other decision-makers are restricted in their access to scientific information by often being provided detailed knowledge of only relatively minor issues – enough to carry out their jobs, but not sufficient for seeing the wider horizon of the problem, or its boundaries. This is another example of power differential. Scientists have the luxury of looking at entire climate and weather systems as well as hydrologic basins. By contrast, water managers are confined by their agencies' missions and constrained by the need to serve political constituencies.

Perceptions about the usefulness of climate information vary not only by the experience of decision-makers and the public with extreme weather events, but according to the economic, regulatory, and institutional settings in which they live and work. Political ideology is also important. If a water manager is put into a position where there are few resources to fortify a region against, say, flooding or drought, or where there are no regulatory or institutional incentives to do so – and s/he tends to be risk averse, then these threats may viewed as lower in priority than more routine management tasks.

Scientists and decision-makers often have very different notions about the reliability of information. For example, as regards climate and weather, scientists are used to dealing with probabilities and comfortable with the idea that uncertainties in prediction are both normal and inherent in the problems they study. In contrast, managers often interpret uncertainty as unreliability. Water managers are also used to dealing with water variability without the benefit of climate forecasts from outside experts. They have their own routines and are much more likely to trust information with which they are familiar. Experience with climate forecasts is recent and therefore less trusted.

Finally, differences over purpose are profound. In climate change debates, three major visions have been advanced in political narratives: (1) that prevailing inequalities among nations lead to unsustainable patterns of consumption and production that require radical reform of political institutions; (2) that weak global governance and planning fail to control global markets and prevent greenhouse gas emissions; and (3) that climate change is little more than scaremongering by

Box 5.3   Climate change as political narrative: Australia

A few years ago the Australian Public Service Commission produced a report chronicling the enormous challenges facing climate change policy in reconciling the sharply divergent story-lines animating debate. In effect, as the three paradigms below suggest, strongly variable worldviews attend the issue of climate change. Each of these has enormous implications for water politics. The three dominant views are as follows:

Profligacy: Prevailing structural inequalities between countries, as having led to increasingly unsustainable patterns of consumption and production. Urgent fundamental reform of political institutions and unsustainable lifestyles is required. Decision-making needs to be decentralized down to the grass roots level. The onus is on advanced capitalist states to take action.

Lack of global planning: This story sees the underlying problem as the lack of global governance and planning that would rein in global markets and factor into prices costs to the environment. No individual contribution will make a difference. Remedying climate change requires all governments to formally agree on the extent to which future emissions should be cut, and how and when (similar to the Intergovernmental Panel on Climate Change).

"Much ado about nothing": Much of the debate as scaremongering by naïve idealists who erroneously believe the world can be made a better place (profligacy story), or by international bureaucrats looking to expand their budgets and influence (lack of global planning). Some holding this view are skeptical about climate change itself; others are convinced that, even if correct, the consequences will be neither catastrophic nor uniformly negative. Technological progress, adaptation, and dynamic markets are the solution (sometimes called a "cornucopian view").

Source: Australian Public Service Commission 2007

naïve idealists (see box 5.3). All three visions are relevant to the politics of water and climate (Australian Public Service Commission 2007).

The first two visions exemplify a growing challenge for water politics – climate change dramatically affects water security (Bakker 2009). These security-related issues shape, and potentially motivate, political action by drawing urgent attention to three major problems. The first is how to manage sea-level rise and its associated impacts including saltwater intrusion. Second, threats to water supply infrastructure from drought and flooding will generate the need for additional water storage impoundments, as well as added measures to fortify sanitation systems that may be already over-taxed (especially in developing countries). And lastly – in many third world cities, larger numbers of low-income people are living on terrain (e.g., hilly slopes, floodplains) especially prone to flooding, storm surges, and other climate-related risks (United Nations Human Settlements Programme 2011).

And, what of vision number three? The view that climate change is a fallacy is an important alternative vision for climate–water politics, which explains resistance to allowing climate issues to shape the water policy agenda, and to encourage continued reliance on conventional water management approaches and profligate water uses. Political debates over water management which take the form of "climate denial," or that are based on the premise that "droughts come and droughts go" have been seen in the Western USA and Southern Australia – among other places. These debates promise to further impede radical action to thwart the threat of climate change – or even to adapt to its impacts on freshwater (Hammer 2010).

Reforming the politics of climate and water: knowledge networks

Knowledge networks are comprised of policy-makers, scientists, government agencies, and non-governmental organizations (NGOs) linked together in an effort to provide close, ongoing, and nearly continuous communication and information dissemination among multiple sectors involved in technological and policy innovations for managing climate impacts (Sarewitz & Pielke 2007). These networks help bridge the gap between knowledge and political action (Jacobs et al. 2005).

In water policy, knowledge networks help ensure that scientific information gets used by tying together information with the needs of the user community. In the US, one of the oldest knowledge networks for water is the long-standing relationship between our excellent system of public-supported land grant colleges, local irrigation district managers, and county extension agents who, among other things, transform highly-technical knowledge about, say, drought, other weather conditions, and the needs of crops and livestock into information useful to farmers, ranchers, local governments, and homemakers. Using this example as an archetype, effective knowledge networks facilitate good communication between those who generate climate information and those, like water managers or members of the public, who need this information to manage drought, alleviate flood damage, water crops, and manage fire hazard risks.

In practice, networks perform this function by holding forums and meetings, permitting person-to-person sharing of information, and allowing water and other resource managers to share what they know about local conditions with what scientists know about, say, climate conditions generally. Networks also encourage good communication through "translation:" taking the technical, difficult-to-understand jargon of scientific forecasting and turning it into useful information for water managers and the lay public. For example, scientists often talk about the probability of floods, the likely severity of drought, and the risk of wildfires. Networks help to translate this complex information into a form that is useful to the types of decisions policy-makers have to deal with by taking information that is shrouded in varying degrees of certainty and, for example, providing decision-makers with various "if-then" scenarios, simulations, and the like.

Finally, networks permit co-production of knowledge – that is, generating new types of useful tools or technologies through the collaboration of scientists and engineers on the one hand, and non-scientists on the other, Such co-production leads to new kinds of models, maps, and other forecast products that can be used to manage real-world problems (e.g., not just knowing "what is the maximum probable flood stage of a river during large rain events?" But, "how many homes and businesses in a community will be threatened if a river crest sat a certain level outside its banks?" Moreover, such dialogue between producers and users allows users to independently verify the usefulness of climate forecast information, and in turn share what they know with scientists so that their knowledge can "feed back" into the process of generating new models. This is what we mean when we say that knowledge networks provide information that is end-to-end useful from creation of knowledge to its use, and even feed back from practical experience into new models.

Theories of network building are important, but by themselves, they tell us little about how to reform science-decision-maker/public communication for water–climate politics. Fortunately, case studies of two climate knowledge networks help to illuminate both the political hurdles – and opportunities – for reform. These cases are based in the Western Hemisphere, and are centered on arid regions – the Southwestern US and Northwestern Mexico, and north central Chile and Argentina.

The Mexico–US dialogue began in 2000 and has devised policy responses to climate variability, water scarcity, loss of rural livelihoods, vulnerability of growing urban populations, and ecosystem degradation. In addition to conducting over 30 workshops and other dialogues attended by some 30–40 researchers and over 300 stakeholders, the partnership has brokered an "urban water governance exchange" between entrepreneurs serving on the advisory council of the Sonoran state capital (Hermosillo) and the City of Tucson's water utility (Scott et al. 2012).

The United States–Mexico case is noteworthy for "the sustained participation of a broad spectrum of stakeholders" including federal agencies, as well as state, municipal, NGO, and corporate stakeholders. The latter have been instrumental in identifying and helping to strategize responses to local problems.

Specific program achievements through these stakeholder dialogues include the establishment of an Upper San Pedro Partnership to encourage sustainable use of the region's groundwater (throughout the cross-border San Pedro/Santa Cruz Basins), a US–Mexico Transboundary Aquifer Assessment Program supported by Mexico's National Water Commission and the Mexican section of the International Boundary and Water Commission, and formation of a regional climate center for the northwest region of Mexico. The latter is charged with encompassing long-term climate change issues into water resources planning. While partnerships with private sector – especially copper mining interests groups – have been less successful, public sector cross-border collaboration has been strongly solidified, and has been assisted by scientists who are eager to be trained in stakeholder engagement.

The Andean knowledge network formed between Chile and Argentina focuses on promoting national mandates to encourage adaptive water management planning. Due in part to Argentina's formal Mendoza Strategic Development Plan, which antedates this network, there is somewhat less flexibility in inviting all relevant stakeholders to participate in the conjoint planning in that nation. Nonetheless, a broad range of local, state, regional, and national agency personnel, bi-national and international organizations, NGOs and other civil society organizations, farmers associations, researchers, and other stakeholders have been involved in this network since 2008 – and in both countries.

Activities include regional drought taskforce planning, water infrastructure project planning, technical design collaboration, and information dissemination – particularly among Chilean stakeholders – on issues pertinent to water services, irrigation, and the environment – with a variety of formal and informal entities, including Aguas Andinas, Santiago's main water utility. While the latter has an acute interest in climate change impact assessment, structural changes in Chile's economy since the 1990s have resulted in the growth of specialized high profit margin "niche" agricultural activities including wine production and fruit growing. The Environmental Commission of the Chilean Congress also is actively involved as a participant.

In Argentina's Mendoza Valley, also a wine-producing region, scientists have played an important role in this bi-national knowledge network. Representatives from over 100 local organizations have produced a set of priorities around water allocation and irrigated-land use, and incorporated social as well as natural scientists in innovative ways – mostly around land-use planning and in ensuring that no legitimate stakeholders are excluded from the dialogue (Scott et al. 2012). The now completed strategic plan encompasses the influence of scientists' perspectives in integrating the interests of elected decision-makers and the local community.

Conclusion – spanning expert and lay audiences

A fundamental challenge in the politics of water and weather extremes has been how to bring diverse interests together around common perceptions of risks, desirable remedies, and goals and aspirations for averting hazards. An elusive goal in the best of circumstances, the crisis nature of drought and flood, and the economic stakes involved, make this aspiration especially difficult to achieve. Some experts suggest the need for novel political entities able to play an intermediary role between different organizations, specializations, disciplines, and practices: sometimes called a "boundary organization." In many forms of scientific endeavor, collaborators come to appreciate the contribution of other kinds of knowledge, perspectives, and expertise and how these can supplement their own labors (Star & Griesemer 1989; Guston 2001).

Boundary organizations perform translation and mediation functions between producers of information and their users. Such activities include convening forums that provide common vehicles for conversations and training, and for tailoring information to specific applications. They do this by "mediating" communication between particular areas of societal concern. In the US, local irrigation district managers and county extension agents often serve this role in agriculture, for example. Such organizations also serve the function of science translation by removing barriers caused by jargon, language, experiences, and presumptions (Cash et al. 2003).

Effective boundary organizations require individuals who are capable of translating scientific results for practical use and framing the research questions from the perspective of the user of the information. These key intermediaries in boundary organizations need to be capable of integrating disciplines and defining the research question beyond the focus of the participating individual disciplines. Table 5.1 depicts some examples of boundary organization for climate change decisions related to water.

Table 5.1 Examples of boundary organizations for climate information support in water politics

Cooperative Extension Services: housed in land-grant universities in the United States, they provide large networks of people who interact with local stakeholders and decision-makers within certain sectors (not limited to agriculture) on a regular basis. In other countries, this agricultural extension work is often done with great effectiveness by local government (e.g., Department of Primary Industries, Queensland, Australia).

Watershed Councils: in some US states, watershed councils and other local planning groups have developed, and many are focused on resolving environmental conflicts and improved land and water management (particularly successful in the State of Oregon).

Natural Resource Conservation Districts: within the US Department of Agriculture, these districts are highly networked within agriculture, land management, and rural communities.

Non-governmental organizations (NGOs) and public interest groups: these focus on information dissemination and environmental management issues within particular communities. They are good contacts for identifying potential stakeholders, and may be in a position to collaborate on particular projects. Internationally, a number of NGOs have stepped forward and are actively engaged in working with stakeholders to advance use of climate information in decision-making (e.g., Asian Disaster Preparedness Center (ADPC), in Bangkok, Thailand).

Federal agency and university research activities: expanding the types of research conducted within management institutions and local and state governments is an option to be considered – the stakeholders can then have greater influence on ensuring that the research is relevant to their particular concerns. The NOAA's Regional Integrated Sciences and Assessments program is an example (see text).

More recently, some have pointed to the NOAA's Regional Integrated Sciences and Assessments teams, or RISAs, as a more experimental form of boundary organization devoted to bridging the gap between science and policy for water and climate decision-making (Feldman & Ingram 2009). The National Oceanographic and Atmospheric Administration (NOAA) formally established RISAs. The ten current RISA teams, located within universities and often involving partnerships with NOAA laboratories throughout the US, are focused on stakeholder-driven research agendas and long-term relationships between scientists and decision-makers in specific regions.

Each RISA builds a regional-scale picture of the interaction between climate change and the local environment from the ground up. By funding research on climate and environmental science focused on a particular region, the RISA program currently supports interdisciplinary research on climate-sensitive issues. In some cases, information

specialists act in place of Agricultural Extension services in respond-
ing to user needs.

A decade ago, a Congressional committee found that the RISA program is a promising means to connect decision-maker needs with the
process of prioritizing research goals, because "(it) attempts to build
a regional-scale picture of the interaction between climate change
and the local environment from the ground up" (Feldman & Ingram
2009). Their experiences point to three factors that are essential to
this collaborative enterprise: leadership, resources, and integration
skills. Specifically, this means inclusive leaders who incorporate the
knowledge, skills, resources, and perspectives of their organizations
and the groups and other entities they serve. Often these leaders
are "change-agents" who have a guiding vision that sustains them
through difficult times, a passion for their work and an inherent
belief in its importance, and a basic integrity toward the way in which
they interact with people and approach their jobs.

While RISA programs have been successful, the RISA model is not
being widely replicated on water-related climate problems such as
coastal areas and floodplains susceptible to flooding. Sea-level rise
and greater snowmelt induced by climate change may exacerbate the
problems faced by this traditional strategy. They are already placing
pressure on the politics of flood decision-making throughout the world.

RISAs embrace the idea that flood, drought, and other wide-ranging
climate phenomena are "normal," recurring events – a point raised
at the beginning of this chapter. An emerging politics of flood and
drought hazard mitigation is beginning to wed locally generated adaptive measures to the science of flood planning. This new paradigm,
as we saw, pursues avoiding flood risks, employing "replaceable" or
low-loss land uses (e.g., don't build homes in floodplains), innovative
forms of flood insurance that reward those who avoid certain risks,
wetlands restoration, and development impact fees. While this newer
paradigm is based on sound science, the gulf between science and
politics on issues of climate remains wide. This is because translating science for policy remains difficult, while the political stakes of
changing current policy are also high. In part, this is reflected by the
slowness of changes in water law – a process that often takes a long
time, even under the best of circumstances.

SUMMARY

- While drought and flood represent extreme variations in water
  availability and its management, climate change represents a trans-

formation in baseline weather conditions that may portend "more extreme extremes."

- Knowledge networks are an important element in the politics of climate and weather extremes – because they influence how science is used for making decisions, as well as who participates in those decisions.
- Climate change has become an ideologically contested issue in the politics of water and weather extremes in many countries. This complicates finding political consensus and makes it more difficult to identify long-term solutions.

RECOMMENDED READING

- Some recent scholarship on water and climate include A. Aghakouchak, D. L. Feldman, M. Hoerling, T. E. Huxman, & J. Lund, "Recognize Anthropocentric Drought" *Nature* (2015), which considers the possibility that drought is a harbinger of longer term climatic changes which will increase the occurrence and severity of such events, and the need for efforts to reduce demands for water – in California and elsewhere. Also, Bellie Sivakumar, "Global Climate Change and Its Impacts on Water Resources Planning and Management: Assessment and Challenges," *Stochastic Environmental Research and Risk Assessment* (2011) tries to bridge science and policy-making on climate change information.
- Various drought mitigation policies have been proposed in recent years. Among the promising studies are K. G. Low, D. L. Feldman, S. B. Grant, A. J. Hamilton, K. Gan, J.-D. Saphores, & M. Arora, "Fighting Drought with Innovation: Melbourne's Response to the Millennium Drought in Southeast Australia," *WIRES Water* (2015), and S. B. Grant, T. D. Fletcher, D. L. Feldman, & J. D. Saphores, "Adapting Urban Water Systems to a Changing Climate: Lessons from the Millennium Drought in Southeast Australia," *Environmental Science & Technology* (2015), which compares the US and Australia.

WEBSITES

- http://www.ipcc.ch/report/ar5/wg2/ (2014) Intergovernmental Panel on Climate Change report.
- http://www.csiro.au/en/Research/Environment/Extreme-Events/ Floods Australia Commonwealth Scientific Industrial and Research Organization (CSIRO).
- http://www.fema.gov/national-flood-insurance-program homepage

for the US Federal Emergency Management Agency's (FEMA) flood information site.

QUESTIONS FOR DISCUSSION

1. How do human actions, choices, and policy decisions exacerbate – or worsen – the effects of flooding and drought?

2. In what ways do drought and flooding have impacts that vary among different groups? What can be done to reduce these disproportionate impacts?

3. Can you identify examples of boundary organizations that bring together scientists and decision-makers around issues of climate, drought, and flood?

CHAPTER 6

Water Rights and Water Wrongs

Why Law Matters

We have thus far discussed law in specific contexts: as a method for allocating water, a set of tools for setting standards with respect to its quality and determining (or regulating) water–energy–food connections, and as a means of protecting, averting, or recovering from the hazards caused by flooding and drought. What more can be added to this discussion? Why is there a need for a separate chapter on water law and politics?

There are four reasons water law is important. First, law is so ubiquitous that we often pay far too little attention to its importance as a factor in the politics of water. The principles of water law identify who possesses power over the allocation of water, and sanctions how beneficial uses are defined. Second, water law shapes and influences the legitimate boundaries for decisions: in effect, the scope of state power over individual behavior with respect to water – what we can and cannot do with it.

Third, when traditional statutory or common law confronts limitations posed by countervailing authority, jurisdictional constraints, or other issues – inhibiting its ability to resolve conflicts – decision-makers must find alternative means to address disputes. These often take the form of novel types of legal arrangements. Because of this, law itself becomes an important political factor in resolving disputes – whether in the form of statute, court decision, or as we will see, negotiated compact: a novel form of law.

Finally, law is the most common, and among the oldest, means of governing water. It determines how water supply is managed, and how its quality is protected from pollution. Competing systems of law that bestow rights to water through land ownership, as well as various regulatory "regimes" that allocate water among jurisdictions, are supposed to ensure that public health is safe, and environmental resources protected.

This chapter focuses on how water law systems ratify power

relationships among users and articulate divergent purpose. We also show how – despite the variety of institutions responsible for making water law – its application and interpretation is often determined by cultural traditions and practices.

While many societies manage water through common law based on tradition, juridical precedent, or practice, the political process of water law embraces a variety of domestic laws, including rules on irrigation, energy, and health. Moreover, while law traditionally has been identified with *government*, it is now very much a part of water *governance* – the global trend toward less formalized approaches to politics wherein decisions are shared by agencies, NGOs, and individuals (Rijke et al. 2012). This makes the process of water law geographically fragmented, multi-level in operation, divided among various types of organizations, interest-driven, and characterized by negotiation, adjudication, and peaceful dispute settlement – as is true for virtually every other component of water politics (Dellapenna & Gupta 2009). We can appreciate this by first looking at water law as an expression of political purpose.

Law as purpose

Water law first arose to formalize, and to institutionally enshrine, how societies should manage a presumably exhaustible resource. This is why law first arose in arid and semi-arid regions. Common to early water law was the inclination to ensure that, above all, human needs were satisfied in its use and management. It is widely believed that codified water law systems first arose, more or less simultaneously, in parts of China, India, and Mesopotamia. In the latter, water law is thought to have emerged as an effort to allocate rights to water as a scarce, seasonally variable resource, especially in the valleys of the Euphrates and Tigris Rivers. Early water law also served other purposes, including adjudicating local disputes and prioritizing socially beneficial uses. In ancient communities generally, water laws were characterized by regulations designed to codify priorities for common, shared public uses, such as growing crops and potable household uses (Boatright et al. 2004; Kornfeld 2009).

This is an important legacy for two reasons. First, despite the wide variety of water law found in both the ancient and modern worlds, certain common characteristics have long been a part of what water law seeks to do, Among these are regularizing claims to access by various groups and resolving conflicts over competing claims. Second, many contemporary arguments regarding the proper purpose of water law are not really new at all – but originated in earlier periods.

An example is the assertion that laws should "do a better job" of acknowledging that water is an exhaustible resource and that access to fresh water should be seen as a basic human right. We sometimes assume these ideas originated with modern-day legal reform efforts such as the 1991 Earth Summit (e.g., the *Rio Declaration on Environment and Development*) or with the 1992 *Dublin Statement*. In one form or another, these aspirations have long been premises of water law.

A second important political legacy of water law's historical anteced-ents is that procedural norms and structures enshrined by common law often serve to protect prevailing water uses – especially those ben-efitting powerful interests, as opposed to those of under-represented groups that are marginalized because of gender, race, ethnicity, or socio-economic background (Mirosa & Harris 2012). In short, while water law has long grappled with the notion that access to fresh water is a human right, it has simultaneously sought to narrowly define access as a form of property right – an entitlement that stems from owning land adjacent to rivers, lakes, or streams, or over-lying a groundwater basin.

In water politics, alternative ways of formulating water rights under reform efforts – for example, defining the "right" to water as entitlement to a healthy environment, or to mitigating water supply burdens upon, let us say, women – are in actuality efforts to use law to reconfigure power relations and access to authority over decisions. Both are increasingly important issues in developing nations.

Common to many reform efforts is recognition that all water law is socially constructed, and emerges from struggles among various groups for control of water and legitimization of claims to use. Thus, changing the balance of equity requires reconstructing power rela-tions so as to permit legal redress, and greater participation by these groups in decision-making – especially participation by indigenous peoples (Tisdell 2003; Boelens 2009; Boyd 2012). This is exemplified in the Andean region of South America (see box 6.1).

A second conundrum revolves around how to protect environmen-tal values and ecological resources, as well as property rights – long a contentious topic in debates over water law. Issues here include non-consumptive or "in-stream" water uses as opposed to so-called "proprietary interests" or rights to using water for economic purposes. It also includes the rights to access of displaced populations (e.g., tribal nations), as well as reserving a certain proportion of water for fish and wildlife habitat and other purposes.

Box 6.1   When water laws and their purposes conflict – the case of rural Chile

In many parts of South America, but especially the Andean region, indigenous peoples have long fought against oppressive laws and practices governing natural resources, from water to mineral rights. For over 60 years, the Likan Antai/Atacama peoples of Alto Loa in northern Chile and the copper mining industry of the area have been embroiled in water rights controversies, complicated, in large part, by laws mostly favoring – until recently – the interests of mine operators.

Because native peoples were long ago dispossessed of their communal property rights, they have also suffered from poverty, been subject to economic exploitation, and have had little control over the resources needed to support their communities. While laws and other policies tended to reinforce these conditions, in the period of military dictatorship following the overthrow of Salvador Allende in 1973, special laws designed to encourage a more liberal, market-oriented export economy created new challenges.

The so-called Water Code of 1981, for example, modified the access and use of water by formally transforming it into private property. Water rights were separated from the property of land and could be freely bought, inherited, or sold. Furthermore, incentives were created to encourage investment and speculation during periods of scarcity due to drought. Initially, water rights were given for free and to private individuals and companies, which, until 2005, were exempt from taxes and not obliged to use the water for productive activities. Allocation did not take their historical uses into consideration and indigenous communities were adversely affected – they lacked access to information about the new conditions of property and use of water, including groundwater. Most water rights were claimed by the mining industry. In 1982, another statute – the Law of Mining Concessions – granted special rights to water for those who put it into productive use on behalf of mining activities.

While these laws reinforced elite political power over water in Chile, following restoration of democratic government, in 1993, a third law – the Indigenous Law – granted native peoples ownership over the ancestral lands, water, resources, and territories they have occupied and established a special commission to compensate them for "historical pilferages" of resources.

Although designed to remedy past harms, it could not be applied retroactively. A slow process of purchasing back land and water rights from private individuals, with meager funds made available by the government, has meant that the state has continued to favor large economic sectors – including the mining industry and water companies that control most of the water rights in the region. Major mine tailing contamination has occurred in the region, further threatening what water rights the indigenous populations control by degrading supplies. In effect, even with nominal reforms, water and mineral laws in Chile continue to reflect the dominance of powerful interests. At the same time, the existence of "overlapping" laws with different goals permits some political space for indigenous groups to make some policy gains when in conflict with these interests.

Source: Gallardo 2016

Third, water law often protects the power and privilege of propertied elites as opposed to the average user. In riparian legal systems, for example, such as those found in the eastern US, Australia, New Zealand, Canada, the UK, and even parts of Africa and India, the role of property rights – versus a broader conception of the public good in water – has long been a source of political friction, as we discuss in the next section. All three of these conundrums can be seen in the example of US water law, where rights-based conflicts have frequently arisen.

American water law – power and competing purpose

The US follows two general systems of water law. Eastern states, for the most part, operate under what is called riparian law. Many of these states have also adopted statutory modifications to riparian doctrine and are thus considered "regulated riparian" states. However, most states west of the Mississippi follow a system of law called "prior appropriation." Prior appropriation law has its own body of common law that has been codified in both state and federal statutes.

Riparian law is very old. Many of its features have their origins in the law that the Romans brought to Great Britain more than 2,000 years ago. Because water, unlike air, is available in only a few places, the legal system of riparian rights responded to this fact by assigning rights to use water to those whose property touched, or overlay, a water source. Water rights are generally described as real property rights. If one owns land adjacent to a watercourse, such as a river, stream, or lake – or that overlies an aquifer – then both local custom, as well as many courts of law, would suggest you have a right to make reasonable use of the water (Tarlock 1997).

In comprehending the connection between land ownership and water rights, it is important to realize that in a riparian system, water rights cannot be sold or transferred other than with the adjoining land, and water cannot be transferred out of the watershed. In fact, riparian rights systems do not afford landowners an absolute right to a given *quantity* of water. For this reason, riparian systems do not easily permit the transfer, through sale or lease, of water from one user to another. Landowners can, however, legitimately seek assurance that these adjacent watercourses are kept reasonably clean and useable by upstream users so as to minimize harm to those users living downstream.

The so-called prior appropriation system, sometimes called the "Colorado Doctrine," in recognition of where it was initially formalized, is a system of allocating water rights where scarcity of water due to aridity and limited stream flow is the norm. While generally used in the western United States, legal details vary from state to state. The general principle – and in marked contrast to riparian rights – is that water rights are unconnected with land ownership, and can be sold or mortgaged like property. The first person to *use* a quantity of water from a water source for beneficial use has the right to continue to use that quantity of water for that purpose. Subsequent users can use the remaining water for their own beneficial purposes provided that they do not impinge on the rights of previous users.

Water rights under a prior appropriation regime differ from riparian law in several ways. First and most important, ownership of land is not the basis for the appropriation water right. One can have a right to water from a watercourse or an aquifer without owning land bordering or overlying the water source. In addition, even if the right to water has been acquired by purchase or other means, water rights exist only when water is appropriated (diverted and used) for a beneficial purpose. In most states following the prior appropriation doctrine, beneficial uses are defined, at least in general terms, by statute. State statutes may provide for preferred uses so that certain water uses are considered more beneficial than others. An example of this is irrigation. Although generally considered a beneficial use, certain kinds of irrigation, such as overflow or natural flood irrigation, have been held to be inefficient and thus can be prohibited (Tarlock et al. 1993).

Because water rights based on prior appropriation are heavily influenced by how arid the climate is – and by the historical fact of water rights being taken into private control by people staking claims to its beneficial use – conflict over water in prior appropriation regions is a frequent fact of life. In both riparian and prior appropriation systems which accord rights to water to individuals, and in *communitarian* water rights systems such as those found among Native American tribes or in tribal cultures in sub-Saharan Africa, there still remains a large *publically-adjudicated* role held by the state – made necessary by the fact that a central government has had to intervene to resolve, or at least referee, these conflicts.

This "adjudicatory" role embraces such issues as determining how and whether water can be diverted between regions; whether large water storage projects for public supply, irrigation, power generation, flood control, and/or navigation shall be built; and, of course, what types of water quality standards shall be imposed to protect public health and afford ecological protection. While the politics of prior appropriation has long determined the allocation of water rights in the west, in recent years – particularly as a result of protracted drought in the region – controversies have erupted over precisely how much water can be diverted for private use, and how extensively appropriation rights extend even to precipitation falling from the sky. At times (see box 6.2), this debate has taken on almost comical form.

Non-consumptive, in-stream water uses have also been enshrined in western water law, however: a reflection, in part, of the value placed on equity, as well as efficiency. The federal government has long held so-called "proprietary interests" in water on or under federal lands. Once these lands were relinquished to states added to the union, the national government reserved water rights to ensure public supplies on military bases, and for fish and wildlife habitat, in-stream flows in national parks and forests and – later – for tribal reservations (*California Oregon Power Company. v. Beaver Portland Cement Company* 1935; *Winters v. United States* 1908).

An ongoing debate within US water law is the question of how much water can actually be "reserved" for these national purposes – partly a matter of water rights seniority, and partly an issue of federal suprem-acy. In the face of increasing drought and diminishing flow, this issue may take on greater importance and lead to pronounced conflicts in the west, as discussed below (Gillilan & Brown 1997).

Debates over power and purpose – the West

In the western US, equity considerations are supposedly built into the prior appropriation system's criterion of "first in time, first in right." This principle predicates that it is unfair to deprive investors of water after they have worked to divert and develop the resource. This princi-ple protects rural farmers who are effectively assured that water will be provided in lean times as well as good ones.

At the same time the growing number of people living in the west made rigid application of prior appropriation law impossible – if equity was going to be satisfied. The needs of many users could not reasonably be accommodated during periods of high variation in stream flow. Moreover, environmental or "in-stream" needs are impossible to satisfy in a system where – in their purest form, water rights are biased toward off-stream and consumptive water uses. These biases of the "first in time, first in right" doctrine have, conse-quently, been reformed on a state-by-state basis over many decades. These reforms, ratified in statutory rules, were prompted by concerns over environmental damage, the need to protect public lands, and

Box 6.2   Are rain barrels an illegal diversion of water? The case of Colorado

Colorado's rain-barrel ban is little known and widely flouted, with rain barrels for sale at many home-gardening stores and commonly used by home gardeners. But the barrels technically violate Colorado water law, which says that people do not own the water that runs on or through their property. "They can use the water, but they can't keep it," the Associated Press has reported. In 2015, Democratic Representatives Daneya Esgar of Pueblo and Jessie Danielson of Wheat Ridge, and Senator Mike Merrifield, D-Colorado Springs introduced House Bill 1259, which would have allowed the collection of precipitation from the roof of a home in up to two rain barrels if certain conditions are met. The measure passed the House in March by 45 to 20 and passed out of the state Senate Agriculture committee but wasn't debated on the Senate floor.

The Colorado State University Extension office reports that water rights in Colorado are unique compared to other parts of the country. "The use of water in this state and other western states is governed by what is known as the prior appropriation doctrine. This system of water allocation controls who uses how much water, the types of uses allowed, and when those waters can be used." Water rights are purchased and many senior rights have existed for a century, so taking this liquid gold from water rights owners is like stealing. As water becomes scarcer and low-water landscaping grows in popularity, rainwater harvesting becomes more attractive and logical. The 2009 Colorado legislative session produced a bill that allows limited rain collection for properties supplied by a well. Even then, residents must apply for a permit to do so. The legislation also allows developers to apply for rainwater collection that will be beneficial, but not essential, to a new subdivision. Only 10 developers were approved for this pilot program. Where does that leave the average city homeowner collecting rainwater? Still a criminal, one supposes.

Source: Kedward 2012; Bartels 2015

growing interests – beginning in the twentieth century, with protecting the interests and traditional rights of tribal nations (Burton 1991; Wilkinson 1992).

In California's San Joaquin Valley, for example, many rural, low-income communities comprised of trailer parks or unincorporated towns receive their water supply from small, private systems or investor-owned utilities. This pattern arose during an era when farm workers were prohibited from living in larger towns, a condition persistent in much of the west before the mid-twentieth century. The result of this segregation was that few water utilities provided service to these under-represented and politically weak communities. As a result, to this day, these communities suffer from a chronic lack of safe drinking water as a result of contaminated farm runoff containing nitrates and pesticides (Environmental Justice Coalition for Water 2005). Moreover, they cannot rely on surrounding communities to finance improvements.

Many western states' constitutions explicitly define water as a "public resource" for which the state is responsible, and for which governance institutions must ensure that water is used in ways that do not harm other water rights' holders, or the environment. However, varying interpretations of these protections make these protections problematic and certainly less than perfect (MacDonnell & Fort 2008). In recent years, this issue has taken sharp focus around the need to regulate groundwater – an increasingly precious and overused resource (see box 6.3).

The Arizona groundwater case discussed below suggests a promising avenue for using law to adjudicate sensible allocation of this precious resource. However, as is the case in most instances where law is employed as a tool to settle conflicts, it is only as effective as the resources available to stand behind its application. In recent years, the agency charged with enforcing the Groundwater Act, the state's Department of Water Resources, has lost nearly half its staff and some two-thirds of its budget, with the result that – some claim – enforcement of the Act is less than adequate (Loomis 2015). Moreover, outside of the original designated "active management areas" or AMAs, significant over-use of groundwater is continuing throughout the state.

As the next section discusses, debates over equity, fairness, water as a property right, and protection of under-represented groups are perennial issues in water law.

Purpose as vision – ancient traditions and water laws

As discussed in chapter 1, purpose can be defined culturally, ethically, or even spiritually. Water law, as a political institution with antiquarian roots, reflects this tendency. Spiritual values have been greatly influential in water law. Two examples from a single region reveal this truism, and its problematical nature – Islamic and Judaic water law. Water law has long been central to Muslim societies in the Middle East and was, from a very early period, closely linked to larger assumptions about the proper path to spiritual salvation. While most water law practices in Islamic societies were relatively informal, it was long considered important that customary approaches to the management, allocation, and protection of the quality of water, especially for human consumption, conform to Islamic principle.

While Islam provides no specific legal sanctions for violating

Box 6.3 Water law reform and groundwater – the case of Arizona

In 1976, cities and mining interests lost an important case at the Arizona Supreme Court when justices ruled a private company (pecan growers) could impose a limit on how much groundwater a municipality (Tucson in this case) and copper mines could pump. The cities and the mines demanded relief from the legislature. In response the legislature formed a 25-member groundwater commission to write a new groundwater law. Three issues were hotly debated:

1. Who should have the right to pump groundwater and how much?
2. What methods should be used to reduce the groundwater overdraft?
3. Should groundwater be managed primarily at the state or local level?

Around this time, Governor Bruce Babbitt convinced the US Secretary of the Interior, Cecil Andrus, to issue an ultimatum: unless Arizona enacted tough groundwater laws, he would refuse to approve construction of the Central Arizona Project. Shocked back to reality, the cities, mines and agriculture asked Babbitt to mediate the discussions. One of the first items of agreement was creation of the Arizona Department of Water Resources.

In relatively short order, what was once considered impossible was a reality. On June 12, 1980, Gov. Babbitt signed the Groundwater Management Act. For the first time, all responsibilities for water planning and regulation (except water quality) were centralized in one state agency. The Act designated four parts of the state where groundwater pumping was heaviest as Active Management Areas (AMAs).

The Department applied more stringent laws and regulations in the AMAs, including the requirement that a developer verify he has secured physical, legal, and continuous access to a 100-year supply of water. Since 1980, the Department has written and executed three of the five management plans required by the Code. The management plans outline conservation goals and methods for various groundwater users in the agricultural, industrial, and municipal sectors.

The Code was the most eagerly-awaited and far-reaching policy initiative ever undertaken by the State. This progressive law granted vast, new responsibilities and authority. In 1986, the Ford Foundation recognized Arizona for its landmark work in water management.

Source: Arizona Department of Water Resources 2015

principles of water stewardship in the Quran, the holy book clearly emphasizes the importance of water as the source of life and on reminding believers that "water is a gift of God, not a mundane thing, and that humans are stewards (*khulafa*) of that life-giving resource."

As one scholar has noted: "Muslim jurists have consistently treated water, land, and crops as indivisible, and water rights have generally been restricted to amounts considered adequate for a given crop area" (Naff 2008). Muhammad himself articulated a number of principles for water stewardship that emphasized balance, harmony, reciprocity, and fairness – ranging from the appropriate amount of water to grow crops, to the allocation of agricultural water among many users, the rights of ownership to springs and wells, and prohibitions on selling water.

Elaborate rules governing water sources and how their uses should be adjudicated were also stipulated and two broad categories of water were established: that which is owned and that which is not (Naff 2008). Earth and its natural resources belong to God, and He has bestowed them as gifts to humans who are, in turn, required: to act as stewards of the earth – obliged to share these resources with other people and species; to protect the interests and rights of others, including the rights of future generations; to respect conservation as a core Islamic obligation; to concede that privatization, if regulated and limited, may play a useful management role; and to uphold the interests of end users. Muslim legal scholars have clearly articulated these principles and they have been increasingly recognized as practically relevant.

Despite this ornate system of spiritually-derived principles, however, the growing secularization of Arab states beginning in the nineteenth century – as well as the susceptibility of the region to Western political authority – led to major constraints on the practice and relevance of *sharia* law. Moreover, despite the retention of the "spirit or sensibility of traditional Islamic water law, and the fact that *sharia* does not acknowledge that any other system of law, canonical or secular, has equal standing with itself," Western legal provisions regarding institutions for water management tended to take precedence (Naff & Dellapenna 2002). This occurred in part because of European colonialism after World War I; certain fundamental *sharia* concepts regarding water remain intact, especially that water is community property (Naff 2008).

Today, all but a few Muslim states impose some form of toll on water and its uses, and despite the political conflicts over water in the Middle East, no Muslim state has invoked Islamic law in contending with another Islamic country (see chapter 7 for examples). This is due to the fact that there is no widely agreed-upon transnational Islamic legal instrumentality for doing so. Nonetheless, in countries like Egypt, for example, Islamic religious rituals had important impacts on water policies, including determining the location of mosques to assure proximity to the Nile, installation of fountains in schools and other public places to allow for ablution (ritual washing) before prayer, public fountains for personal consumption – a practice especially important to Muslims – and special efforts to measure the level of water on the Nile to assure fair allocation of its flow (Gad 2008).

Judaism, with a long and venerable tradition of codified law, faces similar challenges and articulates comparable legal principles for water. The book of Genesis explicitly mentions the importance of water, its magical powers, and the ways its presence constitutes a symbol of life, while the *Talmud* prescribes that those residing closer to a water source have priority rights over those further away – in effect, upstream riparians have prior rights over downstream landowners. Moreover, essential needs of citizens living in a community close to a water source take precedence over those from remote locales (Laster et al. 2008). Comparable priority principles were applied to agricultural usage, with proximity to a water source granting pre-emptory rights.

Scholars note that there is no single orderly set of Jewish water laws or legal principles. As a result, Jewish water law began as a set of rules concerned with water usage in the biblical land of Israel, on national, regional, and personal levels. Later, when the Jews were exiled from Israel, Jewish water law continued to develop, but mainly on a personal level.

Contemporary Israeli water law has little direct relation to Jewish water law. In ancient Israel, constraints of climate led to an impulse to find ways to sustainably manage water sources. There was not much choice, since water stored in cisterns could last from one rainy season to the next, but not much beyond that. Any water source, whether a spring, river, or well was revered and protected.

In modern Israel, however, within a decade of independence (1959), Israel's Water Law also based the supply of water on this notion of sustainability, but without any long-term guarantees as to the amount of water to be supplied beyond essential needs. As we shall see in chapter 9, this one legal principle – that of the state assuring sustainable management of water – and which dates to antiquity, has been instrumental in permitting rapid development of alternative water supply policies.

These two cases exemplify the challenges of using law to protect principles of equity and fairness – whether among people within a society, across societies, or even across generations. They also illustrate a fundamental challenge facing water law generally: the limits of law as a source of durable power and resilient process. Because water laws are based on lofty principles (as in the case of riparian and prior appropriation principles in the US, or ancient laws postulated by Islamic and Jewish traditions), it is subject to differing interpretation and variable application. Moreover, practically by definition, law is limited spatially – to a particular jurisdiction, state, or society. Thus, if conflict arises over the allocation or regulation of water bodies shared across jurisdictions, other legal arrangements may have to be developed – such is the role of discussions of law as process, and the specific role of compacts.

Law as process – compacts and basin commissions

Water laws are for the most part spatially restricted to a given political jurisdiction – a state, province, or nation-state. They also are culturally shaped and animated by lofty, philosophically rooted aspirations that are difficult to fully implement. While there are many "process" aspects to water law, one of the most generally innovative legal processes has been the emergence of the so-called water compact – a specially empowered legal entity designed to provide *comprehensive, trans-boundary governance* of river or groundwater basins.

Compacts manage water allocation and, in some instances, regulate water demand and quality and even build and operate water projects. Compacts seek to develop a system of equitable, fair, publically acceptable management by consulting with public officials, and how they try to *independently verify* how much water is actually used.

One of the world's oldest, and the first river basin compact in the US, is the Colorado River Compact, concluded in 1922 (although one member, Arizona, did not ratify it until 1944). In many respects a model for how compacts generally work, the compact also exemplifies the controversies and intense political debates involved in allocation agreements. Negotiated by Arizona, California, Utah, Wyoming, Colorado, Nevada, New Mexico, and the federal government, the Colorado River Compact allocates water in two ways: between upper basin states (i.e., Colorado, Utah, and Wyoming) and the lower basin states (the remainder – with New Mexico being considered a part of both sub-basins).

Division between sub-basins was one of the most contentious elements of the compact's negotiation, largely because before states' allocations could be defined, agreement had to be reached on the need to give states in the upper basin rights to the full flow of the water in the tributaries located there, as well as half the total flow of the river at the point where the upper and lower basins would be divided – Lees Ferry, Arizona (Hundley 2009). Adding to the difficulty, some flow (as it turned out, some 1.5 million acre-feet) had to be left over for Mexico – a non-signatory of the compact, but an international riparian with long-standing uses of the river for agriculture. As difficult and time-consuming as this set of negotiations proved to be, the allocation of water to individual states also proved to be a political

Box 6.4   Compacts and the emergence of a "Law of the river" – the case of Arizona vs. California

In actuality, the Colorado River is managed and operated under numerous compacts, federal laws, court decisions and decrees, contracts, and regulatory guidelines collectively known as the "Law of the River." While the Colorado River Compact of 1922 is the cornerstone – defining the relationship between the upper basin states, where most of the river's water supply originates, and the lower basin states, where most of the water demands were developing. Each sub-basin has the right to develop and use 7.5 million acre-feet (MAF) of river water annually.

Perhaps the most important legal regime governing the river system, however, is the US Supreme Court Decision in *Arizona v. California* of 1964. In 1963, the Supreme Court issued a decision settling a 25-year-old dispute between Arizona and California. The dispute stemmed from Arizona's desire to build the Central Arizona Project so it could use its full Colorado River apportionment. California objected and argued that Arizona's use of water from the Gila River, a Colorado River tributary, constituted use of its Colorado River apportionment, and that it had developed a historical use of some of Arizona's apportionment, which, under the doctrine of prior appropriation, precluded Arizona from developing the project. The Supreme Court rejected California's arguments, ruling that lower basin states have a right to appropriate and use tributary flows before the tributary co-mingles with the Colorado River, and that the doctrine of prior appropriation did not apply to apportionments in the lower basin.

The 1964 decree enjoined the Secretary of the Interior from delivering water outside the framework of apportionments defined by the law and mandated the preparation of annual reports documenting the uses of water in the three lower basin states. In 1979, the Supreme Court issued a Supplemental Decree that addressed present perfected rights referred to in the Colorado River Compact and in the Boulder Canyon Project Act. These rights are entitlements essentially established under state law, and have priority over later contract entitlements.

Source: US Bureau of Reclamation 2008

compromise of the first order, as it was based on prior use priorities and estimated future needs.

Commitment to a compact by these seven states ensured that the federal government would fulfill its commitment to build one or more dams to ensure priorities and future needs could be met (e.g., the Hoover Dam in 1928). Negotiators also assumed rather optimistically a total average annual flow of between 14–17 million acre-feet (MAF) of water, with the midpoint for purposes of allocation assumed to be 16.5 MAF, or 7.5 MAF in each sub-basin, with 1.5 MAF left for Mexico.

In theory, agreements such as the Colorado River Compact are supposed to anticipate and resolve conflicts over water allocation that regular water laws cannot effectively address. In practice, however, this is not always the case. Prior to the severe drought that has affected the Colorado River over the past half-decade – and which has exposed the seven-state region's dependence on the river and its principal tributaries for water supplies – there has been a long-standing dispute between Arizona and California over the allocation of lower basin supplies (see box 6.4) which was supposed to be settled by adjudication, but whose legacy still resonates throughout the region.

While there is a growing consensus that the river system cannot continue to support municipal, agricultural, and hydroelectric demands, actual cuts in use are strongly dependent on law. For example, in states like Arizona – which under the Colorado River Compact would be subject to the largest reduction, cities such as Phoenix could be facing severe challenges, because cuts would not apply to all users equally.

Phoenix might have to recycle more wastewater for potable use while rural communities such as Yuma may not experience any cuts at all due to their legal priority to the water of the river. Farms in that region have been drawing water since the late nineteenth century, which earned the area the most senior rights in Arizona and some of the most senior in the basin. Nearly 1 MAF out of the total of 15 MAF annually allocated under the compact (or 7 percent of the total) are allocated to just 150,000 acres of farmland. Unless the parties here can find an amicable solution, as drought worsens the federal government may intervene (Yardley 2015).

Similar challenges face compacts in other societies. The Niger Basin Authority, comprising Benin, Burkina Faso, Cameroon, Chad, Cote d'Ivoire, Guinea, Mali, Niger, and Nigeria, functions primarily as an organization to promote cooperation among members. Its goals revolve principally around integrated development of water-related activities including energy, water resources, agriculture, and forestry management.

Moreover, as in other places, the Niger River Compact overlaps jurisdiction with other compacts – including the Lake Chad Commission which shares four member states from the former: Niger, Chad, Nigeria, and Cameroon. Formed in 1964, the Lake Chad Commission has designated legal authority to prepare regulations in support of its multinational convention. The commission collects, evaluates, and disseminates information on projects prepared by member states and recommends common projects and research programs. The Lake Chad Commission also has a role in ensuring efficient use of basin waters, regulating navigation, and resolving conflicts (Hooper 2005).

The Mekong River Commission, whose members include Vietnam, China, Thailand, Laos, and Cambodia, faces extraordinary challenges revolving around the development of hydropower resources in the region. While its mission is to "promote and coordinate sustainable management and development of water and related resources" for the benefit of its member states, differences among these states has made its mission anything but easy, particularly since its powers are not binding – only advisory. Amidst efforts to articulate a coherent vision of several lower Mekong mainstream dams, the Mekong Commission also undertakes flood forecasting and warning, water balance studies, water quality monitoring, salinity control in the Mekong Delta and studies of the impact of multi-purpose dams planned for construction. The last of these issues is by far the most politically contentious.

As of 2015, the Mekong has some seven upstream dams built by China with 21 more under construction and, in the near future, some 11 additional dams to be constructed by Laos and Cambodia along its 2,600-mile course. The existing impoundments have already had a profound impact on local economies and the riparian environment, disrupting fish migration and spawning and forcing thousands of residents to switch to farming. This is no mean adjustment: Cambodians and Laotians catch more fish per capita than residents of any other country (Nijhuis 2015). These projects have also led to rapid electrification of the region: an effort applauded by the International Energy Agency due to projected increases in energy demand in Southeast Asia by some 80 percent by 2035.

A further challenge faced by the Mekong Basin Commission is geopolitics. China, the country building the greatest number of dams in the basin, and by far the strongest member of the compact, is not a full member of the commission and does not have to consult with other members before undertaking its development activities. Moreover, full members such as Laos, in the process of building the Xayabari Dam – financed by Thailand which will be a major consumer of its electrical power – has gone ahead with its plans to impound the Mekong despite recommendations by the Mekong Basin Commission against building the project due to its projected adverse environmental impacts to fisheries and in-stream flow.

These trials underscore the political challenges facing Mekong River Basin Compact negotiation and implementation. While the compact seeks to develop equitable arrangements for management by consulting with political officials and stakeholders, providing independent verification and monitoring of water allocation and plans for river development, and enforcing allocation decisions through a common framework – its power and authority depends on the extent to which collaborating parties can forge a political consensus over common objectives.

What makes reaching consensus difficult is precisely the fact that such "common objectives" are elusive. Each national party has development objectives that take precedence, in their view, over those of their neighbors. Moreover, when negotiating compacts, countries are aware that once rules for allocation are forged, they are likely to be difficult to "undo" or re-negotiate if stream flow or water uses should change. This is because the original formulation of such rules is an arduous, painstaking process. This dilemma is a conundrum all compacts face.

Are there political "levers" that can help facilitate consensus over objectives? One remedy that has been suggested is that the institutions that permit and finance large river basin schemes – especially hydropower developments such as those in the Mekong basin – require that protagonists undertake basin-scale environmental assessments. Such assessments might account for cumulative ecological and social impacts, as well as climate change. The logic of this suggestion is that it links the economic "power" of funders to the objective of considering a range of social and environmental objectives, as well as alternative sites for hydropower projects (Winemiller et al. 2016).

We explore these and related issues associated with transnational water problems in the next chapter. An important facet of this issue is the relationship between these objectives, and the trust and confidence among parties negotiating compacts.

Conclusion – What gives water law its power?

Water law is neither "self-enforceable" nor by itself a source of power. Systems of laws and formal rights do not necessarily reflect or determine actual practices by governments any more than self-professed values reflect the actual behavior of people. The principal reason for this is that law itself, as we have seen, is constantly evolving, making it difficult to locate the actual or legitimate sources for the authority of a law's enforcement. This is also true for compacts (Boelens et al. 2010). Moreover, laws and legal regimes are not only diverse, but each legal system has its own sources of authority, and all have their own culturally specific definitions of – and standards for – equity and justice.

The role of law in water politics is intrinsically connected to power. In riparian legal systems, for example, such as those found in much of the US, Australia, New Zealand, Canada, the UK, and even parts of

Africa and India, if one owns land adjacent to a watercourse, such as a river, stream, or lake – or that overlies an aquifer – then both local custom, as well as many courts of law, would suggest you have a right to the use of that water. In effect, the power of property ownership often defines the authority of water law. Moreover, property owners can claim further assurance that these adjacent watercourses are to be kept clean and reasonably useable by upstream users so as to minimize harm to those living downstream. At the same time, riparian rights systems do not afford landowners an absolute right to a given *quantity* of water. For this reason, riparian systems do not easily permit the "transfer," through sale or lease, of water from one user to another.

Law and power are also connected through moral authority. Both the Muslim and Jewish traditions of water law, as we have seen, are guided by a strong spiritual basis for adjudication of water conflicts, for allocation of water rights, and for the governance of water quality. While Muslim water law is guided by *sharia*; literally, the moral path for access to drinking water, covenantal traditions of water quality, purity, and access also characterize Jewish water law. In fact, both systems share many traditions in common as regards the fundamental importance of stewardship over water resources – traditions that are important for understanding contemporary water conflicts in the Middle East, for instance (Laster et al. 2008; Naff 2008).

Finally, in *communitarian* water rights systems such as those found among Native American tribes or in tribal cultures in sub-Saharan Africa – there is a large *publically-adjudicated* role held by the state which embraces such issues as determining how and whether water can be diverted between regions; whether large storage projects for public supply, irrigation, power generation, flood control, and/or navigation should be built; and what types of quality standards best protect public health and afford ecological protection.

Another policy constraint is the rise of disputes that challenge the legitimacy of existing water allocation regulations. Such disputes may become so intractable as to impede any compact authority becoming trustworthy enough to serve as an arbiter. Current water disputes in the southeastern US, prompted by drought, urbanization, and the need for three riparian states to share the same sources of water, exemplify this problem.

Since the 1980s, there has been sharp disagreement between Georgia, Florida, and Alabama over the Apalachicola-Chattahoochee-Flint (ACF) river basin and the Alabama-Coosa-Tallapoosa (ACT) river basin, resulting in a so-called "tristate water war." The water war erupted when the city of Atlanta sought a permit from the Corps of Engineers to retain 529 million gallons of water each day from the Chattahoochee, Flint, and Coosa Rivers, and store it in Lake Lanier, a primary source of drinking water for north Georgia. Atlanta officials believed this was a necessary and legal method of acquiring adequate quantities of water essential to support their projected population growth. The plan would increase withdrawals from the Chattahoochee and Flint rivers by the year 2010.

Alabama and Florida viewed Atlanta's request as a major threat to their own drinking water supply and to protection of fish and wildlife habitats. They also feared it would increase pollutants in their water supply due to decreased water flow necessary to dilute and minimize the severity of pollution. Interstate water disputes such as this are generally resolved through the use of the United States Supreme Court or Congressional allocation.

In retaliation, these states filed suit in federal court to prevent implementation of the Corps' plan for Atlanta. In 1997, before a ruling was issued, the three states agreed to enter into two separate interstate compacts that would allow each state's governor and a federal appointee to negotiate an allocation system for the ACF and another for the ACT. These compacts were the first of their kind in the southeast (Environmental Protection Division 2007), and they have attempted to reconcile water quality, supply, and in-stream flow issues (Ruhl 2005).

As discussed earlier, the Clean Water Act requires that states determine designated uses for streams and then establish criteria necessary to support those uses. Alabama, Florida, and Georgia have supported designated uses for fish, wildlife, and other aquatic life in the ACF system, including tributary streams. Since the Clean Water Act predicates "the protection and propagation of fish, shellfish, and wildlife, and provides for recreation in and on the water be achieved," it is the obligation of the federal government and states to arrive at a solution that protects water quality for human health needs – regardless of what type of allocation agreement is reached – as well as minimum in-stream flow.

Reconciling agricultural, industrial, and public supply activities has been an especially difficult challenge in this dispute. Agricultural activities affect the health of aquatic life in these rivers. In addition to the commercial fisheries that depend on an adequate supply of fresh water, low flows and waterborne pollutants jeopardize the survival of ecologically important aquatic biota. These issues are still being debated.

The ACF dispute exemplifies the way global trends we have discussed

in this book can sometimes converge in ways that are difficult to reconcile. In short, rapid urbanization, diminishing supplies due to stream
and aquifer depletion and deteriorating or poorly maintained urban
water infrastructure, and agricultural demands can quite suddenly
generate regional conflict over the control of water (Postel 2000).

In developing nations, disputes over water rights, if not resolved
"can debilitate civil society and erode ... trust-building processes"
(Homer-Dixon 2000). While the consequences of such disputes are not
as dramatic in developed countries, their resolution is equally difficult. The key claim is avoiding practices that overexploit or deplete
aquifers and rivers (e.g., groundwater over-pumping, irrigating crops
in arid regions, and construction of large-scale, inefficient hydraulic
infrastructure that destroys habitat and disrupts in-stream functioning of aquatic and riparian ecosystems) and adopting a new paradigm
for management based upon conservation, reuse and recycling, and
other remedies designed to reduce water use and hasten more sustainable use of supplies.

Avoiding such practices – between different countries – requires
a negotiating environment able to foster high levels of confidence,
participation, and shared power. Successful achievement of these
objectives is the ultimate goal of dispute resolution at the international level. It is also an elusive goal, as we discuss in the next chapter.

SUMMARY

- Water law is the product of legislation, administrative fiat, tradition, and cultural norms. It takes many forms, including compacts
  and basin commissions.
- With respect to purpose, an important issue is: what, and who, is
  law for? To ensure equity in use and allocation; protect nature; or
  ensure adequate supply?
- With regards to power, laws favor certain interests and considerations over others. How they favor these interests is a contentious
  topic.
- Compacts are widely used to coordinate trans-boundary water
  sources. As modified versions of law, they are subject to contention
  over how they allocate water.

RECOMMENDED READING

- Good analyses of water law as political instruments are J. W.
  Dellapenna & J. Gupta, *The Evolution of the Law and Politics of Water*

(2009). They analyze the evolution of water law in a variety of geographical contexts. A. D. Tarlock, *Law of Water Rights and Resources* (1998) and A. D. Tarlock, J. N. Corbridge, Jr. & D. H. Getches, *Water Resource Management: A Casebook in Law and Public Policy* (1993) examine riparian and appropriation systems.

- Comparative studies of water rights are offered in L. L. Butler, "Environmental Water Rights: An Evolving Concept of Public Property," *Virginia Environmental Law Journal* (1990). Also, J. W. Dellapenna, "Rivers as Legal Structures: The Examples of the Jordan and the Nile," *Natural Resources Journal* (1996). An interesting study of water rights in the Andean states of Latin America is found in R. Boelens, "The Politics of Disciplining Water Rights," *Development and Change* (2009).

- B. Hooper, *Integrated River Basin Governance: Learning from International Experience* (2005), discusses legal and political entities of compacts, while the classic study of the Colorado River Compact and the political process leading to its consummation is N. Hundley, Jr., *Water and the West – the Colorado River Compact and the Politics of Water in the American West* (2009).

WEBSITES

- http://ssrn.com/abstract=1025849. Water privatization and law
- http://www.usbr.gov/lc/region/g1000/lawofrvr.htm Law of the Colorado River
- http://www.colorado.edu/law/research/gwc Natural Resources Law Center, University of Colorado

QUESTIONS FOR DISCUSSION

1. Distinguish the major differences of riparian, appropriation, and traditional water law – how does each system allocate water, and set priorities for use?

2. What kinds of processes are employed by river basin compacts to enforce water allocation agreements and the distribution of water supplies? Are they effective?

3. Why aren't water laws self-enforcing? How do geopolitics and differences in power affect their enforcement and effectiveness?

CHAPTER 7

International Cooperation

Global and trans-boundary issues

Freshwater management has increasingly become a trans-boundary challenge. Over the past century, countries have amplified their collaboration in order to resolve quality and supply problems they are unable to solve by themselves. The need to do so is underscored by the fact that much of the world's freshwater is shared by two or more riparian states. Thus, problems requiring conjoint management include allocating rivers and groundwater equitably; avoiding depletion or undue diminution of shared sources of supply; managing fisheries, habitat, and other freshwater resources; and averting and mitigating pollution. While this chapter examines means for cooperation, chapter 8 examines sources of disputes.

Some of the first laws allocating water among different countries were developed and implemented some 5,000 years ago between two Mesopotamian city-states that lay in close proximity to one another as upper and lower riparians. These states often clashed over water apportionment and ratified one of the earliest water treaties in order to peacefully resolve their differences (Dinar 2013).

Students of international water politics recognize that there is no single, unified process for resolving transnational disputes, or cooperating on solutions to trans-boundary problems. Many freshwater problems manifest in one place are caused by actions originating in another – including downstream depletion caused by upstream diversions, as well as point and non-point pollution. While this compels cooperation, it also suggests that cooperative solutions must be tailored to specific cases.

Another issue that has arisen in our era is that some freshwater problems have become, in effect, global issues that are not limited to riparian states. Instead, they are planetary in scope. Examples include the commercialization of water in international trade, debates over water access as a human right, and the transfer of technology and know-how for climate adaptation. These issues often pit the interests

144

of more developed countries in the global "north" against developing nations in the Southern hemisphere.

Trans-boundary and global water problems share a number of *political* characteristics in common. Above all, cooperation between countries is far more difficult than among political entities within a single country. The roles of power, process, and purpose are fundamentally different in the international arena in three major respects.

First, nation-states are unequal in power. Those that are stronger in their ability to marshal economic, legal, or even military power can often bend decision-making outcomes to their will. The result is that weaker countries engaged in negotiation – or who are asked to collaborate with stronger powers – may harbor mistrust and jealousy. This not only inhibits cooperation, at least on the most divisive issues, but it also makes identifying mutually satisfactory solutions difficult.

Secondly, there is no authoritative process for dispute resolution in the international arena that has binding power to resolve conflicts. This is one of the fundamental ironies that compels nations to work together to manage trans-boundary water problems. In effect, the lack of an authoritative process to resolve conflicts forces countries to work together toward amicable solutions. At the same time, mistrust and unequal power make reaching compromise difficult (Hamner & Wolf 1998; Conca 2006).

On balance, however, as one set of observers has noted: "Contrary to received wisdom, evidence proves this interdependence (over water) does not lead to war . . . (in fact) water is a greater pathway to peace than conflict in the world's river basins" (Wolf et al. 2005). The resulting institutions riparian countries establish to manage water are often durable enough to endure even during regional wars. This has been the case, for instance, for the Committee that manages the Mekong River Basin, whose member states even shared data throughout the Vietnam War. To some extent, it has even been true in water conflicts between Israel and Palestine, as we will discuss (Wolf et al. 2005).

Thirdly, and adding further irony to the international politics of water, nation-states have divergent goals toward the use of shared waters. This divergence exacerbates pre-existing sources of distrust, and fosters a lack of confidence toward one another's willingness to cooperate fully. India and Pakistan, for example, are currently embroiled in a dispute over development of hydropower dams at remote upstream reaches of the Indus basin, with each country hoping to complete a full range of projects accruing to its advantage before the other does so (Tirmizi 2011).

Long-standing enmity between these two countries has forestalled full cooperation over a conjoint solution to their dispute. Nonetheless, the Indus River Commission continues to cooperate on water management issues. Why? Because rather than sabotaging cooperation, under the right conditions distrust hastens efforts to design agreements that foster information sharing, provide transparency through joint monitoring and verification of state actions, and that are based on governance arrangements that build confidence through encouraging a shared vision regarding the value of the resource they share (Sadoff et al. 2008).

We now analyze two international systems for collaborating on water issues that illustrate problems characterized by unequal power, disjointed decision-making process, and divergent purpose. They are (1) formal international "regimes" (e.g., river basin compacts or other agreements enshrined in treaties) for the governance of shared, trans-boundary surface waters or groundwater basins; and (2) non-governmental or civil society networks comprised of water experts, environmental advocates, and, occasionally, local officials who exchange knowledge and information and establish common standards for water management.

Overcoming barriers – the art of confidence building in formal regimes

Confidence building is a key to formal systems of international as well as global cooperation over fresh water. It is especially important in agreements between countries that allocate water supplies, commit member states to reduce pollution, or bind countries to conjoint watershed or fisheries or other resource management. Confidence building is the process by which one nation complies with certain agreed-upon goals as a signatory to an agreement, with the understanding that other countries to such an agreement are expected to do the same.

To ensure confidence three conditions must be met. First, the goals of a transnational water agreement must be formally codified in a treaty – so that conditions being agreed are clear and transparent. Secondly, there must be a means of deterring parties from circumventing the terms of these agreements – ways to prevent cheating, in other words. This condition requires some form of third party or independent verification of compliance behavior. Finally, each party to an agreement must receive tangible benefits by complying – for example, an allocation of a river's flow on an annual basis, limits on harvesting of forests in shared watersheds, promises of improvements to water quality, and the like (Sadoff et al. 2008).

Key to understanding confidence building in practice is recognizing that it as an ideal that is rarely, if ever, fully achieved. While confidence building is required to make agreements work, treaties among countries are, at best, approximations of this goal because of the divergent interests of negotiating parties and other barriers to compliance capacity – especially among developing countries.

Thus, we distinguish three basic models of confidence building in this chapter, characterized by their degree of cooperation. We call these: low cooperation/low confidence, partial cooperation with partial confidence, and high confidence with robust cooperation. A fourth model, evolving cooperation with partial confidence is exemplified by the Nile Basin Initiative (see box 7.1). In the Nile region, local communities, NGOs, scientists and aid organizations are working together to design solutions, identify funding sources, and share information regarding adaptive solutions within the region's *sub-basins* to improve international support for irrigation efficiency, groundwater management, and rural electrification.

Low cooperation/low confidence

While many international agreements aspire to build confidence among parties, a number of factors impede full cooperation in resolving thorny and divisive issues. An example of such a low cooperation/ low confidence model would be governing agreements for the Tigris-Euphrates river system. In 2008, after decades of negotiation, at times mediated by the former Soviet Union, Iraq, Syria, and Turkey agreed to establish a Joint Trilateral Committee (JTC) for managing the Tigris–Euphrates basin. The JTC agreement was preceded by a series of unilateral efforts undertaken by each country to construct water projects for hydropower and irrigation on the main stems and tributaries of the Tigris–Euphrates. These unilateral efforts, without full consultation or accommodation of mutual interests, led to threats of wars, sporadic skirmishes between Iraq and Syria, and tensions between Syria and Turkey.

In addition, separatist movements of various kinds, occurring simultaneously but not directly related to water, made these disputes more intractable. Syrian support for Kurdish separatists in Iraq and Turkish military support for Israel, for instance, served to effectively erode trust among these countries' efforts to negotiate their water policy goals. Tensions flared between Turkey and Iraq in 1997 after Turkey

Box 7.1   "Living on the Nile" – accord without agreement

In 1999, ten African countries: Kenya, Burundi, Rwanda, Tanzania, Eritrea, Ethiopia, Sudan, Egypt, Uganda, and Congo agreed to form the Nile Basin Initiative, an effort to produce a binding compact to allocate water to 160 million people. Thus far, an allocation agreement remains elusive in part because Egypt and Sudan, the largest countries in the basin by population, and downstream riparians, refuse to relinquish power to *upstream* countries over determination of appropriate withdrawals. Ironically, and contrary to riparian traditions (chapter 6), a 1929 British mandate, when both these countries were British colonies, granted rights to withdraw a larger volume of water than upstream countries.

Compounding the difficulty in developing a binding allocation agreement is the fact that Ethiopia, an upstream riparian, is engaged in completing a number of large water and hydroelectric projects on Nile tributaries in its territory (the Gilgel Gibe project) which gives it de facto power to control and regulate flows on the Nile and, thus, creates additional political friction in the basin. Added to this are the visible effects of climate change (chapter 5) which is causing drought throughout the basin – Lake Victoria, a major source of the Nile, is falling 2.5 meters every three years, while Nile Delta farmers are forced to conserve water by planting fewer acres of rice.

While it is not surprising that a durable solution to the allocation problem remains elusive, the Nile Basin Initiative is having some success in "evolving" toward a framework of confidence: this is exemplified by its oversight and supervision of a basin-wide strategic planning process which is being operationalized within the Nile basin's sub-basins: the main Nile, Baro-Akobo-Sobat and White Nile, Tekeze-Atbara-Setit, and Blue Nile sub-basins. Within these sub-basins various stakeholders are coming together, including community leaders, scientists, and NGOs, to identify problems related to irrigation and groundwater management and, rural electrification, as well as joint investment projects and funding sources. Sharing of information among these stakeholders – and conjoint decision-making – is building confidence in the capacity of communities to resolve fundamental problems through amicable collaboration.

Sources: Fleishman and Linthicum 2010; Nile Basin Initiative Secretariat 2014; Nile Basin Initiative 2016

invaded northern Iraq to attack Kurdish rebels. Moreover, construction of the Keban Dam in southern Anatolia by Turkey in the late 1960s and early 1970s, and Tabqa Dam in Syria during the same period heightened regional tensions (Lowi 1991; Wolf & Newton 2007a).

What prompted a shift in attitudes among protagonists was Turkey's proposal, beginning in the 1980s, for a Southern Anatolia development project named "GAP" – a massive irrigation and hydroelectric power scheme on the Tigris and Euphrates Rivers that would construct some 21 dams and 19 hydroelectric plants as well as the cultivation of some 1.65 million hectares of farmland. While periodic and intermittent discussions between all three countries took place through the early 2000s to try and find common ground over this project's impact, and ways of reducing adverse effects, serious discussions only began following a joint Syria–Iraq water coordination committee convened in Damascus.

These economically and militarily weaker riparians agreed on the criteria for fair distribution of the Euphrates and Tigris between all three countries. Iraq and Syria also agreed to coordinate their negotiating positions with Turkey. In the event, by the early 1990s, Turkey's response was that an equitable allocation should be based on cultivated land (understandable given the objectives of GAP), while Syria proposed an absolutely equal division of water among all three nations (Gruen 1993).

After a series of on-again, off-again talks, interrupted by major wars in the region (including, eventually, the fall of Saddam Hussein's regime during the US-led Iraq War), in 2008, all three countries agreed in principle to fairly allocate the rivers' flows in due course, and to engage in prior consultation with one another before undertaking any major water project impacting the others. Iraq also agreed to trade petroleum with Turkey and to help curb Kurdish separatist activities.

In April 2014, however, Turkey began unilaterally reducing the flow of the Euphrates – which rises in Turkey – into Syria and Iraq, cutting much of the river's flow: to Iraq by 80 percent, to Syria by 40 percent. This was done in part to hasten the completion of key elements of the GAP project by 2017. The Euphrates now effectively terminates at the Turkish–Syrian border. Once finished, it is projected that the project will withdraw up to 70 percent of the flow of the Euphrates: 90 percent of its flow originates in Turkey.

The prognosis for this conflict, in one of the most politically volatile regions on the planet, is impossible to predict. What we know for certain is that low confidence of the tri-lateral agreements to resolve differences over management of the Tigris–Euphrates system is the result of three political factors. First, lack of trust has been exacerbated by ethnic conflicts and foreign policy differences among the three countries. This has also made the articulation of a conjoint *purpose* for management elusive. Second, differences in the military and economic *power* of the three countries has made collaboration difficult, and for Turkey, largely unnecessary. It was able (and clearly willing) to risk armed conflict to develop the GAP project. Finally, protagonists have had difficulty resolving differences due to a lack of any established compact or other structural means for cooperation. As of this writing, armed conflict among irredentist forces remains a reality in the region, and it would not be an exaggeration to state that water has even become a weapon (see box 7.2).

Partial cooperation – weak confidence

Two examples of partial cooperation and weak confidence are Haiti and the Dominican Republic over watershed management, and Israel and Palestine over domestic water supply. While vastly different in context – the former case revolves around economic development efforts while the latter is connected to providing water security in a hostile political environment – they share a number of features in common. These include an approach to cooperation that closely conforms to the *realist* paradigm often espoused by students of international relations. This position sees trans-boundary cooperation between non-friendly rivals as only possible if parties focus on areas of what might be termed apolitical or "functional" practices – such as reforestation, water system engineering, and infrastructure maintenance.

Haiti is one of poorest countries in the Western hemisphere. Its extreme poverty and lack of economic opportunities have long imposed severe impacts on its land and water resources, creating, according to the United Nations, "pressure on their land, [and] pressure on their economic space, [resulting in] a competition between Haitians and Dominicans" (Gronewold 2009). The former has lost some 98 percent of its forests to clear-cutting for charcoal production as well as land clearing by local squatters seeking cultivable acreage. Rampant forest clearing has also occurred in the Dominican Republic, in part due to an exploding illegal market for charcoal to serve the needs of Haitians and Dominicans alike. The former receive some 60 percent of their energy supply from charcoal, and even though production is illegal in the Dominican Republic, many Haitians risk their lives to acquire it (UNEP 2013).

The environmental impacts of deforestation on both countries have been enormous, affecting the health of several watersheds due to siltation of streams and precipitous declines in fisheries. Along the Massacre River, which forms part of the boundary separating these countries, Haiti's wildlife habitats have been severely damaged with 25–30 tributary watersheds largely degraded or permanently altered.

In 2007 both countries issued the *Declaration of Santo Domingo* under which they vowed to establish a series of greenhouses to produce some one million seedlings for a bi-national reforestation program. With

Box 7.2   Iraq and Syria – water as a weapon

"The outcome of the Iraq and Syrian conflicts may rest on who controls the region's dwindling water supplies. Rivers, canals, dams, sewage, and desalination plants are now all military targets in the semi-arid region that regularly experiences extreme water shortages," says Michael Stephen, deputy director of the Royal United Services Institute think tank in Qatar. "Control of water supplies gives strategic control over both cities and countryside. We are seeing a battle for control of water. Water is now the major strategic objective of all groups in Iraq. It's life or death. If you control water in Iraq you have a grip on Baghdad, and you can cause major problems . . . ISIS rebels now control most of the key upper reaches of the Tigris and Euphrates, the two great rivers that flow from Turkey in the north to the Gulf in the south and on which all Iraq and much of Syria depends for food, water, and industry.

"Rebel forces are targeting water installations to cut off supplies to the largely Shia south of Iraq," says Matthew Machowski, a Middle East security researcher at the UK Houses of Parliament and Queen Mary University of London. "It is already being used as an instrument of war by all sides. One could claim that controlling water resources in Iraq is even more important than controlling the oil refineries, especially in summer. Control of the water supply is fundamentally important. Cut it off and you create great sanitation and health crises.

Securing the Haditha Dam was one of the first objectives of the American Special Forces invading Iraq in 2003. The fear was that Saddam Hussein's forces could turn the structure that supplies 30 percent of all Iraq's electricity into a weapon of mass destruction by opening the lock gates that control the flow of the river. Billions of gallons of water could have been released, power to Baghdad would have been cut off, towns and villages over hundreds of square miles flooded and the country would have been paralyzed.

"The use of water as a tactical weapon has been done by both Isis and the Syrian government," says Nouar Shamout, a researcher with Chatham House. "Syria's essential services are on the brink of collapse under the burden of continuous assault on critical water infrastructure." The deliberate targeting of water supply networks "is now a daily occurrence in the conflict."

Source: Vidal 2014

Canadian cooperation, they also formed the *Artibonite River Management Initiative* to raise awareness about managing water and conserving of soil in order to restore the economies of the border region, create jobs, and improve human health. Finally, these countries are also pursuing a $3.5 billion watershed restoration project, funded by Norway's development agency, UNDP, UNEP, and the World Food Program. The partnership trains local authorities and farmers to manage natural resources sustainably, including revamping irrigation systems as well as improving sanitation in the region, further aiding watershed

health and restoration while contributing to community development efforts (Government of Canada 2016).

The reason for calling this initiative a partial confidence building
approach is because of the lack of national capacity to fully achieve
its ambitious goals. Unlike the "low cooperation" model afforded
by the Tigris-Euphrates case, however, Haiti and the Dominican
Republic – with massive third party assistance – have created a durable process for managing environmental restoration, and identified
resource streams to support its objectives. This process has, among
comparably weak powers, helped to generate a modicum of trust and
an acknowledgement of the need for pursuing common purposes
– including public education and outreach. Only time will tell,
however, if these efforts have been successful. Much will depend on
supporting efforts to institute alternative energy sources for families
and communities.

The so-called "Joint Water Committee" (JWC), comprised of Israeli,
Jordanian, and Palestinian officials, was established to manage water
infrastructure in the West Bank and Gaza as a result of the Oslo Accord
(phases I and II) of 1994–5. The JWC is another example of partial cooperation and partial confidence building connected to a realist model
of cooperation.

Its charter seeks to remove water and wastewater from the region's
cycle of violence, while also undertaking mutual steps to provide
stable, safe water supplies to local communities, especially in the
West Bank. The latter is promoted by agreement to operate and maintain water and wastewater treatment infrastructure, and to mutually
respond to community demands to repair water and water treatment systems. The two sides also agree to provide water and sewer
services to communities in their respective political jurisdictions,
to make repairs anywhere in the settled regions, and not to harm or
disrupt anyone engaged in operating, maintaining, or repairing water
works. In effect, harm to the water works of one side or the other
harms both – while assistance to one renders assistance to all.

The agreement does not seek – and is clearly not empowered – to
address larger questions of water sharing, sovereignty, or control: or
even to curtail the right of further Israeli settlement, which some vigorously argue is the agreement's most fundamental shortcoming – and
the principal reason it has not generated a high degree of confidence
(Selby 2013). Instead, efforts are focused on minimizing the sources of
conflict that lead to uncontrolled hostility by treating the water supply
systems of Israel and the West Bank as "intertwined and inseparable."
While the agreement forming the JWC does seek to estimate use,

availability and recharge rates for the complex aquifer system of the region, and to estimate future needs and uses, it also acknowledges that the region's surface waters have been fully "appropriated."

Critics also note that inequities in national allocation and sharing of water supplies remain, and that data on water availability remains opaque, with a lack of policy coordination for the areas in greatest need (e.g., Gaza), and over the Jordan River (Ehrenreich 2011; Selby 2013). While the agreement is the culmination of a process that began in 1995 with an Israeli promise to increase water supply to Palestinians by some 25 percent, disputes over water supply still persist (EcoPeace Middle East 2009).

Power over water decision-making between the two sides is clearly unequal, with Israel holding most of the control over the aquifer system shared by the two countries. Moreover, the process governing decisions depends almost wholly on the trust and confidence of local officials who operate within national governance systems that lack strong, formal diplomatic ties. Common purpose – aside from the pragmatic goal of protecting water delivery and treatment systems – is virtually absent.

On the other hand, the JWC does provide a means for ensuring basic *compliance and verification* and a structure for discussion and policy implementation. Each side has three members, and there is no "third party" mediation. Instead, differences are resolved by negotiation within the JWC itself (Shamir 1998). Each side knows, at the local level, how much water is being consumed, and for what purposes, while international donor aid has been attracted to the region for JWC-supported water projects, in part, because of confidence in the pacification of water as an issue.

Wisely, perhaps, negotiators deliberately "bracketed out" larger issues such as what constitutes a fairer allocation of total water supplies among the two nations, knowing that this issue is probably impossible to resolve in the current political climate in the region. Until such issues are resolved, however, no lasting peace agreement is possible. Certainly, and sadly, no such pending agreement over water looms on the horizon.

High confidence and robust cooperation

High confidence and robust cooperation over water is exemplified by a handful of agreements among nation-states sharing roughly the same level of economic development; which are mostly democratic; and which have extensive involvement by civil society groups in domestic water management. Care should be taken in not confusing high confidence and robust cooperation with freedom from conflict (see box 7.3 – US and Canada). Nor should it be assumed that a regime that has high confidence always resolves the problems it was founded to address – the management of the Rhine River exemplifies many of these characteristics.

The International Commission for the Protection of the Rhine (ICPR) provides a forum for member countries to address water quality issues; a vehicle for public participation in helping design anti-pollution policies and programs; a system of river monitoring stations; a knowledge network (see chapter 5) for exchange of information on best practices in water quality abatement; and, most importantly, a platform for ongoing negotiations over trans-boundary issues. Its core functions include improvement of water quality, flood control, guaranteeing the use of Rhine water for drinking water production, improvement of the sediment quality in order to enable the use or disposal of dredged material without causing environmental harm, flood prevention and environmentally sound flood protection, and improvement of the North Sea quality in accordance with other measures aimed at the protection of this marine area (Hooper 2005).

The ICPR's evolution illustrates the challenges in achieving high confidence, as well as the arduous means for doing so. Early industrialization along the Rhine and its tributaries caused devastating pollution. In 1901 a cynical German Reichstag seriously considered legally designating the Rhine a sewer (Schulte-Wülwer-Leidig 2008). A treaty among several Rhine riparian nations in 1886 sought protection for economically valuable salmon fisheries but was too ineffective to prevent their near extinction (Huisman 2000). Moreover, The Netherlands, a downstream nation enduring the majority of pollution damage, prodded other countries to enact a more forceful international pollution agreement, but to no avail.

In 1950, ICPR was finally established under the aegis of an existing Navigation Commission – a body charged with removing snags and other shipping hazards but which was thought to have the administrative capacity needed to provide oversight of a pollution abatement system. Initial signatories included the Netherlands, Germany, France, Luxembourg, and Switzerland. A 1963 treaty concluded in Berne, Switzerland, created a permanent secretariat but did not establish explicit emission goals (Mostert 2009). Until the mid-1980s in fact, ICPR could be considered little more than a "paper" vehicle for protecting water quality with little actual authority to reduce chemical pollution or formulate enforceable emission standards.

Box 7.3   The US, Canada, and Trans-boundary Water Management – "friendly" rivals?

Relations between the US and Canada have long been amicable. Thus, any hint of discord over water is difficult to fathom. Yet in recent years, a proposed expansion of an existing US water project – the so-called Garrison Diversion Unit – did exactly that: it caused intense and for a time intractable conflict over water management and environmental protection in the northern plains of the US, and in Manitoba, Canada.

In 1909, a Boundary Waters Treaty was forged between the two nations to ensure, as stated in Section IV of the covenant, that "the waters herein defined as boundary waters and waters flowing across the [US–Canada] border shall not be polluted on either side to the injury of health or property on the other." While rarely invoked, an International Joint Commission charged under the treaty with adjudicating disputes that may arise was called into action nearly a whole dozen years after the US Congress authorized the Garrison Diversion Unit (GDU). An ambitious irrigation scheme, the principal purposes of GDU were conceived as (1) irrigating some 250,000 acres of arable land in North Dakota, (2) providing water for municipal and industrial use in 14 communities, and (3) enhancing recreational opportunities and fish and wildlife management programs within, and adjacent to, the canals and reservoirs resulting from its construction. The project was to be financed by hydropower sales from Lake Sakakawea, created when Garrison Dam was completed in 1956.

Canadians, especially residents of Manitoba, feared that return flows from the project would provide a direct route into the Red River of the North, introducing invasive species that could disrupt fisheries and inflict other damage. Concerted litigation, Canadian opposition, and federal budget cuts have sharply reduced the size and scope of GDU since the mid-1980s. Its irrigable acreage has been reduced by over 50 percent, a principal feeder reservoir has been eliminated, and provision of municipal and industrial water delivery has been moved from second to first priority by a Congressional commission.

The controversy illustrates the consequences of the lack of a coherent environ-mental agreement between two friendly nations that not only shared watersheds but, theoretically at least, have a high confidence arrangement for resolving differences. The impact of GDU would have extended to Canada, yet there has been little agreement between the two nations over what values should guide trans-boundary water resources development in this region. Moreover, the two countries – and residents of Manitoba and North Dakota, respectively – defined the issues differently. To US proponents, the project was compensation to an entire region for losses of land associated with the original construction of Garrison Dam. To many Canadians, the central issue was balancing potential negative impacts against benefits. Neither view can alone encompass the range of social, economic, and environmental consequences of complex river basin development – the reason for having a trans-boundary agreement in the first place.

Source: Feldman 1991

In 1986, a major chemical spill in Switzerland led to a massive fish and eel kill, bans on potable water use throughout the basin, and public outrage. The latter led to demands for concerted action from the 10-nation secretariat. In 1987 a Rhine Action Programme (RAP) was developed. Since then, modest water quality improvements have been made. Oxygen levels are improving and heavy metal pollution has been reduced.

On the negative side of the ledger, salmon have not re-appeared in significant numbers and serious runoff pollutants persist. In 1999, a set of ambitious water quality goals were promulgated and ICPR began to be widely viewed as a model of international collaboration. In fact, the RAP has remained no more legally binding than its predecessors due to national resistance to granting the Commission independent enforcement or investigative power.

So, how can we characterize this regime's confidence as high? Strong knowledge network collaboration among member states has led to a gradual harmonization of national standards toward the regulation and management of pollution. These have proven to be more important to the ICPR's pollution abatement outcomes than any central enforcement mechanism.

The Rhine Action Programme has encouraged an active sharing of knowledge among country negotiators and civil society groups – especially technical "sub-groups" that have been formed to investigate the causes, consequences, and possible remedies of specific water quality problems. Robust knowledge sharing, in turn, has been facilitated by three factors unique to ICPR countries: high levels of economic development, strong economic interdependence (a function of European Union membership for most ICPR signatories except Switzerland), and the fact that democratically-elected leaders are more responsive than autocrats to water quality and allocation issues (Pfeiffer & Leentvaar 2013). The ability to share and exchange information has indirectly forced a set of common pollution policy processes among ICPR member states, ensuring over time the development of adequate safeguards (Pfeiffer & Leentvaar 2013).

While other transnational water quality regimes have tried to achieve similar objectives (e.g., the Danube Convention), significant obstacles to their success include their reliance on voluntary harmonization of standards by countries both less economically developed or economically integrated than those in ICPR, and a lack of strong democratic traditions. Decades of neglect of water quality concerns by authoritarian Communist governments made the Danube a virtual open sewer for its 80 million residents. Inadequate water treatment facilities, a lack of best management practices to retard runoff from farms (and a proliferation of large-scale, inefficient collective farms), and persistence of inter-country rivalries such as that between Hungary and the Czech Republic on the need for a new dam to furnish water for irrigation and public supply, all contributed to the basin's degraded water quality.

Progress has begun to be made – in part due to the same type of knowledge propagation and dissemination programs used by the much wealthier Rhine basin states. The Danube River Protection Convention, or ICPDR, has focused on generating baseline data to help reduce point source pollution, and to focus its limited response capabilities on so-called "hot spots" centered on cities, manufacturing centers, and agricultural districts. Gradually, wastewater treatment, conservation easement programs, and wetland restoration programs are improving river water quality and reducing hypoxia zones in the Black Sea (Gils & Bendow 2000; ICPDR 2005).

In sum, getting countries to appreciate that their water security is inter-linked is not merely a function of being "hydraulically connected." Common purpose and a process able to forge constructive ties are needed to develop confidence. While this process can be hastened by support and resources furnished by states external to the region (as with Israel and Palestine and Haiti and the Dominican Republic), ultimately, hydraulically connected states must recognize that it is in their national self-interest to collaborate (Tir & Ackerman 2009). This lesson is true among high confidence states, as in the Rhine basin, and it is also true for low confidence situations – as in the Tigris-Euphrates region.

Non-governmental networks – "soft" power and cooperation

In recent decades, freshwater problems have increasingly manifested themselves as global political issues that transcend hydrologically connected countries. Examples include demands by less developed nations for climate adaptation technologies, and pleas for reallocation of resources to address community-level water problems.

While confidence building remains key to successful problem solving in this global context, two additional issues have been introduced into the arena: a desire on the part of developing countries to shift control of the resources used to manage these problems from the more developed countries to themselves, and a growing sense of vulnerability on the part of localities – including provinces, states, and even cities, to the impacts of climate change. Another important issue has arisen in the past decade: frustration with inaction (or seemingly inadequate action) on the part of national governments to address these issues (Rabe 2004; Selin & VanDeveer 2009).

Significantly, change has been brought about not so much through the traditional levers of international politics – economic compulsion, diplomatic influence, or even military action, but through the exercise of what political scientists call "soft power" – persuading actors to modify their values through encouraging them to emulate the success of others.

Three general sets of actions have resulted from the introduction of these issues into global debates over freshwater management. First, since the 1980s, many UN-affiliated organizations that support climate adaptation and funding for community water and wastewater treatment infrastructure have come under pressure to become less "owned" by the wealthy, powerful nations of the Northern hemisphere and more sensitive to the interests of the developing countries of the global "south." Examples include UNESCO, UNEP, UNDP, the World Bank (especially its Global Environment Facility, which funds climate change adaptation projects), and the Intergovernmental Panel on Climate Change (IPCC) (Schneider 1987; Young 1989).

Second, beginning in the early 1990s, the United Nation's Conference on Environment and Development's (UNCED) Local Agenda 21 Program, and Article 10 of the Rio Declaration on Environment and Development, encouraged developing countries to restructure their national development plans to better embrace local-level decision-making programs that foster resilience. The goal is to ensure that investments made by UN-affiliated organizations are vetted through local NGOs and community groups that may not be adequately represented at *national* levels of decision-making. The hope is that this can increase their capacity to leverage development funds to tackle issues related to sea-level rise and comparable problems affecting freshwater systems (United Nations Division for Sustainable Development 1992; Grubb et al. 1993).

Third, these initiatives gradually encouraged the growth of so-called "locally enhanced plans" for integrated watershed activities to forestall erosion and deforestation, encourage sound land uses, and ensure the participation of indigenous populations in water resource decisions. These local plans emphasize "de-bureaucratization" of decisions, and devolution of authority to local governments. They also have contributed to the advent of a number of civil society and local government "networking" efforts that foster innovation diffusion.

One example of such networking efforts is a series of international conferences on water and human rights: the Dublin Conference of 1992 being one example. Other networking meetings have followed suit, including various World Civil Society Forums, as well as Stockholm Water Symposia (Coulomb 2001; Delfino 2001; World Civil Society Forum 2002). Common themes expressed at these gatherings include urging attendees to lobby for universal access to drinking water, encourage investment in local water management, and shield vulnerable communities from untoward efforts to privatize water provision systems, especially in poorer rural communities. Stockholm symposia have encouraged more local "knowledge networks" to check the power of private water interests.

One of the most significant networking efforts with respect to urban water is ICLEI – The International Council of Local Environmental Initiatives for Sustainability, a loose confederation of some 1,000 local governments engaged in sustainable development efforts, based in Germany. ICLEI is best described as an information and innovation dissemination network. Its goal is to help local communities and especially cities engage in climate change reduction, mitigation, and adaptation activities. Formed in 1990 at the conclusion of the World Congress of Local Governments, its charter is predicated on the idea that locally designed initiatives best provide effective, cost-efficient ways to achieve sustainability. ICLEI provides consulting, training, and other services to build capacity, share knowledge, and support local governments in implementing sustainable development innovations. It publicizes and awards notable "success stories," an example of the use of "soft power" to institute change (Nye 2004).

While much of ICLEI's efforts focus on energy use and waste management – especially reducing greenhouse gases – water services have gradually become a larger part of its suite of activities (ICLEI 1995). In 2007, for instance, ICLEI-USA initiated a Climate Resilient Communities program to help communities become more resilient to the impacts of climate change on water (ICLEI 2007). Strategies that ICLEI has endorsed and helped communities develop include better means of integrating climate preparedness strategies into existing hazard mitigation plans, reduce the costs associated with disaster relief, and prioritize vulnerabilities such as infrastructure, zoning, and water supply capacity.

Moreover, ICLEI-USA partnered with the National Oceanic and Atmospheric Administration's (NOAA's) Regional Integrated Sciences and Assessment to help local experts from universities and research organizations provide direct guidance to local communities seeking to increase climate resilience.

Finally, in the early 2000s, ICLEI developed a Global Water Campaign to help cities adopt low impact development projects to improve water quality and help conserve supplies by harvesting rainwater, improving water use efficiencies, and recycling wastewater. A keystone of this campaign was to assist smaller cities – such as those in South Australia suffering from the effects of the mid 2000s Millennium Drought – to adopt methods proven elsewhere by working together to affordably introduce costly innovations (ICLEI 2006).

An indirect result of such efforts has been the growth of "mini-networks:" regional consortia comprised of NGOs and, in some instances, public agencies, to further sustainable water management among countries. One of the best examples is the European River Corridor Improvement Plans project (ERCIP), formed in 2011 by nine partners from the UK, Germany, Italy, Romania, and Greece.

ERCIP's mission is simple yet ambitious: to connect the European Union's ambitious Water Framework Directive – which articulates guidelines for improving riverine quality by prescribing means for stream restoration – with local efforts to improve the management of river catchments (ERCIP 2014). Financed largely by the EU's Regional Development Fund, ERCIP encourages individual member states to develop locally-viable restoration plans, which range from improving recreational tourism and river corridor protection in Greece, to water quality improvements to rivers and "thermal waters" in Romania, improving communication and marketing campaigns for riverine tourism and restoration in Germany and Italy, and reducing the impacts of urbanization pressures in the UK. Like ICLEI, ERCIP disseminates innovations among members, promotes "best practices," and produces an easily understood guide to other national and regional authorities to use when undertaking comparable efforts.

It remains to be seen if such efforts can address the type of water resource problems their benefactors – including Local Agenda 21 – hoped they would address. What is clear is that these efforts are based on a new paradigm for global water politics: connecting locally-generated innovations in one place with local needs in another, and doing so through direct local government-to-local government, NGO-to-NGO collaboration – often, without the benefit of national-level intervention.

Conclusions – new challenges in trans-boundary accord

The lack of any prescribed process for international water management has, in recent years especially, given rise to the concern that regional disputes could arise over water that might lead to larger and increasingly intractable conflicts. In February 2012, the US intelligence community issued a report on *Global Water Security* commissioned by former Secretary of State Hillary Rodham Clinton.

The report concluded that by mid-century, serious bouts of flooding and drought were likely to occur, most especially in the developing regions of North Africa, the Middle East, and South Asia as a result of acute climate variability. These and related problems "will hinder the ability of key countries to produce food and generate energy, posing a risk to global food markets and hobbling economic growth" (Defense Intelligence Agency 2012).

Various methods for improved water management, which will be discussed later, such as investments in technologies to reduce water use by agriculture, may partly alleviate these problems. However, when the water problems these countries face "are combined with poverty, social tensions, environmental degradation, ineffectual leadership, and weak political institutions," the net result are societal disruptions that may result in state failure, even with the introduction of water innovations.

This combination of problems – while unlikely to lead to war – will produce chronic, low-intensity conflicts. Although the report is not precise as to what "chronic" conflict might look like, examples we earlier explored in the Middle East – as well examples we will examine in the next chapter – provide a fairly well rounded picture of the possible political scenarios we may expect to occur with greater frequency.

The final, and perhaps most sobering challenge in the report is that improved water saving and conservation approaches, as well as wastewater and other water reclaiming technologies, can address some of these issues – but are not panaceas. Continued population growth and demands for more food and energy will severely tax the world's fresh water and – axiomatically – will demand some kind of global prescription for its management (Defense Intelligence Agency 2012). To ponder what that solution might look like, we first have to understand the "realpolitik" of water politics – or, in other words, the actions that cause, and the consequences that result from, water disputes. We take up this issue in chapter 8.

SUMMARY

- Because watersheds and aquifers do not respect political boundaries, governance methods based on cooperation and accord must acknowledge national sovereignty.

- A key to cooperation is confidence building – countries comply with agreements out of the belief that others will do so, and that non-compliance can be deterred.

- While cooperation provides common mutual benefits and shared decision-making processes, power differentials among countries remain significant barriers.

RECOMMENDED READING

- A historical view of water conflicts among countries and the institutional frameworks developed to abate these disputes is found in: A. Dinar, S. Dinar, S. McCaffrey & D. McKinney (eds.), *Bridges over Water: Understanding Transboundary Water conflict, Negotiation, and Cooperation* (2013).
- A good chronicle of efforts at developing international river basin agreements with a comprehensive bibliography can be found in: J. Tir and J. T. Ackerman, "Politics of Formalized River Cooperation," *Journal of Peace Research* (2009).
- An excellent examination of the role of knowledge networks in the development of strong confidence building systems for river basin management can be found in E. Pfeiffer and J. Leentvaar, "Knowledge Leads, Policy Follows?" *Water Policy* (2013).
- Dinesh Kumar's *Managing Water in River Basins* (2010) is a comprehensive river-basin management text that ranges widely between hydrology, economics, and law and politics to dissect the complex politics of water management.

WEBSITES

- http://www.transboundarywaters.orst.edu/research/case_studies/index.html Program in Water Conflict Management and Transformation, Institute for Water.
- https://www.globalpolicy.org/security-council.html The Global Policy Forum.
- http://jpr.sagepub.com/content/46/5/623 article on formalized river cooperation.

QUESTIONS FOR DISCUSSION

1. What factors contribute to building strong confidence in international agreements among countries negotiating treaties or other agreements to manage water?

2. What processes are employed by compacts, commissions, and other entities to enforce allocation agreements and distribution of supplies? Are they effective?

3. What ideals do compacts seek to achieve? Why are these ideals so difficult to achieve in practice, and how do process and power affect their achievement?

CHAPTER 8
Water Conflicts

What causes water disputes?

While countries, or regions within them, rarely come to blows over how water is used, efforts to harness rivers, streams, or groundwater basins – or to acquire access to a water source – often result in conflict. Moreover, changes that affect quality and availability – such as the building of dams – may dislocate people from their homes or dispossess them of their means of livelihood or ancestral lands. Such actions adversely affect cultural as well as economic goals and purposes.

In short, using, moving, impounding, and polluting water may result in disputes that involve the use of *power* (sometimes exercised unequally); embrace various dispute-resolution *processes* that can employ law, regulation, voluntary collaborative agreements, or litigious exchanges between parties; and have as their *purpose* protagonists' desires for solutions accruing to their divergent interests.

While freshwater disputes have numerous causes, three distinct activities most often precipitate major conflicts. These are: *diversion* – the transferring of water from one basin to another; *depletion* – using up available ground or surface water without replenishment; and *degradation* – reducing the healthy functioning of a water body through pollution, channelization of streams, impoundment, and other alterations.

Ironically, these practices may arise because rules governing the use of water in a region encourage its depletion, degradation, or over-use. Examples include laws that inadvertently promote groundwater overdraft or off-stream over-allocation. Even when these laws, rules, and regulations change, their legacy persists in the form of irreversible impacts. Groundwater basins cannot easily recover once depleted; and channelized streams cannot be easily restored once modified. To compensate, we may engage in practices that impose different harms.

Diverting water – power, process, purpose

Diversion is often undertaken in regions where water is in short supply and where competing demands are acute. In such instances, proposals to move water great distances are introduced to replenish dwindling supplies, or supplement existing but inadequate supplies. This can be done within countries, or among them. Recent diversion projects in China and India exemplify both.

In North China, serious groundwater depletion has led to the water table around Beijing falling some five meters per year. Wells must be drilled up to half a mile in depth. Serious shortages have left smaller cities without adequate drinking water and deferred plans for growth. By World Bank estimates, the aquifers beneath the North China Plain – which provide 60 percent of the supply for the 200 million residents of the region, and encompass the provinces of Hebei, Henan and Shandong as well as the cities of Tianjin and Beijing – will be depleted by 2045 (Wong 2007).

Problems first became dramatically apparent after the 1949 Communist revolution. Water use in China increased five-fold, while the growth of cities as a result of rapid industrialization led to the building of massive dams and canals to permit the storage of water for their benefit, while bypassing rural areas. To compensate, farmers increased their use of groundwater in an effort to help China become agriculturally self-sufficient. This rapid development also promoted inefficient and environmentally questionable water use. While Chinese industry uses 4–10 times more water than industrialized countries, agricultural water use efficiency is about 40 percent compared to 75–80 percent in the US. Farmers pay for water based on area irrigated, as opposed to the amount of water they use – further contributing to inefficiency (Wong 2007).

To rectify the problems generated by rapid development, Chairman Mao himself conceived of a "South–North Water Transfer Project." This $62 billion scheme is designed to transfer 12 trillion gallons of water per year via three canals from the Yangtze River in the South to the Yellow River basin in the North, using in some cases existing canal infrastructure – and all primarily for the benefit of cities and industry (see figure 8.1). When completed, the eastern route will provide water for domestic and industrial use for Shandong and Jiangsu provinces, while the central route will provide supplies for more than 20 cities, including Beijing and Tianjin.

As in many major water projects conceived by governments, proponents have heralded its perceived benefits and downplayed both its

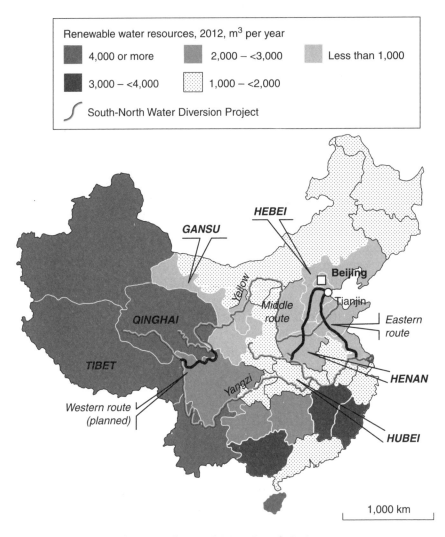

Figure 8.1 *China's South-to-North Water Transfer Project*

risks and possible alternatives that could have been adopted. It has been widely asserted that the project would mitigate conflicts caused by competitive uses, avert over-exploitation of groundwater reserves, and make it possible to fully meet agricultural demands.

As portions of the project have been completed, however, the government has had to backtrack on some of these claims, acknowledging that water quality along the eastern canals and riverbeds may worsen because these watercourses may become conduits for runoff pollution from industry and agriculture. Other adverse environmental and social impacts have also arisen.

Communities along the project's middle route have faced massive relocation of families – some 180,000 people have been moved within Hubei Province and another 150,000 to Henan Province. Massive impacts to cities such as Danjiangkou City, where large storage reservoirs for the project have been built, are reminiscent of the relocation that accompanied construction of the Three Gorges Dam a decade ago. And, as in that case, some claim that relocation estimates issued by the government have been considerably lower than the actual numbers (Barclay 2010; Economist 2014; Chen 2015). As a result, questions have been raised over the project's ultimate purposes and the power conferred by its differential benefits on some groups. The hierarchical and non-inclusive process used to make decisions regarding the project's construction has also come under scrutiny.

In Beijing, the fastest growing water demands that are reliant on the project's completion stem from luxury gardens, swimming pools, and high-rise apartments. The city's two major reservoirs have already been reduced to less than 10 percent of their original storage capacities (Barclay 2010). As of 2014, the project has annually drawn some 9.5 billion cubic meters of water from the Han River. With some 25–30 percent of the river's total flow being diverted, the river's middle and lower reaches will be damaged through depletion of flow, greater concentrations of pollutants, fewer navigable days, loss of fishery breeding grounds, and other adverse impacts. The majority of expenditures for the eastern route have been earmarked for pollution control facilities (Wong 2007; China Daily 2012).

The project's costs, as well as growing demands for water conservation, are also leading to higher charges for project water. Some cities and provinces are beginning to balk at paying higher fees, and higher charges for agricultural irrigation water have begun to reduce water use for lower value crops such as grain. While increased water tariffs may become a sound, long-term alternative for managing the country's water, an irony in all this is that it has taken a very expensive diversion project to spark serious proposals for its introduction.

If China represents the politics of large-scale diversion in a country facing diverse water needs, India's conflict with Pakistan over plans to develop a portion of the upper Indus basin represents a similar set of issues in a transnational context. Since 2009, India has been constructing a hydroelectric project with a planned capacity of 330 MW by diverting the waters of the Kishanganga-Neelum River – a tributary of the Jhelum River in Kashmir.

The name Kishan Ganga is applied strictly to the Indian side of the valley, while Pakistan refers to the tributary as the Neelum: this differential nomenclature underscores the depth of division between the two nations. Diversion will be achieved through a 23-km-long tunnel planned for completion in 2016. The goal of the Kishanganga-Neelum hydro project (or KHEP) is to generate electricity for India's rapidly growing, power-hungry economy (Tanoli 2015). Thus, like China's South-to-North Water Transfer Project, the project's primary purpose is fostering economic development.

At the center of the conflict is Pakistan's fear that the KHEP project could allow India to reduce flows on the Kishanganga-Neelum. Such a reduction in flow would threaten downstream agriculture, which accounts for 25 percent of Pakistan's economy and employs nearly half the country's population. As far back as the 1990s, when India first announced its plans for KHEP, Pakistan raised concerns over what it calls "inter-tributary diversions," formally barred by the 1960 Indus Water Treaty which established a bi-national commission for governing allocation and management of the Indus system.

In effect, Pakistan argues, its existing uses of the Neelum are legally protected under the treaty while the KHEP would deprive Pakistan of the river's natural flows. The project would adversely affect irrigated agriculture in the Neelum valley. Pakistan has raised other objections, including the project's draw-down technology to flush sediments, which could prove injurious to Pakistan's own plans to construct the Neelum-Jhelum hydro-electric project (NJHEP) at Nowshera. The latter would be built with assistance from a Chinese consortium and have a planned electrical output three times greater than that of India's KHEP project – see figure 8.2 (Grover 2014).

In May 2010, Pakistan filed a brief with the Permanent International Arbitration Court to stop the KHEP project on grounds that inter-tributary diversion is illegal under the Indus Treaty and that India's draw-down plans would reduce the power output of Pakistan's NJHEP. The Arbitration Court directed the case to the International Court of Justice on the basis of several clauses of the 1960 Indus Basin Treaty, the International Convention on Environment Change, the Kyoto Protocol on Climate Change, and the Ramsar Convention on Wetlands (Tanoli 2015).

In February 2013, the court ruled that since the KHEP is a "run-of-the-river" project, India might divert water from the Kishanganga-Neelum River for power production. In addition, while India's plans for river development were certain, Pakistan's were more tentative, exemplified by the latter's lag in planning and implementation of the NJHEP. Consequently, in the Court's opinion, India's plans took priority over Pakistan's – a not uncommon principle in international law.

Figure 8.2 *Kishanganga–Neelum river basin*

The country that carries out its plans first exercises its claims most convincingly (Grover 2014). The Court urged both nations to use the Permanent Indus Commission – the governing body of the Indus Basin Compact formed in 1960 – to revisit the case seven years after the KHEP is completed, in order to consider whether diversion is having negative impacts.

On one level, the verdict would appear to be a clear legal victory for India, and a diplomatic and economic loss for Pakistan. Politically, it solidly legitimizes India's aspirations to continue to develop hydropower projects on the Jhelum and Chenab Rivers. On another level, however, the Court tried to ensure that India operate the KHEP in a manner less environmentally harmful than might otherwise have been the case.

The Court ordered India to strictly respect Indus Water Treaty limits on water storage behind impoundments; to adopt methods other than low gates to flush silt from its dams on future run-of-river projects; and to protect in-stream flows by providing for minimal releases that would reduce electricity production at the KHEP by nearly 6 percent annually. Despite these safeguards, the project will ultimately reduce the flow of water for Pakistan's NJHEP, reducing its power production by some 20 percent, and resulting in significant revenue losses that – during periods of drought – could total over $0.5 billion annually (Grover 2014).

There is a second interpretation of this case, however, that may be equally warranted. While India "won," the Court's verdict incorporates into the Indus Treaty means to avoid – or at least defuse – serious basin conflicts between India and Pakistan in the future. For one thing, while India can develop hydropower projects in the western portion of the basin, it must do so "under a set of well-defined constraints on the amount of storage as permitted in the treaty" (Grover 2014). For another, in August 2014, India agreed to re-visit Pakistan's objections over the design of KHEP and four other power projects on the Jhelum and Chenab rivers through bi-lateral talks between teams of negotiators under the Pakistani and Indian Commissioners to the Indus Water Commission (Hasnain 2014).

While no changes in the ICJ's decision have been made, the case remains significant in what it says about the importance of legally defined environmental obligations and the adequacy of international courts and other tribunals to settle complex disputes. Clearly, India and Pakistan would prefer a peaceful – if not entirely amicable – arbitration to this dispute, as opposed to the kind of contentious and unpredictable political alternatives large dam projects often generate.

What of the politics of diversion more generally? China's South–North Transfer project and the India–Pakistan KHEP–NJHEP projects offer three important lessons regarding the roles of process, power, and purpose in the politics of diversion. First, economic development pressures are hugely influential in proposals to divert water. A sense of crisis, or at least of an impending and urgent set of demands, tends to propel diversion projects forward. These interests exercise greater power in part because they ally themselves with public agencies that also have an interest in building large-scale projects to advance regional economic development, and so as to justify the programs and philosophies of their agencies, which tend to favor big engineering approaches to problem-solving.

Second, the processes by which diversion projects are undertaken are often narrowly conceived, hierarchical, and involve sharply truncated participation. This is reflected in the fact that they often fail to capture environmental or social equity issues when proposed, implemented, or – in the case of India and Pakistan – appealed to an international tribunal. When policy reforms are advanced to try and rectify these concerns, they often propose changes in decision-making processes that force consideration of water conservation programs or, at the very least, changes in the manner in which diversion projects are operated.

Third, at a critical juncture in diversion disputes – usually when their potentially adverse consequences become apparent – demands arise to include alternatives in decision-making. These demands do not necessarily prompt debates over the fundamental purpose of diversion, unless one side or the other claims harm and, thus, disagrees over its goals. The early twentieth century dispute over the diversion of the Owens Valley in the Eastern Sierra to provide water supply for a growing Los Angeles exemplifies disagreement over diversion centered on divergent purpose (see box 8.1).

By contrast with the Owens Valley in the early twentieth century, Pakistan and India today both aspire to develop hydropower, and in the same basin. They disagree over the need to protect their own economic interests as a result of the other side's efforts to achieve the same objective. This suggests that even when purpose is shared, other differences may still be manifest unless countries choose to pursue their comparable purposes conjointly.

Depletion – what happens when water is used up?

The political challenge of depletion is that water policies designed to regulate water withdrawals in order to sustain regional economic activities may result in the opposite: over-drafting of groundwater and depletion of stream-flow. Exhaustion of surface water and groundwater supplies is becoming a fact throughout the world. An increasingly common denominator of these problems is the promotion of regional economic development through a combination of private and public capital investment in exploiting water resources. While states in these instances may be strong enough to provide direct subsidies or licensing of certain activities, they are often too weak to avert the harms that result. In short, they lack power to regulate or enforce withdrawal limits. A good example of these policy challenges can be seen in groundwater depletion in the Ojos Negros Valley in Baja California (Mexico) and bottling of beverages in India.

Since the 1980s, increased pumping of groundwater for farming in the Ojos Negros valley has seriously depleted the regional water table, which now lies at more than 30 meters in depth. Over the past century

Box 8.1   An old diversion whose legacy remains – Los Angeles and the Owens Valley

As Los Angeles' population doubled during the 1890s, from 50,000 to 100,000, and then doubled again within five years, all but depleting local groundwater, and threatening to deplete the Los Angeles River, civic leaders sought a permanent remedy. Fred Eaton, one-time city engineer during the 1890s, mayor from 1899 to 1901, and superintendent of Los Angeles' municipal water system, conceived of an Owens River aqueduct in the early 1900s. Initial challenges proved to be fiscal, not logistical. Voters were persuaded to acquire public ownership of the vast, fragmented, and poorly maintained private network of water providers in 1902. Following consolidation of legal control over water in its immediate vicinity, the Owens Valley project was pursued. In 1904, William Mulholland – a protégé of Eaton and now city engineer – asked his mentor to "show me this water supply" in the Owens Valley about which Eaton had often spoken. Following an intrepid journey both took through the region, which included a preliminary survey of an aqueduct route, events moved quickly. In September 1905, voters approved by a 10-1 margin a $1.5 million project to acquire right-of-way, and to build an aqueduct that would stretch from north of Independence some 234 miles southeast to the San Fernando Valley – a recently incorporated area of the city.

At the moment political forces in Los Angeles maneuvered to acquire Owens Valley water rights, the newly-formed US Reclamation Service drafted a plan to irrigate the valley by constructing dams. As a federal agency mandated to promote irrigation, the Service was inclined to support valley residents against those of a large city seeking to augment its water supply. However, the Reclamation Service's southwestern regional chief, Joseph P. Lippincott, served (secretly) as a paid consultant to Los Angeles, abetting the city's plans, since Lippincott advocated for the city's interests in Washington, DC, not those of the Owens Valley. Lippincott helped ensure that, while valley lands would be set aside for public purpose, no land rights would be secured. This aided Eaton's efforts to set about buying up options on lands for aqueduct construction. A campaign to obtain Congressional approval of the City's application to build the aqueduct was effectuated in 1906; while in 1907, Los Angeles voters approved a second bond measure authorizing $23 million for aqueduct construction. Construction began in 1908, and the project was completed in 1913.

The virtual draining of Owens Lake as a result of the opening of the first Los Angeles Aqueduct exposed the alkali lake-bed to winds that lofted toxic dust clouds containing selenium, cadmium, arsenic and other elements throughout the region. Airborne particulates were often suspended for days during excessively dry periods – and have long posed a health hazard to local residents. They have even posed risks to communities further to the south. These issues came to a head in the 1990s through public protest, litigation, and federal intervention. In 1994, a settlement was reached between Los Angeles, Inyo and Mono Counties, and the US EPA, and was enforced, in part, through a series of massive fines levied upon the Los Angeles Department of Water and Power (LADWP). The settlement forced the agency to restore 62 miles of the lower Owens River, to "re-water" portions of Owens Lake and to allow the return of flows through Owens Gorge, and to restock bluegill, largemouth bass, fingerling trout, and other aquatic species – although a final negotiated solution was not consummated until 2014.

Sources: Kahrl 1982; Davis 1993; Mulholland 2002; Los Angeles Department of Water and Power 2010

or more, the valley has become a major agricultural production region, largely due to irrigation. Ranching – mostly drylands pasturing – is also increasing. While farming and ranching have expanded the regional economy, they have taken a toll on the environment in several ways, including an increase in evapotranspiration, humidification of the local climate, and depletion of wetland and riparian ecosystems, including drying out of the Ojos Negros marshes – a significant habitat for bird species (Ojos Negros Research Group 2012).

Ordinarily, adverse impacts on irrigated agriculture from depletion might have been expected. However, low energy costs (subsidized by the Mexican government) not only encourage groundwater pumping, but compensate for the greater relative effort required to recover groundwater in support of agri-business in the valley and for the large numbers of *ejido* proprietors. The latter is a type of collective, communal farming enterprise unique to post-1910 revolutionary Mexico. In essence, low user costs contribute to their over-exploitation of groundwater.

As one study has suggested, Ojos Negros is a classic "tragedy of the commons" (Ojos Negros Research Group 2012). Aquifer regulation, probably in the form of a strictly enforced withdrawal permitting system, is needed to rectify this situation. This, however, would require a system of rigorous groundwater monitoring to assure that data on depletion rates are made available to regulators and the authority to impose penalties for over-use.

Mexico's national water commission (Comisión Nacional del Agua, or CONAGUA) has authority to enforce the 1992 National Water Law – the federal legal code that protects the water rights of rural residents – sets water quality discharge standards, and oversees municipal water authorities. It also administers all financial resources pertinent to water in Mexico, from user fees to World Bank loans (Medellin-Azuara et al. 2013), and is empowered to monitor water use from all sources. While also having an extensive network of regional offices corresponding to hydrologic regions, it faces considerable hurdles in the Ojos Negros Valley.

Underreporting, as well as "illegal water use, poor surveillance and lack of enforcement" (Medellin-Azuara et al. 2013: 21) is among the nationwide institutional deficiencies in water resources management it faces – especially in the Ensenada region. While recognized by the government as a challenge, serious reform is probably beyond the capacity of a political system with a weak regulatory state and a tradition of clientele politics.

In recent years, more frequent droughts have taken a special toll on ranching. Despite government subsidies available for groundwater pumping – many ranchers simply have no wells, or only small ones. CONAGUA also supplies farmers and ranchers with seminars and other sources of information as means of coping with these problems, and the Mexican government has subsidized the shipping of hay from Mexicali to Ojos Negros during droughts. Nonetheless, longer-term solutions such as rainwater harvesting through retention structures, dikes, dams, or reservoirs have not been widely initiated. As for groundwater generally, most believe water supply rationing is the only viable solution (Ojos Negros Research Group 2004). Efforts to devise integrated resource management plans have been undertaken in the region and may, over time, pay off.

If Baja, Mexico and the Ojos Negros symbolize the challenges of a "weak" state to regulate groundwater depletion, the extracting of groundwater for beverages in India exemplifies the challenges entailed when industrial-scale bottling encompasses multiple levels of governance, differing views of the public interest, and a political disconnect between governmental and corporate power in an international regulatory context.

In 2003, a PepsiCo bottling plant in the rural community of Pudussery in Kerala state, India, and another owned by Coca-Cola in nearby Perumatty, had their water-use licenses revoked and not renewed, respectively, due to citizen complaints that their operations were seriously depleting local groundwater supplies. A high court in Kerala reversed the decision against Coca-Cola, but the controversy remains unresolved because Coke and Pepsi together dominate the country's $1.2 billion market for soft drinks, one of the world's fastest growing. They also compete to sell bottled water.

Vocal and well-organized groups in both communities continue to criticize these companies for "exploiting" local water resources in the face of drought. However, local, state, and national elected officials want to strengthen trade with the US in order to promote job opportunities – thus, they stand opposed to the goals of protesting groups in this matter. For their part, Pepsi and Coke claim to maintain a vigilant watch over the environmental impacts of their operations (Rai 2003).

Most problematic of all, it is unclear to what extent if any trade in bottled water can be regulated by binding international agreements. Currently, free trade agreements are structured so as to inhibit national regulations of commodities in trade (such as bottled water and soft drinks). Moreover, these agreements tend to be stronger than local laws designed to protect sustainable water use. And there are currently no internationally binding agreements that can restrict trade in those instances where the bottling of water has been proven to adversely affect local water systems (Hoekstra 2010).

Both of these disputes exemplify the kind of conflicts engendered by connections between groundwater use, subsidized rural electrification, and groundwater-dependent economies discussed in the UN's *World Water Development Report* briefly discussed in chapter 1 and, to an extent, the challenges facing the water–energy–food nexus discussed in chapter 4. Three lessons are paramount. First, the ability of strong public concerns to institute reform is circumvented by weak states with low enforcement capacity – neither India nor Mexico are able to exert much restriction on groundwater withdrawal activity due to economic pressures to continue this activity.

Second, the lack of consensus across jurisdictional levels also impedes efforts to avert depletion. In Mexico, many local farmers and ranchers oppose continued unregulated withdrawals – but some constituencies who benefit from continued over-drawing do so with impunity. Likewise, in India, while local communities often oppose withdrawals, state and national levels of governance support them.

Finally, international entities have both positive and negative roles in these conflicts. In India, as we saw, rules governing water in trade make vigorous regulation on water bottling difficult. In Mexico, however, there has been some discussion around establishing a regional "Water Fund" to solicit international donor support as well as local user fees for the Ojos Negros region in order to fund irrigation efficiency improvements, water infrastructure, and education and training programs. It remains to be seen if such a fund can actually be established and effectively deter over-drafting (Medellin-Azuara et al. 2013).

Degradation – dysfunctional waters in dispute

Degradation entails reducing the capacity of a water body (i.e., a lake, river, stream, or aquifer – an underground reservoir) to sustain life-giving functions. This condition may be caused by introduction of contaminants or pollution from heat, chemicals, or radiation. It may also be generated by infestations of "non-native" predator species that feast on the fish and other aquatic life native to a particular water body. Finally, it also can result from construction of dams or levees that impede, alter, or obstruct the natural flow of a stream, creating in their stead impoundments or channels that transform rivers into still-bound reservoirs or floodways.

In many developing nations, dam building is viewed as an enormous incentive to economic development – especially for vast interior regions. Thus, the risk of degradation is often considered a worthwhile gamble, at least on the part of political leaders who promote and oversee the development of such projects. Brazil's Itaipu Dam (see box 8.2) exemplifies this political phenomenon.

Forms of degradation at least as severe, if not more so, can occur through diversion. The Aral Sea is a fitting example of the politics that produces such outcomes. Located on the border of current day Kazakhstan and Uzbekistan, until the early 1970s, it was the world's fourth largest saline lake. Its environmental demise began in the early 1960s when the former Soviet Union diverted the Syr Darya and Amu Darya – the principal tributaries feeding the Aral with seasonal runoff – to irrigate cotton farms and row crops in its vicinity. The goal of agricultural self-sufficiency was so compelling at this time, that Soviet leaders ignored warnings of possible irreversible environmental damage to the Aral. Unfortunately, these warning were all too prophetic.

After diversion of these twin rivers, problems arose almost immediately. Under pre-diversion conditions, the Aral normally received about 20 percent of its water supply via rainfall, with the remaining 80 percent provided by inflow from the Amu Darya and Syr Darya rivers. So long as inflow from these sources exceeded the rate of evaporation, naturally high in this semi-arid landscape, the Aral was sustainable. Diversion caused a steadily increasing imbalance, causing slow desiccation of the sea.

While the diverted water was routed into canals for irrigation, the majority (perhaps 25–75 percent) was soaked up by the desert and never served the needs for which it was intended (The Aral Sea Crisis 2008). The water level in the Aral Sea started drastically dropping from the 1960s onward, while the sea's salinity rose from 10 grams per liter to over 100 grams, killing off most fish species.

Impacts on human health in the region were even more adverse. Salt and dust-laden air have exacerbated respiratory ailments, including

Box 8.2 The benefits of dams come with many costs – Brazil's Itaipu Dam

Itaipu was completed in 1984, and took over a decade to build. Constructed on the Parana River on the border on Brazil and Paraguay – and just upstream from Argentina, the project is the second largest hydroelectric facility in the world – just behind China's Three Gorges Dam. The project generates approximately 14,000 MW, or as much as nine nuclear plants, and accounts, by itself, for fully 20 percent of Brazil's and 94 percent of Paraguay's electrical power. It has fostered considerable economic and political cooperation between Brazil and Paraguay, in part because the project was jointly built by both nations, and because a bi-national commission that markets the project's electrical power conjointly manages it.

While Itaipu has encouraged foreign investment in aluminum smelting, a user of the cheap power, especially by Argentine, Italian, and US industrial concerns, the project has also generated considerable environmental and other impacts that must be weighed against its benefits. Over 700 kilometers^2 of old growth tropical forest was destroyed, mostly on the Paraguayan side of the reservoir, as a result of the reservoir's filling and the need to clear-cut vegetation. Some plant species, including a rare orchid unique to this region of the South American rainforest, became extinct during construction. Moreover, some 59,000 people, many of whom were members of native, indigenous tribes, were relocated from the reservoir area.

As a result of both international pressures and domestic concerns expressed by environmental groups, a bi-national effort was undertaken to preserve many endangered plant species, and to salvage as much old-growth rainforest as was feasible. It has been estimated that over 50 percent of the forest cover in the region that could have been lost remains as a result of mitigation measures adopted during the building of the project. Considerable environmental planning was undertaken by both governments to monitor and prevent further damage to the impounded region's flora and fauna. One innovative measure was a special effort to minimize the effects of reservoir flooding on the fauna of the region by catching certain species of animals and releasing them in specially established biological reserves away from the reservoir area. The long-term success of this effort has not been easy to measure because some species may take decades to adapt to their new habitat.

Source: Wolf & Newton 2007b

asthma. Anemia, cancer and tuberculosis, and allergies are frequent in the region, and NGO activists who monitor local conditions allege dramatic increases in typhoid fever, viral hepatitis, tuberculosis, and throat cancer that, in many areas, are as high as three times the national average (Aral Sea website – maintained by NGOs in Kazakhstan). The application of pesticides into the rice and cotton fields irrigated by the Amu Darya and Syr Darya's flows have led to seepage of chemical residues back into these rivers, heavily contaminating local water supplies in communities living along their banks – these polluted flows make their way into the remnants of the sea.

If decisions leading to the Aral's demise can be characterized as risky and abusive – as some observers contend – then the policies to rectify and repair the damage can best be described as deliberately benign. Even after the effects of degradation became obvious to the landscape and local population alike, the Soviet regime ignored the need for restoration. When the sea split into two segments in the early 1990s, Russia, Kazakhstan, and Uzbekistan began to seek remedies. However, while formally establishing a joint restoration fund set at 1 percent of their annual GDP, failure to seed this fund led to a failure to take significant action for decades.

Local officials and villagers undertook initial restoration efforts. In the 1990s, they constructed a small dam to stabilize the remnants of the northern Aral. While eventually abandoned, it preserved enough of the Aral to make possible a World Bank-funded project to rebuild the canal system and construct a dam with Kazakhstan to raise the northern remnant of the Aral by 13 feet: deep enough to drop salinity to biologically sustainable levels, and to allow native fish to repopulate the sea. This $85 million project also improved irrigation structures upriver. This not only improved agricultural efficiencies but also led to restoration of local fauna and, amazingly by 2006, some spillover of water from the northern to the southern Aral (Conant 2006).

Politically, the Aral crisis comprises a complex intersection of local, national, and international actors and divergent political agendas. The power of the former Soviet state to undertake a series of steps to promote irrigation, at what proved to be at reckless expense to the Aral Sea, was eventually countermanded by local and individual country actions once the Soviet system collapsed. Nevertheless, a lack of dedicated national resources produced a diffuse, largely locally directed restoration effort that became linked principally to internationally funded efforts to undertake a more professional repair effort.

Even now, only Kazakhstan, with World Bank assistance, has taken an active interest in restoration – with Uzbekistan making no contribution. This contrast in effort is due, at least in part, to the former's growing reliance on a petroleum-driven economy as opposed to one wholly dependent on agriculture – allowing it to afford Syr Darya and northern Aral restoration. By contrast, with a quarter of its economy dependent on cotton, Uzbekistan has shown less interest in restoring the South Aral.

In 2006, as if to further ratify international political interest in the Aral Sea and what its restoration symbolizes, UNESCO granted it the status of "World Heritage Site" in an effort to compel partial restoration of the southern part of the sea. One political scientist has suggested that partial restoration would not only alleviate some of the region's health and environmental problems, but bring about a more sustained international effort to force governments in the region to cooperate on mitigating the problems of poor air quality caused by desiccation (Glantz 2007).

If the Aral represents the degradation through diversion producing desiccation of an inland sea, the Chesapeake Bay Program affords a good example of a multi-jurisdictional effort to reverse the effects of non-point pollution (see chapter 3) in order to try to restore the biological health of a major estuary impacted by diverse economic activities. Beginning in the early 1980s, Maryland, Pennsylvania, Virginia, the District of Columbia, the Chesapeake Bay Commission, and US EPA joined together to sponsor a government–private sector restoration partnership to abate and reverse water quality declines – including an acute, hypoxic dead-zone – and other threats to fish and wildlife in the Chesapeake Bay estuary. The outcome was the creation of the US Chesapeake Bay Program. A water body holding some 15 trillion gallons, embracing a 64,000 mile^2 drainage basin, fed by some 150 streams, and populated by over 15 million, the Bay is also home to some 3,600 animal and plant species, including seafood resources that have considerable economic value to six states, including parts of Delaware, Maryland, New York, Pennsylvania, Virginia, and West Virginia.

Initial restoration efforts largely began with a broad-based, citizen-led social movement beginning in the early 1970s that promoted a series of fact-finding efforts which led to the establishment of both the Chesapeake Bay Program and three agreements – in 1983, 1987, and 2000 – known as the Chesapeake Bay Agreements. In effect, a multi-stakeholder partnership, these agreements committed partners to a cooperative, integrated approach to protect the shared resources of the Bay and to restore it to productivity. Key to this approach is acknowledgement that the estuary is fed by major streams (including the Susquehanna and Chesapeake Rivers) that support numerous agricultural, industrial, and urban uses vital to the region's economy and ecosystem.

Water quality strategies have included reductions in point source pollutants and targeted cooperative and voluntary landowner participation programs to address non-point runoff, including a variety of growth-related initiatives to deter pollution. These landowner participation programs embrace a number of protected lands, including public, private, military, and agricultural easement lands: properties that are protected through a variety of conservation preservation measures.

There have been a number of political challenges to making this partnership – in actuality, a power-sharing agreement – work effectively. Foremost among these are the lack of firm, enforceable standards which hamper the ability of local and state governments to require as much pollution reduction as is needed to recover the bay's ecological health. Other issues include divergent standards for permitting new development, and – as one major study concluded – the inability of state governments to institute effective regulations to decrease nutrient pollution. Consider, too, that many of the pollutants affecting the bay originate in watersheds far upstream. The geographic disconnect between those generating pollution and those affected by it has exacerbated concerted opposition by both agribusiness and urban development interests (Ernst 2003; Chesapeake Bay Program 2010).

Nitrogen and phosphorus levels in the bay remain high, while overall water quality remains low. State officials continue to rely on public education and underfunded incentive programs to induce adoption of "best management practices" to alleviate runoff-induced pollution. While the Chesapeake Bay Agreements could be viewed as anchors of an incremental and inclusive process, it must also be conceded that little progress has been made in cleaning up the bay. Political resistance by established land users has reduced the effectiveness of efforts to implement best management practices to alleviate runoff containing contaminants that threaten the bay's ecosystem. Moreover, land use controls that could limit development in sensitive areas or reduce pollutant sources rely almost solely on voluntary efforts as opposed to regulatory or other binding measures (Martin 2010). As a result, the quarter-century campaign to restore the bay has been revealed as a costly failure.

In 2014, the American Farm Bureau Federation joined with other agricultural NGOs in a suit against the EPA, contending that it had exceeded its authority by developing a complex "pollution budget" and allocating responsibility for reducing inputs of nitrogen and phosphorus by the eight states in the basin. While the Third Circuit Court of Appeals upheld the EPA's policy, as of this writing, the case is pending on appeal before the US Supreme Court (Parenteau 2016).

Conclusion – can divergent interests be reconciled?

The water disputes we have examined in this chapter share many factors in common, including the exercise of centralized *power*, sometimes by a few agencies and other times by multiple stakeholder groups, that in one form or another lead to adverse environmental and social outcomes affecting some region, groups, and set of resources. Asymmetries of power are also characteristic of each of these disputes; with some agencies of government, stakeholder groups, or entire nations able to exercise greater authority in both causing environmental changes and, in some cases, resisting changes in policy direction so as to satisfy the concerns of parties who have been harmed.

They also share *processes* of decision-making that may be described as mal-adaptive, resulting in decisions that are inflexible, costly, and result often in an over-reliance on large public works or other actions that serve practical ends but may result in adverse environmental or economic consequences. Whether the activities chronicled here are long or short distance water diversions for water supply or power (China, India–Pakistan), depletion of groundwater for agriculture or other commercial activities (India, Mexico), or degradation caused by un-planned pollution or diversion of rivers for irrigation, they impose nearly irreversible commitments of time, money, and other resources. This is what leads to the disputes resulting from these activities.

The irreversibility may take the form of forced migrations in the path of a project's construction, as in China's South–North transfer project; fear that one country's hydropower project will adversely impact another country's contemplated project in the same basin; exhaustion of local groundwater supplies, leading to a contraction of a region's economy over time; or so severely degrading a region's water supply and quality as to transform its ecology and threaten human health. The latter is exemplified in different ways, and to different degrees, in the Aral Sea and Chesapeake Bay.

What about purpose? The activities leading to dispute in these cases are largely animated by efforts to improve the economic performance of various provinces, states, or entire nations – by providing additional water supplies and/or hydropower, to satisfy the needs of agriculture or global trade; or to provide more irrigable acreage, or adding nutrients to crops to increase their yields. Ironically, however, these purposes, while predicated on creating permanent infrastructure that will yield dividends to future generations, may lead to adverse impacts on the future that are difficult to rectify.

In the next chapter, we discuss the implications of efforts to provide additional supplies of water, and to manage currently available supplies more efficiently and fairly, through more adaptive and resilient solutions. These approaches aspire to a low probability of failure, and to rely on flexible, multi-pronged solutions. They also seek to generate fewer negative consequences that are costly to mitigate, to help conserve resources for renewal and innovation, and to incorporate lessons from previous experiences, including experiences of failure.

As we shall see, such innovations come with a price of their own, and generate political contentions unique to their costs, risks, and public perceptions. Most importantly, their effective implementation relies on institutional as well as engineering or economic reforms.

SUMMARY

- Disputes have one of three causes, often in combination – damming and diverting water; depleting availability; and degrading water's ability to sustain health.
- Making disputes intractable is the fact that power is often asymmetrical – one party possesses more authority to act than another, making amicable resolution difficult.
- The process for resolving disputes is complex and multi-faceted – sometimes employing formal instruments such as treaties, mutual agreements, or litigation.

RECOMMENDED READING

- A historical view of water conflicts and the institutional frameworks developed to abate them is A. Dinar, S. Dinar, S. McCaffrey & D. McKinney, *Bridges over Water: Understanding Transboundary Water conflict, Negotiation, and Cooperation* (2013). Dinesh Kumar's *Managing Water in River Basins* (2010) is a comprehensive text that ranges between hydrology, economics, and law and politics to dissect the complex politics of water management – and does so in a multi-issue-focused manner.

WEBSITES

- http://www.columbia.edu/~tmt2120/introduction.htm Aral Sea degradation crisis
- The Ojos Negros Research Group. Sustainable Management in Ojos Negros basin.

- http://ponce.sdsu.edu/ojosnegrosreportexecutivesummary.html Ensenada region groundwater basin dispute
- http://www.hindustantimes.com/chandigarh/impact-of-verdict-on-kishanganga-project/story-A7t55uqlwMDmFnfqyM1V3O.html Upper Indus dispute
- http://www.wsj.com/articles/cities-in-chinas-north-resist-tapping-water-piped-from-south-1429781402 China's North–South diversion project
- https://www.globalpolicy.org/security-council.html The Global Policy Forum

QUESTIONS FOR DISCUSSION

1. How is power exercised in disputes over diversion, depletion, and degradation? Are governments or interest groups more influential in these disputes?

2. What roles do international bodies, such as courts, NGOs, aid agencies, or other entities, have in causing – and preventing, averting, or reducing – water disputes?

3. To what degree do NGOs and citizen groups exercise similar – and different – strategies to protest activities that cause water disputes?

CHAPTER 9

Tapping into Toilets: New Sources of Water

Introduction – the politics of water alternatives

Numerous methods – some novel – have been introduced to address water shortages and enhance water quality. These methods – ranging from reuse of wastewater for potable as well as non-potable uses to desalination, storm-water harvesting, and bio-filtration of pollutants – are all technically feasible to one degree or another. Their actual adoption, however, hinges on their costs and perceived benefit; the ability to mitigate any risks they may engender; the degree to which they can be made to "fit" within certain urban planning constraints; and, ultimately, their public acceptability. The latter, we have learned, depends upon political processes that embrace these concerns and engage various stakeholders in decisions to adopt them.

There is considerable debate over all these issues. For instance, the economic costs of desalination are often difficult to precisely calibrate because these costs depend to a large extent on the price of energy (desalination is a particularly energy-intensive technology). This varies considerably from place to place and from one source of energy to another. Likewise, debates over the health risks of recycled wastewater – while the overall technology has been deemed safe – are not without some contention. For instance, not every potential contaminant that might be present in reclaimed wastewater intended for potable use is sufficiently chronicled for regulation – and while some states in the US are prepared to regulate reuse, for instance, others are not. The same problem is true elsewhere (NRC 2012).

The one issue over which there is agreement is that many parts of our planet are reaching a point at which traditional water supply options are not, by themselves, adequate to satisfy demand. In addition, we may need to expand how we think about both "supply" and "demand" – away from costly, centrally managed approaches and toward a more diverse portfolio of sustainable options (Pacific Institute 2014). Preference for distributed as opposed to centrally-controlled and managed water sources and options are to a large extent based on cultural preferences as well as ethical notions regarding the importance of access and control – not just efficiency of service.

In short, every option has potential advantages and disadvantages. These include cost, energy use, environmental impact, and public confidence and trust. Rather than look for the "best" option, we contend that a fundamental lesson from debates over water alternatives is the need to seek the most *adaptive and resilient* solutions. Such solutions are unlikely to be found in a single panacea. No one approach can fit all problems or meet every political objection. Instead, approaches need to be adopted that have a low probability of failure. Such options would rely on flexible, multi-pronged solutions, generate few negative consequences that are costly to mitigate, help conserve resources for renewal and innovation, and incorporate lessons from previous experiences. This chapter addresses these issues through a discussion of the politics of various unconventional approaches.

Is there a political process for adopting alternatives?

While thought of as a largely technical and apolitical process, there is a politics of water alternatives. This political process begins when a new or unconventional approach is initially conceived. Following this conception, most freshwater supply methods are then introduced on a small pilot scale, and subsequently offered to decision-makers and communities after they have been established as proof-tested and cost-effective alternatives to conventional water supply methods.

These alternative methods range from ocean desalination, to reclaimed or re-used wastewater, captured or "harvested" storm-water runoff, and various methods for substituting low-quality treated water for non-potable needs of industry, agriculture, energy production, and other economic sectors. All these methods depend on various forms of government promotion – as well as regulation – of their health, safety, and reliability. Oftentimes, government-sponsored research and development programs help subsidize the development of various technologies and the science underlying them. Moreover, governance decisions must be made to determine whether, how, and where to actually introduce a new method, as well as how to finance it.

A fitting example is China. It is widely recognized that the potential water savings from rainwater harvesting are enormous. What makes the Chinese case instructive is that harvesting rain is an old and venerable practice in that nation for agriculture, but has only recently gained attention as a possible large-scale urban water strategy. In the past, rainwater harvesting relied on techniques such as soil terracing and plastic covers to conserve water on farms. Currently, reliance on underground storage tanks made from modern materials, as well as more efficient irrigation techniques are in vogue in places such as Gansu province (Cook et al. 2000).

Proponents of rainwater harvesting in China view it as an innovation that can be adapted to current water needs in creative and multi-faceted ways. Currently, over 21 million Chinese harvest rainwater to meet their domestic, household needs. Beijing has some 55 pilot projects encouraging the use of rainwater harvesting. However, the Beijing Municipal Water Authority estimates that 230 million cubic meters of rainwater could be used annually. Recall from chapter 8 that Beijing faces severe water supply challenges resulting from local groundwater depletion, and which – in part – are to be rectified by the great South-to-North water transfer project.

The special appeal of rainwater harvesting in Beijing and other Chinese cities, as some Chinese academics have noted, is that it not only saves water but also abates urban flooding, groundwater deple-tion, and rainwater runoff pollution. It can also improve the health of urban ecosystems (Wong 2007). In essence, for urban water man-agement, rainwater harvesting can help address a number of water quality as well as water supply needs, as well as help attenuate the effects from the types of climate variability we discussed in chapter 5 (e.g., flood and drought). Moreover, unlike conventional pollutant treatment methods or flood abatement strategies, rainwater harvest-ing is a relatively low-cost tool for addressing China's various water crises – and it potentially fits into the notion of a multi-pronged approach to addressing pollution and water supply issues.

A number of political questions arise from its application. These include: will the price of water charged to consumers be calibrated in such a way as to encourage conservation as well as adoption of rain-water harvesting, especially for easily substitutable non-potable uses? Also, will decisions regarding its adoption be made in a thoughtful manner to ensure that some harvesting "solutions" do not exacer-bate water problems in the future (Wong 2007)? And, is the process through which rainwater harvesting is adopted subject to broad public and policy-maker discussion?

Regardless of the technical prowess of unconventional methods for managing or obtaining fresh water, there is another set of process considerations important for their adoption: legal requirements for environment, health, and safety. These include compliance with public health and environmental standards that – over time – tend to become more stringent. As we will discuss later on through an example from

Australia, a potential conflict that often arises within these governance processes when approaches are under scrutiny is between the quest for policies that "streamline" and expedite permitting, licensing, and/or approval in order to incentivize their development on the one hand, and pressures to carefully vet their impacts by members of the public on the other. Efforts to balance these two aspirations are especially pertinent in debates over wastewater reuse, rainwater harvesting, and desalination (Farrelly & Brown 2011; Keremane et al. 2011).

Desalination – purpose, process, and power

Desalination is an increasingly popular alternative for addressing water needs in arid and semi-arid regions, as well as in coastal communities facing water stress. While an energy intensive and, therefore, relatively expensive means of providing fresh water, methods to both reduce these energy costs – and to abate adverse environmental impacts – are being introduced through, for example, adoption of renewable energy technologies (Goosen et al. 2011).

Concerns with desalination tend to revolve around its potentially negative environmental effects. Aside from energy consumption, some of the most significant of these are associated with the construction of marine structures, seawater intake, and brine disposal (Palomar & Losada 2011). In various parts of the world where desalination has been proposed for adoption, additional site-specific issues that are often raised – and have become significant political issues – include siting and habitat disruption, public access, aesthetics (including noise), public health impacts, land use implications, and concerns that the availability of additional water can induce greater demand by attracting more population growth.

Given these potential impacts, what is the purpose of desalination? The obvious answer is the world's need for new sources of freshwater water. A case for this purpose has been made by Elimelech and Phillip (2011) who argue that providing ample and safe drinking water is "complicated by population growth, industrialization, contamination of available freshwater resources, and climate change" and that, despite our best efforts to conserve, repair leaky infrastructure, and improve watershed capture systems, there are likely to be only two major sources – globally – for increasing potable supplies: desalination and water reuse. Options for desalination are wide-ranging and include seawater desalination, a virtually unlimited water source, and desalination of brackish groundwater: a possible option for regions well inland of ocean coasts (Elimelech & Phillip 2011: 712).

Advocates of desalination, however, recognizing its potential environmental risks, often caution that this overall purpose – alleviating water stress – should be measured against other societal considerations. In effect, the process by which desalination is adopted should reflect, to the extent possible, the need to encompass these contending concerns and to develop a palatable way to assess them. In practice, this has led countries that adopt desalination to implicitly amend its purpose to be considering this option as one among several methods, and to view it as part of a portfolio of water supply options. Only for those water-scarce countries that have already implemented all other practical methods should desalination be viewed as the *only* viable option (Elimelech & Phillip 2011).

Israel's experience illustrates the dynamics of process and purpose for desalination. It also illuminates the role of power in moving desalination to the forefront of water supply options. In Israel, provision of reliable, safe fresh water has long been a matter of national security and national survival. Following nationhood in 1948, Israel embarked on three major tracks: conveying fresh water from the north to cities and farms in the south; harvesting rainwater; and reusing wastewater.

A major aqueduct system completed in 1964 (the National Water Carrier) delivers water from the Sea of Galilee (also known as Lake Kinneret), as well as other water sources, to population centers near the coast. Since the early 1990s, reliance on reused effluent for agriculture has also increased dramatically – climbing from some 300 million cubic meters per year in 1993 to 400 million cubic meters per year in 2015 – and it is expected to more than double by 2025 (Dinar 2016).

Following a severe drought that began in 2000, a committee of the Israeli Knesset concluded in 2002 that the country not only faced an urgent water shortage, but a political crisis caused by fragmented bureaucratic responsibility for water management (i.e., separate agencies charged with issues of public health, environmental protection and water, and agriculture), and a lack of centralized coordination for overall policy. The committee's final report made no effort to mask its frustration, stating in the report's introduction that: "The crisis is so deep, and the shortage in the interim period will be so grave, that the ability to maintain the provision (of) vital services is placed in great doubt" (The Parliamentary Committee 2002). Emergency powers were requested to allocate water and oversee new projects, and a recommendation to "establish an independent, professional water authority" led to formation of the Israeli Water Authority, an interministerial committee with super-ordinate powers, in 2007.

Several measures to reduce water demand and augment supply were immediately pursued. The price of water was increased by an average of 40 percent and – in response to serious depletion of the country's mountain aquifer system – an aggressive program of desalination of Mediterranean seawater was pursued in tandem with renewed efforts to recycle wastewater (Kershner 2015). Between 2009 and 2015, desalination capacity went from two plants producing 152 million cubic meters per year to five plants with a capacity of 550 million cubic meters per year – and is expected to exceed 750 million cubic meters per year by 2020.

To set the stage for adoption of desalination, an aggressive program was begun to cut annual water quotas for farmers, ending decades of subsidies. The National Water Authority also adopted a two-tiered household rate system: those who use more pay slightly more per unit (discarding an antiquated tax on surplus household uses). Water-saving devices were freely distributed and a major institutional change was introduced: municipal utilities are no longer responsible for maintenance of local distribution systems. Local private corporations have been formed, and monies collected are directly invested in infrastructure improvements.

Israel has undergone great changes in water use since enactment of these measures. Desalination and wastewater reuse account for half of Israel's domestic water supply, and wastewater reuse accounts for 55 percent of agricultural supply. The country reuses 86 percent of its wastewater (Kershner 2015). While the role of crisis cannot be discounted as a driver of changes which simplified the process of coordinating policy, coalesced national purpose around emergency measures to counteract the drought's impacts, and concentrated power in the hands of a single agency with virtually unlimited authority to enact measures, the high degree of political consensus over the urgency of the crisis as a national security issue is probably of paramount importance to the state's capacity to act.

By contrast, California – facing a protracted period of drought, a number of institutional and attitudinal hurdles in adopting novel supply methods such as reuse and rainwater harvesting, and with five times the population of Israel – has also seriously contemplated – but failed to adopt – desalination on a wide-scale basis. At its root, while there has been some movement toward desalination adoption, there is as yet neither the broad consensus, nor the possibility for institutional centralization, afforded in Israel (see box 9.1).

Box 9.1 Desalination in Southern California – a lengthy build

Poseidon Resources, a corporation with investors in Japan and Israel, completed a $950 million desalination plant near Carlsbad, California, in late 2015. Designed to produce some 50 million gallons per day and serve the needs of some 300,000 people in north San Diego County, the product of the plant is hardly inexpensive. At a cost of some $1500–2000 per acre-foot, the water is considerably more expensive than water from other regional sources. On the other hand, as project proponents have often noted, there are no other plausible options. The region has no access to additional water from the Colorado River, no groundwater, and – although there have been discussions about this alternative – no moves to adopt direct potable re-use have been taken as of this writing.

The project was built following years of public debate and partly hinged on the sale of public bonds by the Metropolitan Water District of Southern California. The "Met" financed the project – in part because the project's benefits are seen as regionally beneficial. The project is energy-intensive, consuming some 33 MW of electricity, enough to power some 20,000 homes. And, like all desalination projects, how to safely dispose of its brine is an important issue.

Poseidon is seeking to duplicate its success by building another plant further up the coast in Orange County. Many of the same issues have arisen – most of all, will municipal water districts line up to buy the water that is produced, and can they legally connect their distribution systems to the plant? These are issues that, while not unique to California, do make this case different from that of Israel, where concerted national policy change could trump such local issues.

Supply approaches and fairness

Recycled wastewater use presents several political challenges. It can reduce the need for imported and diverted fresh water, thus alleviating pressure on supplies controlled by others as well as a major source of water disputes. It also can reduce wastewater-generated pollution by alleviating the need to dispose of "dirty" water unfit for potable use in rivers and streams.

In considering whether the use of recycled water is fair, it is important to recognize three impacts. The first is the so-called "*toilet to tap*" issue: the perception that people are being asked to use water that quite readily has been taken from the wastewater stream and is almost immediately being used as tap water. Many reuse schemes are indirectly potable – purified wastewater is injected into groundwater basins and later pumped for use.

A second impact is that greater reliance on water re-use and wastewater recycling to enhance and recharge groundwater resources and for prescribed potable and non-potable uses may encourage additional population growth. Opinion surveys find that it is often viewed as an indirect *subsidy* for unwanted additional population and residential and business growth (Boberg 2005; Groves et al. 2008).

Third, while a number of studies stretching back to the 1970s indicate that potable re-use is safe, doubts have arisen over safeguards. Important to the environmental justice debate is that perceptions of safety are associated with a sense of inclusion in decision-making. In less affluent areas and in communities or neighborhoods suffering from ongoing water-related environmental legacy issues (e.g., abandoned hazardous waste sites, contaminated aquifers) proposals for re-use arouse suspicion and widespread mistrust.

In light of these concerns, there is growing agreement that in order to make unconventional approaches acceptable, decision-makers must focus on the local community and local water provider level. It is at these levels that power to influence changes in land use regulations and other built-environment concerns, and to build public confidence, will most effectively take place. Decentralized approaches are favored with state-level attention focused on regulatory reform and establishment of more uniform human health and environmental risk standards.

The ultimate goal of reuse, as for other supply-side approaches, is to build water resilience – the ability to adapt to environmental and social conditions different from those originally in existence at the time a community's water provision system was established (Benson & Craig 2014). In governance terms, resilience requires that agencies and river basin or watershed authorities have the capacity to adapt to severe environmental change. Agencies possessing flexible, decentralized operations and that are able to negotiate with other entities to informally accommodate new and unforeseen needs or problems, are resilient. This means gathering the input of multiple stakeholders who collaboratively engage in solving problems (Carpenter et al. 2001; Dietz et al. 2003).

Generally, alternative approaches, as well as genuine innovations, are easier to introduce in a political environment that promotes entrepreneurial activity. Israel is an example – and not just with respect to desalination or reuse. Think tanks, industrial inventors, and others have developed an array of innovations, including microscopic sewage scrubbers and smart water networks to detect leaks and avert waste through distribution system losses. Another part of this entrepreneurial culture is economic conditions – including price mechanisms that encourage conservation and punish or deter waste (Little 2015). Some large cities (see box 9.2) that promote innovation illustrate how this political climate can be encouraged.

Box 9.2   Innovations in mega-cities: Tokyo

Tokyo has some 13 million residents. Population growth, changes in lifestyle, economic growth (which has become practically incessant since the end of World War II), and uncertainties affecting supply are having significant impacts on the city. Despite a growing appreciation for the long-term effects of climate change on the city's water supply, demands for water continue to increase (Tokyo Waterworks Bureau 2013).

Practically from the moment Japan sought to modernize its society, it also sought to modernize and develop its provision of urban water supplies. During the early period of the Meiji restoration (1898), the city of Tokyo's waterworks began supplying water from a modern treatment facility, the Yodobashi purification plant. Today, the city has one of the world's most sophisticated and "smart" metered and regulated water supply systems. Tokyo's waterworks are among the world's largest, and are noted for reliance upon the highest levels of technology.

After World War II, rapid in-migration and economic growth dramatically increased water demands at the same time planners decided to pave over small waterways to facilitate urban expansion. Increased consumption led to declines in groundwater and land subsidence. Since the 1980s, climate change concerns, including local "heat island" effects from urbanization leading to additional energy use, have prompted introduction of large-scale wastewater reuse, non-potable storm-water harvesting, groundwater withdrawal restrictions, and aggressive conservation. As a result of the city's efforts to foster conservation, it has been estimated that per capita household demand will plateau within the next decade.

Tokyo's Metropolitan Waterworks Bureau has sought to develop new projects through active international cooperation, and from an international perspective – both to help institute globally recognized standards for engineering, and to model approaches that can be exported to less developed nations where needs for clean water in urban areas especially are crucial (Tokyo Waterworks Bureau 2013). It has implemented a variety of innovations to conserve as well as protect potable water supplies. Highly advanced water treatment systems have been installed in virtually all the city's potable water treatment plants – particularly in the large Tonegawa River system, and an extensive public education and outreach program, Tokyo Tap Water's "Water for Life," has been introduced to help customers better understand their role in conserving water and protecting its quality, and to comprehend how waterworks services operate.

Source: Tokyo Waterworks Bureau 2013

Demand-side measures – do they really work?

Aside from supply-side approaches, inducing residential and other sources of conservation has been a growing method of water management by water providers. A number of strategies are being employed. These strategies range from incentives to install water-saving landscape to indoor water-appliance standards and special rebates or loan programs to adopt these methods to various water pricing schemes. In the Western US, California included, such programs were introduced beginning in the 1970s in response to protracted drought. Municipalities adopted metering, incentives for adopting drought-tolerant landscaping, aggressive public outreach programs, and water appliance standards, and also resorted to a number of water-pricing schemes to induce conservation (Gleick 2003; City of Los Angeles 2008; Hanak et al. 2011).

Demand-side reforms usually depend on some type of conservation pricing scheme. Three approaches to pricing predominate among utilities: uniform, decreasing, and increasing bloc rates. While, in general, increasing bloc rates – a method whereby consumers pay more per unit volume of water once their use exceeds a nominal "conservation" threshold – can induce water savings, considerable variation has been found. There is broad agreement that the overall price of water influences demand. However, there also remains wide debate over the comparative effectiveness of different approaches to this goal and, ultimately, what factors encourage users to place a high economic value on water and, thus, to save it.

Residential consumption varies as a result of climate, square footage of lawns and general landscape preferences, home size, income, and aggressiveness of public education and outreach – making any one-size-fits-all policy solution impossible (Nieswiadomy & Molina 1989; Nieswiadomy 1992). Moreover, rate structures are usually so complex – combining fixed and variable charges in different combinations – that ascertaining exactly how a particular price structure affects consumption is, to say the least, difficult (Arbues et al. 2003; Doig 2012).

The advent of social media, data-driven technology innovations, and the proliferation of personal mobile devices have provided individuals with direct, immediate access data, allowing them to manage their water consumption more effectively. Many of these tech-based opportunities have teamed up with local water agencies to provide individuals with updates about new water-related rebates, high-consumption and leak alerts, and helpful water conservation tips (Wang 2014).

Social normative marketing approaches have been shown to be politically effective in both Australian and American contexts. The long-standing "Don't be a Wally with Water" marketing campaign began in 1984 to change Melbournian's attitudes toward wasting water by branding those who used more than their fair share a "Water Wally." This campaign again proved successful during the

Millennium Drought (1997–2012) and was resurrected in 2013 by a major newspaper in Melbourne to temper a spike in water consumption during a heat wave (Dowling 2013).

Some critics argue that social normative marketing, by relying on neighbor comparison, is a "Big Brother" approach and inconsiderate of individual household needs (Hoffman 2010). Nevertheless, outreach in the form of educational and information campaigns, as well as physical and behavioral water efficiency demonstrations, are major components of many water agency conservation strategies, as well as the focus of recent academic studies (Dolnicar et al. 2010).

Purpose – are demand-side measures fair?

Mandated conservation measures that compel replacement of water appliances such as low flow toilets and showerheads and water meters may adversely affect low-income populations at the same time as they save water. There is no consensus regarding how to institute conservation innovations with principles of political fairness and equity. In part, this is because many international agreements pertinent to water view the provision of water as a basic human right. In effect, water should be provided to people regardless of their ability to pay. In developing countries especially, as we discussed in chapter 2, efforts to increase charges for water use or water access may lead to vigorous protest. With respect to conservation, an example of this is metering.

Metering measures water consumption at the point of consumer use. In developed countries such as the US, introduction of metering for domestic uses where it has not been employed previously (such as in multi-family apartment complexes) has in some locations led to water savings of as much as 20–40 percent compared with previous volumes (Hanak et al. 2011). However, metering may penalize lower income residents for the simple reason that the type of residential housing stock that lacks metering, and for which it is prescribed, may be apartment buildings and other domiciles that disproportionately house lower income groups. For people on fixed incomes, moreover, it may be burdensome if the costs of installing meters are passed down to residents.

Attempts to install water meters in parts of Argentina found that public resistance in Salta province led to vandalism of newly-installed meters, protests, and refusal to accept metering at neighborhood meetings. These were prompted by the fact that metering was introduced at the same time as aggressive enforcement of bill payment, "tiered" rates, and household charges for meter installation. A larger fear was that meters would not be accurately read and that residents would be charged for excess water usage when, in fact, the culprit was poorly-maintained, leaking plumbing systems (Post 2009).

Lowering water demands can be a hugely contentious undertaking. During drought, for instance, attempts to suppress demand may lead to bitter conflicts among water use sectors. We also know that general public apathy or even resistance to lowering demand can be a barrier to demand-side management because the time horizons needed for planning supply resilience on one hand and demand attenuation on the other requires action before the onset of an actual drought. Ironically, however, during non-drought periods, the political will to prepare may be absent due to lack of public attentiveness and interest in drought (Gleick & Heberger 2012).

Conclusions – when is an alternative a positive innovation?

To successfully introduce alternative water supply and demand approaches successfully, decision-makers must engage users in their introduction. This objective is vital if their goal is to encourage long-term policy change. Decision-makers also need to undertake partnerships and agreements that foster equitable management, administration, benefit allocation, and sharing of the burdens and risks entailed in innovation (Huitema et al. 2009; Kallis et al. 2009). For water conservation, reuse, and desalination, these are arduous tasks for two reasons. First, the perceived benefits and risks from these innovations are socio-economically cross-cutting. While conservation and metering may adversely affect lower income communities, recycled water and desalination are perceived – fairly or not – as negatively impacting communities at every income level, as well as under-represented populations.

Second, impacts from all these innovations are perceived as long-term and chronic, rather than short-term and acute (e.g., community stigma, diversion of "hard earned tax dollars" to special interests). Thus, they tend not to produce the types of political mobilization associated with hazardous waste or contaminated water supplies – protagonists express concerns through the media or via surveys and polls.

To say that these "newer" conflicts are low intensity, however, is not to ignore that they represent a growing source of dispute. The need for fair, open, and transparent decision-making processes in which all groups affected by water decisions can equally participate, and where no relevant constituency is excluded, is essential. Such processes must embrace four characteristics. First, they must be proactively pursued. Decision-makers must reach out to disaffected groups to inform them of the reasons these technologies are being endorsed, to educate and inform them, and to elicit and respond to their concerns.

Second, these innovations require that attention be paid to compensating those less able to afford the distributional burdens of their adoption. Implementation should be calibrated according to affordability. Affordability is affected by factors over which the poor may have little control – such as special health needs and care for small children or the elderly. For its part, questions of risk and potential health concerns regarding innovation require an adroit ability to understand complex principles. Audiences who lack the technical skill to decipher environmental documents will need assistance in doing so (Environmental Justice Coalition for Water 2005).

Third, potable water innovations such as wastewater re-use and desalination could benefit from national-level water supply certification standards that assure protection of in-stream flow and health safeguards. These would affirm that their advantages are independently validated, and strongly resonate with the notion of *stewardship* (Miller 2006). All three must be embraced to overcome public inhibitions toward adopting these innovations.

Finally, as we discuss in the book's final chapter, it is important to identify opportunities for greater participation, for broadening opportunities for inclusive decision-making, and for embracing the special challenges facing communities of color, as well as the needs of other under-represented groups. It is also important that alternative approaches be sensitive in their implementation to a variety of environmental impacts in order to be politically acceptable (see box 9.3). If these challenges can be met – and meeting them requires attention to political factors as well as to technical ones – we may then say that an alternative approach is innovative.

In sum, debates will continue to arise in a variety of political arenas regarding, the impacts of various supply-side innovations to environmental amenities (such as coastal zones in the case of desalination); the acceptability of other innovations to under-represented groups suffering from environmental justice issues (in the case of plans for recycled wastewater plants); and fairness to middle-income farming communities (in the case of water transfers to protect endangered or threatened species). Making options acceptable will require changes in public confidence and the perceived competence of those responsible for managing them (Po et al. 2005). Without these changes, prospects

Box 9.3 "Newer" approaches – the politics of pushing the envelope

In many arid regions, untapped sources of "new" water are sometimes available, such as groundwater basins deep underground. In California's Mojave Desert, some 200 miles east of Los Angeles, lies such a source. The Cadiz Project is a proposed groundwater mining effort that began some 25 years ago with the purchase of some 45,000 acres in eastern San Bernardino County. The essence of the project is to intercept groundwater flowing off the Cadiz Valley before it reaches the dry lakes beds at the center of the valley – and pump it 43 miles to the Colorado River Aqueduct – an existing water diversion system. One water district in Orange County has signed a contract for some 5000 acre-feet of water from the project, while seven other water agencies have expressed their intent to do so if the project actually is able to open.

The project is fraught with controversy. Proponents claim the water recharging the basin – left alone – eventually rises to the surface of the dry lake beds and evaporates at the rate of some 32,000 acre-feet per year (enough water for some 100,000 homes for many years). Allowing it to evaporate is "wasting" an economical source of water, say proponents. Others argue that the water is contaminated with naturally occurring chromium 6, a known carcinogen that would first have to be removed before the Metropolitan Water District (whose aqueduct Cadiz plans to use) would allow access – and for which Cadiz would have to pay a use fee.

Others point to the hydrological assumptions being used to support the project. Cadiz claims the aquifer recharges some 32,000 acre-feet annually but is planning to divert as much as 50,000 acre feet – by including in plans the intercepting of water before it slowly migrates from upslope areas to the lake beds. Several environmental organizations and academic researchers claim, however, that actual recharge rates are far less than even the 32,000-acre-feet annually: and more on the order of one-fifth to one-sixth this volume. Moreover, desert ecosystems currently supported by the project – springs supporting a variety of flora and fauna – would severely suffer. There is another set of embedded issues surrounding the project. Would its water supply – if competitive in price – merely drive more development that is unsustainable, and is the aquifer system really replenishable at predicted use rates?

The overall purpose of the project is itself difficult to fathom – to provide a novel source of "new water" through a type of untapped resource for which there are few precedents (clearly, the desire of investors to make money from their speculation could be described as another purpose, critics contend). The power to decide these issues is reposed in a host of agencies, as well as state regulatory oversight bodies that will have to permit the project and approve of its environmental impacts before it can proceed.

Source: Orlowski 2015

for long-term erosion of public trust, confidence and civility over water issues – and even political gridlock – is not unlikely.

SUMMARY

- Many novel approaches to supply are low impact developments – based on small-scale, locally-based as opposed to large-scale, centrally-controlled methods.
- While technical feasibility is important, adoption of any approach requires that proponents prove affordability, fairness, and mitigation of adverse impacts.
- Psychology is critical in supply-and-demand innovations – the public must be engaged in decisions and tactics to address perceived risks must be acceptable.

RECOMMENDED READING

- A good summary of rainwater harvesting is contained in S. Cook, L. Fengrui, & W. Huilan, "Rainwater Harvesting Agriculture in Gansu Province, People's Republic of China," *Journal of Soil and Water Conservation* (2000).
- While much investigated, clear, lay accounts of seawater desalination are rare. A good account can be found in M. Elimelech & W. A. Phillip, "The Future of Seawater Desalination: Energy, Technology, and the Environment," *Science* (2011).
- For a discussion of reuse in Australia, see M. Po, B. E. Nancarrow, Z. Leviston, N. B. Porter, G. J. Syme, & J. D. Kaercher, J.D. 2005, *Predicting Community Behaviour in Relation to Wastewater Reuse: What Drives Decisions to Accept or Reject?* (2005). Also, K. G. Low, D. L. Feldman, S. B. Grant, A. J. Hamilton, K. Gan, J. D. Saphoresm & M. Arora, "Fighting Drought with Innovation: Melbourne's Response to the Millennium Drought in Southeast Australia," *WIRES Water* (2015).

WEBSITES

- http://www.nytimes.com/2015/03/30/world/middleast/water-revolution Israel and desalination.
- http://www.nap.edu/catalog/13303/water-reuse-potential-for-expanding-the-nations-water-supply-through Water reuse in the US.

QUESTIONS FOR DISCUSSION

1. How is governance important in adopting innovations? How is politics a factor in determining the feasibility of innovations?

2. What makes a water innovation fair and publically acceptable? Do these issues depend on the process of decision-making. If so, how?

3. How does conservation pose differential impacts on water users? What role does governance have in mitigating these differential impacts?

CHAPTER 10

Toward a Water-Sensitive Future

Introduction – paradigms and politics

Water politics is the process by which societies provide safe, secure fresh water and also satisfy demands for food, fiber, and energy. Since ancient times, nation-states, regions, and cities have engaged in water politics in order to maximize their ability to compensate for the impacts of drought and flooding while addressing competing demands – including those from other nation-states.

Given these purposes, it is not surprising that water politics has often been focused on formulating and implementing plans to alter rivers, harness groundwater basins, and treat wastewater through large-scale public works designed to protect societal assets, irrigate farms and slake thirsty cities, and generate economic benefits to entire regions. While some of these goals have changed over time, this primary approach to water politics has persisted. This explains the dominance of what we have called "path dependency" – the tenacious hold previous decisions have over current policies – long after the reasons giving rise to original decisions cease to be relevant.

While present-day water politics continues to be shaped by this path-dependent paradigm, other forces have emerged to challenge it. The urgency of climate extremes (i.e., longer and more extreme droughts punctuated by periods of intense flooding), as well as growing clamor for more inclusive and democratic decisions has led to the emergence of a new paradigm. We glimpsed elements of this new paradigm earlier in our discussions of the water–energy–food nexus, efforts to incorporate climate information in water policies, the pursuit of green infrastructure solutions to water quality problems, and in novel methods of collaboration taking place at the transnational level by intergovernmental "networks" comprised of NGOs and local units of governance. We also saw elements of this new paradigm in our discussion of demands for incorporating public concerns when adopting alternative water supply approaches.

These earlier glimpses were tantalizing but incomplete. This chapter seeks to fill in the details regarding this newer water politics paradigm; one that is characterized by two broad strategies. First, its central tenet is *integrated water resources management* (IWRM). IWRM not only stresses novel approaches to water provision and management such as wastewater reuse, rainwater harvesting, non-structural floodplain management, drought adaptation schemes, better water conservation, and "green infrastructure" approaches – but it conceives of fresh water as an irreplaceable, precious, and diminishing resource that must be governed as a renewable, re-useable resource.

From the standpoint of politics, IWRM considers water that is saved or conserved to be a potentially "new" source of water supply, possibly obviating the need for imports or diversion from other places, for example. In addition, the long-standing practice of regulating water as a series of separate, segmented domains – as wastewater, storm-water, surface water, groundwater, and the like: with their own sets of policies, programs, and management "silos" should be abandoned in favor of a more comprehensive approach which treats supply and demand management as integrated.

Integrated water management also implies, as we discussed earlier, greater reliance on weather and climate knowledge networks that connect water users and weather information generators as means of making better decisions. These efforts also attempt to span the domains of local and expert knowledge in order to help societies adapt to environmental changes affecting water. Cases we earlier discussed involving the southwestern US and northwestern Mexico, as well as north central Chile and Argentina, exemplify this kind of effort.

Second, the new paradigm for water politics embraces greater public participation, engagement, and inclusion not only as practical means to facilitate adoption of innovative approaches to water management – and, thus, to encourage integrated water management – but as socially just goals in themselves. This is especially important in light of the growing uncertainties associated with water availability worldwide. In short, adaptive and democratic management of water and other vital resources help people better cope with the unanticipated consequences of future environmental pressures – including climate change, urbanization, and growing demands for food and energy.

These enhanced forms of participation, engagement, and inclusion start from an ethical premise: everyone who wants to should be included in water politics – at least at levels of decision-making appropriate to their lives. For many, especially in developing nations, perhaps the single most important domain is that of one's household or land parcel. Often, in these societies, water is either self-supplied or provided to an entire village or neighborhood via a single, local source.

This "inclusionary" argument contends that differences of race, ethnicity, income, and especially gender – a topic we discussed earlier – should not be barriers to having influence over the allocation, protection, or provision of water. Moreover, to assure that these barriers are removed, community-based politics for water – a concept also discussed earlier – should be assertively re-introduced in ways that make sense in light of "newer" problems: needs for removing contaminants, the provision of affordable and accessible infrastructure for water supply, and the like.

Participation, engagement, and inclusion are not only good for society, in that they maximize opportunities for all relevant groups to have a say in vital water decisions – but they are also good for the environment. They empower each and every member of a society to become a steward of water, and to have a stake in its future condition. As we discussed, creative forms of public and NGO engagement committed to these ideals were seen in Australia, northeast Brazil, Taiwan, and other places suffering from drought, as well as in parts of India grappling with local issues at the nexus of water, food, and energy. Many other forms of participation are also important in helping communities both large and small in sharing innovations, ideas, and experiences with respect to water, as we saw in our discussion of innovative global cooperation.

Achieving the new paradigm – resistance

Path-dependent views toward water resource management will continue to complicate the achievement of political consensus and make difficult the attainment of long-term solutions with respect to water quality, additional water supplies for both mega-cities and rural areas, and in managing the effects of climate variability on water. This assertion is borne out by continued resistance to newer approaches to water politics. This is exemplified by the conservatism of many water agencies that remain tradition-bound, risk-averse, and resistant to change (Kiparsky et al. 2013).

Despite this persistence, path-dependent politics probably will not entirely thwart the success of this new paradigm – even if it slows its adoption. Societies can be located along a water-resilience–water sustainability spectrum: from continued reliance on traditional hard-engineered "plumbing" solutions at one extreme, to a focus on integrated water management at the other. Likewise, participation and engagement often vary within societies, depending on the seriousness of water issues they face.

The exact location of a society along this spectrum is partly shaped by its level of economic and political development, as well as by the openness of decision-makers toward participation and innovation. Elements of the newer paradigm are favored by groups traditionally "locked out" of previous decisions, or who have been less successful in benefitting from policy outcomes that tended to favor more powerful interests.

Few if any societies have achieved the goal of a "water-sensitive" politics. Fewer still have pursued this aspiration through a fully inclusive and democratic process. To cite but one example, while Australia has made tremendous progress in drought response and adaptation, some of the political innovations of the past decade have now been abandoned. In 2014, for example, the Office of Living Victoria was reorganized into the Department of Environment and Primary Industries and shortly thereafter eliminated entirely (Low et al. 2015). Opinions vary as to whether this is a concerted abandonment of democratic engagement and innovation, or just a cost-saving measure and a means of administrative simplification.

Moreover, the rapid adoption of "new" approaches may not always be the result of greater inclusiveness or participation. In Israel, again – as just one example of a challenge – while considerable investment in a variety of innovations has been pursued in response to drought and growing agricultural and urban demands, how inclusively overall water policies are made in that country is an issue many accounts of water politics have raised. As we discussed earlier, it is legitimate to ask, for instance, what are the limits as well as the opportunities for shared engagement among both Palestinians and Israelis on water issues? Is investment in desalination the result of a bottom-up process of decision-making or a more "top-down" approach? These are difficult questions to answer (Zeitoun 2007; Ehrenreich 2011; Selby 2013).

The claim that the new paradigm requires political process changes such as a growth in democratic engagement; a lessening of economic disparities among members of a community's population; and the capacity of civil society groups to freely articulate their needs is an easy one to make. Achieving these changes remains very difficult, however. If there is an emerging consensus, it is that integrated water management, and an inclusive means to bring it about, both require a new form of water governance: one predicated on responsiveness to public concerns; legal reforms that permit broad participation; and a willingness on the part of decision-makers to share power. Even international forums are beginning to acknowledge this.

In 2012, the United Nations published a new edition of its *World Water Development Report*. The fourth in a series that first appeared in 2003, this project is an effort by dozens of organizations to assess the condition of the planet's fresh water. Its contributors include a host of UN agencies and a wide array of experts from universities, think tanks, and national environmental agencies. Subsequent reports devoted to water and energy and water and sustainability were published in 2014 and 2015, respectively. While important analyses in their own right, they may be regarded as extensions of the wide-ranging 2012 report (UN Water 2014d; 2015).

The contributors to these reports differ in their emphasis on certain issues, and they do not always agree as to how they should be addressed (UN Water 2012). Nonetheless, the reports are sober, carefully vetted studies on the scope, magnitude, and consequences of freshwater problems. And, they acknowledge the importance of governance in their calls to action. A "foreword" to the 2012 report by UNESCO Director-General Irina Bokova contends that responsibility for water resource management is too often fragmented and that true reform will require "*governments*, the private sector and civil society to work more closely together and to integrate water as an intrinsic part of their decision-making" (UN Water 2012). The report's executive summary further states:

> Managing water well requires appropriate *governance* arrangements that move considerations of water from the margins of government to the center of society. On national and local scales, appropriately funded infrastructure and adequately funded robust *governance* mechanisms are required to protect water resources and ensure sustainable development and the equitable distribution of water-derived benefits. (UN Water 2012)

But what would an "appropriate governance arrangement" look like? Here, the report waxes in lofty but disappointingly inexact prose. As Erik Swyngedouw suggests, the report "depoliticizes" water by assuming that the involvement of multiple stakeholders alone "would lead to better outcomes for all . . . a largely unexamined hypothesis" (Swyngedouw 2013: 823). Reminding readers that "calamitous conditions with respect to water access are sufficiently known and understood," and that deaths from contaminated water are easy to remedy, Swyngedouw criticizes the *World Water Development Report* for skirting the actual political causes of these problems and employing veiled language to sanitize indefensible policies on the part of financial institutions, private investors, and various multilateral agencies (Swyngedouw 2013).

In short, while governance crises are, indeed, at the root of global water problems, solutions are not to be found in technical framing – as the *World Water Development Report* stresses. Instead, efforts to rectify the unequal power relationships that currently govern water allocation and management must be undertaken. Governance of a special kind is needed – one based on freedom, as well as economic and political equality.

Finding viable governance – the limits of markets

In short, as critics contend, one troubling issue with the UN's water report is its easy acceptance that markets have an important role to play in governance. This raises the ire of detractors of neoliberalism who, we will recall from our earlier discussion at the beginning of this book, contend that dispossessed citizens in many developing nations are subject to exploitation by corporate interests that control water services, and who over-charge for them while also monopolizing available water sources (Samson & Bacchus 2000; Swyngedouw 2005; 2007; Baer 2008; Shiva 2009).

To achieve the paradigm shift we have been describing requires overcoming bureaucratic inertia on the part of multilateral aid agencies and international financial institutions that have generally insisted that developing countries shrink the size of their public sectors in order to reduce government deficits. Such a strategy includes "outsourcing" water and other vital services. In addition to reversing this trend, reforms also will require harnessing private developer concerns with returns-on-investment with public and community interests in affordability of service and guarantees that water will be provided as a fundamental need, regardless of peoples' ability to pay for it.

While privatization of water services may make sense in certain instances in order to improve the quality of water provision and treatment, making privatization work fairly requires oversight mechanisms that permit ratepayers and others affected by a firm's operations to hold these service providers accountable. As we previously discussed, making such arrangements feasible will require empowering local institutions as well as civil society groups with authority to regulate and oversee such enterprises (van de Meene et al. 2011). Moreover, within these civil society groups, there must be fair representation of all affected citizens – this requires acknowledging the importance of gender, culture, and community management in their internal operations.

Process and power – gender, culture, community

The roles of gender, ethnicity, shared interests and experiences, and community-based institutions have frequently been cited as important factors in explaining behavioral outcomes related to water. The complexity of water use and the inclination to accept demand-side measures, for example, are to a large extent shaped by gender (Sofoulis & Williams 2008; Supski & Lindsay 2013). And, in recent years as we discussed, gender has been recognized as an important factor in water governance. Worldwide, women have far less power and influence over the determination of water use and management than do men (Van Koppen 2002; UN Women 2009; Balana 2016).

If water governance is to be reformed in such a way as to permit greater freedom and equality, this "gender gap" must be bridged. A number of studies undertaken in sub-Saharan Africa, South and Southeast Asia, and elsewhere suggest that keys to this reform include improving women's access to water by removing physical impediments to irrigation and other water systems; and reforming land tenure systems so as to ensure women can inherit and manage land as well as obtain collateral such as livestock, financial resources, and lines of credit. Most importantly, structural obstacles to water rights must be removed. This requires legal reforms that ensure women are invited to participate in irrigation collective meetings, and to hold leadership roles in farm decision-making and other activities vital to water management, such as water user associations (Van Koppen 2002; Zwarteveen 2012; Balana 2016).

Reforming gender-based access to water will require embracing cultural politics notions of authority as well. As we previously saw, cultural politics considers the ways in which the management of water resource problems is tied to socially constructed notions of nature, resource management, land tenure, and kinship (Peters 1994; Bolding et al. 1995; Gilmartin 1995; Mosse 2008). While gender biases in water management are sometimes attributed to traditionally based water management systems, studies of rural communities in developing societies suggest that equal access to water and water rights is possible if traditional systems of community management are joined to modern approaches that facilitate access and convenience.

A simple but telling example is Ghana, where the provision of small reservoirs in rural areas has been found to make small-scale irrigation and livestock watering more accessible to women. This is especially the case in those places where built-in canals that deliver water to farmers' fields allow for water to be diverted to individual plots using gravity instead of pumps. Such a small innovation requires significantly less physical labor and, thus, equalizes gender accessibility (Balana 2016).

Community-based water management has other implications for water governance and the promotion of a new paradigm. As we have already seen, the aspiration for community-based control of water on the part of rural villages can help us better understand how to meld traditional values and practices to contemporary needs for potable water – and the importance of local capacity building through fiscal accounting systems that allow for accountability and enforcement of rules over funding, operations, maintenance, and repair (Davis 2014). It also serves to explain the resistance that arises when state-centered and/or corporate-backed efforts seek to exploit water resources through: privatizing local supplies; using local water sources to bottle soft drinks and other beverages; or building large water projects that store and divert water for the benefit of distant, affluent, and more powerful urban centers.

In recent years, the advent of so-called bioregional approaches to watershed management suggest that community-based approaches which draw on powerful cultural identities can also encourage trans-boundary water stewardship and promote a "multinational" consciousness toward water quality protection based on a sense of common regional identity. One locale that has been held up as exemplary of such a coherent identity is the New River watershed that straddles the desert region of Baja California Norte and Southern California along the Mexico–US border (Dicochea 2010).

Proponents describe this sense of identity as a kind of "bioregional" consciousness which facilitates trans-boundary plans to conjointly manage water pollution; encourages sharing of cleanup activities and their associated costs; and enables the mobilizing of citizen groups and NGOs around watershed restoration activities. This bioregional consciousness is strongly coupled to a common trans-border legacy of poverty and lack of economic opportunity that has generated the sense among residents that they comprise a coherent, victimized community historically suffering despair, loss, and exclusion related to water (McGinnis 1998; Dicochea 2010). While bioregionalism may serve as a powerful driver of trans-boundary water governance – especially given the large number of developing countries facing trans-boundary water quality problems – it also reminds us that there must be transnational institutions available to build and sustain a capacity for action. As we shall see, at what scale such institutions should be built remains a challenge.

Purpose – improving governance through appropriate scale

Geographers, economists, political scientists and others have long debated the appropriate spatial scale for water governance. Concepts such as "polycentric governance," "conjoint management," and "inter-jurisdictional partnership" have often been tossed around with little thought given as to precisely how they apply to particular water problems, or how best to match the scale of governance to these problems. It is not our intent here to critique or embrace these concepts. A considerable body of research has been undertaken on their purported advantages for social learning and democratic engagement (e.g., Dietz et al. 2003; McGinnis 2005; Lebel et al. 2006; Ostrom 2010; Smith & Stirling 2010).

What we are concerned with here is a larger question *not* fully embraced by these concepts – the interrelationship between power, process, and purpose on the one hand, and spatial scale on the other. Recent research by Emma Norman and her colleagues suggests that, while scalar reforms that devolve authority for water management to local levels of governance are important means of increasing citizen participation, fostering watershed-level collaborations, and encouraging novel methods of decision-making, these "re-scaling" efforts by themselves do not enable the new political paradigm we have been discussing (Norman et al. 2012).

Effective water governance that embraces inclusion, participation, and innovation entails understanding the ways in which spatial scales are themselves "socially constructed." In a diverse series of cases, Norman and her colleagues show how relocating the locus of authority for decisions to more locally constituted levels of authority does not inherently lead to greater inclusiveness or more democratic decisions. Moreover, no amount of tinkering with scale-based reforms can eliminate the fact that the most important factors determining the power of water institutions and practices are not linked to scale at all. Instead, they are based on long-established beliefs and political practices. These include water rights systems and assigned bureaucratic responsibility for managing water infrastructure. Finally, so-called "hydrologically-based" governance entities such as river basin authorities intended to foster "holistic management" afford water users, at best, mixed results because they often subdivide various water management functions among non-holistically-inclined agencies, thereby strengthening environmentally adverse activities (Norman et al. 2012). Some of these issues can be seen in two developing country cases: Honduras and South Africa.

Honduras manages water supply through a decentralized approach. The Minister of Health is responsible for overall supply issues at the national level, but local institutions are responsible for policy implementation. A national council for water and sanitation is in charge of policy development and planning, while a separate regulatory agency sets potable water standards and performance criteria for water companies. Some years ago, local utilities established an autonomous coordinating agency for water supply and sewage treatment – the Servicio Autonomo Nacional de Acueductos y Alcantarillados or SANAA (Lockwood & Smits 2011).

Rural water supply is fairly well managed for a developing country, with SANAA overseeing support to municipal sectors. However, in small, widely dispersed communities of fewer than 300 people, water is essentially self-supplied and there is no national support program in place. As a consequence, Honduras faces vast gaps in water supply and sanitation in rural areas. The Global Partnership on Output-Based Aid (GPOBA), a collaboration of various NGOs, has funded an innovative outcome-based aid project to improve access to water and sanitation to 15,000 low-income families in Honduras. Finding that low tariffs are at least partly to blame for local municipalities' inadequate water quality, GPOBA suggested strengthening local government leadership. In 2003 new legislation decentralized responsibility to local municipalities in gradual steps over the course of 10 years and provided new funding as a means of encouraging harmonization between water management sectors (One Drop 2014; Water for People 2014).

From 2008 to 2010 GPOBA signed two contracts with SANAA and Aguas de Puerto Cortes (APC) to provide funding to improve water quality and sanitation services. In 2005, the World Bank approved a rural infrastructure project with the objective of improving access, quality, and sustainability of infrastructure services for rural poor in Honduras. Water and sanitation were included among the services to be improved in the project. In March 2014, the World Bank released an evaluation of the progress of the project. Over 60,000 rural residents now have access to improved water sources, with many new piped household water connections as well as rehabilitated water connections and latrines systems built.

While significant progress on improving rural infrastructure has been made, rural needs have not been totally met for two reasons. First, the resource base for reform is inadequate. In Honduras as in most developing countries, poverty remains the single greatest determinant of water quality and plentiful supply. Second, the prospect of connecting rural water providers is constrained by spatial inaccessibility. Honduras' smaller rural communities are remote, isolated, and communications remain difficult.

By contrast, South Africa faces herculean natural challenges as regards water supply – and enormous opportunities. With a population of some 52 million and an average annual per capita GDP of US$7,460, South Africa is an upper middle-income country. However, income inequality remains profound, especially between whites and blacks. The country receives little rainfall, and suffers from high evaporation rates. Its per capita water availability is lower than neighboring Namibia, a desert nation.

South Africa's Department of Water oversees overall policy and assists local utilities, while local governments are responsible for service delivery and access. With the end of Apartheid, the government instituted the *Free Basic Water Policy* in 1997 to effectively guarantee the universal right to a basic water supply, regardless of ability to pay. The policy prescribes 6,000 liters of clean water to be provided to each household each month (National Water Resources Strategy 2013).

Implementation of the *Free Basic Water Policy* has been gradual. By 2002, the Department of Water Affairs and Forestry reported successfully providing free water to some 27 million South Africans, or roughly half the country's population. As of 2012, 88 percent of the rural population in South Africa had access to improved water. This translates to almost 46 million people (World Bank 2014).

The challenges in meeting the objectives of this ambitious policy are formidable. First, rehabilitation of water infrastructure and service is a critical need. In 2008, South Africa applied for a US$36 million loan from the World Bank to improve water infrastructure services. For undisclosed reasons, however, this project was cancelled in 2011 (World Bank 2014).

Another challenge facing efforts at reform is a chronic legacy of corruption, particularly for large water projects. Many groups forced to relocate from water project construction have not been fairly compensated, and inequitable pricing schemes remain in operation in some regions – reinforced by a lack of political transparency and accountability of those profiting from these schemes (Bond 2002).

South Africa's significant hydrological challenges have led to a movement toward aggressive use of reclaimed water for non-potable purposes such as irrigation and industrial cooling. Since 1999 a public–private partnership in the Durban region has been supplying reclaimed water to industrial sectors. At the World Summit on Sustainable Development (WSSD) held in Johannesburg in 2002, a plan was proposed to link water sustainability with industrial development and poverty eradication – in part to demonstrate government commitments to improve citizens' quality of life through continuing to supply free water to its populace (UNWWDR 2006).

Three major lessons emerge from South Africa's experiences that bear upon the new water politics paradigm. First, while the country's social justice aspirations with respect to water provision are bold and ambitious, without the capacity of multiple levels of governance – and the likelihood of significant civil society collaboration around these aspirations – accomplishments will continue to fall short of goals. Notably, the most successful partnerships have been over reclaimed wastewater – in part because the primary goal around which industry and the state were able to rally was economic and business development.

Second, the lack of financial resources remains formidable. Frequent media reports over the past several years underscore the major challenges in upgrading as well as maintaining the country's water infrastructure, which has long been founded on massive water transfers from water-rich to water-needy areas.

Third, water governance in South Africa, especially with respect to the *Free Basic Water Policy*, is a confusing and often dysfunctional amalgam of rules, permits, and highly detailed regulations. Not only is access to water prescribed in detail, but it is also the responsibility of municipalities to ensure that the water can be provided. While the Department of Water Affairs provides some funding for this, allocations to municipalities are provided by special licenses that prescribe exact amounts of water to be allocated by way of local Water Service Authorities. In effect, local governments ultimately control where the water goes, how it is used, and the condition in which it is treated and reused, which varies enormously from place to place (Kings 2012).

Detailed investigation of one set of projects – in the Olifants basin – shows that efforts to develop basin resources on behalf of formerly excluded and often impoverished regional residents are made more arduous by the persistence of antiquated systems of legal entitlements. Categorically defined "Historically Disadvantaged Individuals," or HDIs, have yet to benefit from efforts to divert water to productive uses through direct user access – with some HDIs actually losing access rights. In addition, the persistence of poverty, ineffectual administrative authority from the center, resistance to collaboration by key groups, and – most of all – a simple backlog of claims and water service delivery needs has worsened this problem. Moreover, there is concern that the remaining water resources to be exploited – and the infrastructure to provide them – may soon become exhausted (Van Koppen 2008).

The white supremacist system established under Apartheid produced systematic exclusion of black South Africans from water decision-making and access to public water supplies. Despite enormous progress, reform efforts since the 1990s – including the National Water Act and accompanying water strategy – have failed to fully bring about the redress they have promised.

Conclusions – new approaches, old problems

In Honduras, South Africa, and elsewhere as we have seen, traditional problems of water availability, demand management, economic development, and poverty continue to affect all aspects of water politics. Moreover, patterns of traditional decision-making persist due to established law and the habits of long-standing practice. This makes radical alterations of policies difficult.

There is no ideal set of responses to these conditions, nor is there a simple solution to these problems. Inclusiveness and participation are important avenues toward finding solutions, however, for one basic reason. Both of these reforms acknowledge – as we have stated throughout this book – that no single group, leadership elite, or expert cohort has a monopoly of knowledge about water. Broader political participation heightens the opportunity for adaptive solutions to water problems (i.e., solutions that are small-scale, incremental, and reversible if they fail). They also help to ensure that all forms of control over water are likely to be tempered by fairness and accountability. If any group or interest believes they are excluded from decision-making, they will likely resist prescribed outcomes and – with democratic processes of inclusion available to them – they can do so peacefully.

How to design a new water politics that accommodates these aspirations will remain a formidable challenge. As we have seen, however, there are numerous examples of adaptation to these challenges worldwide – and they generally take the form of collaborative efforts, often in smaller regions and water basins, where local communities, NGOs, scientists, and aid organizations are working together to design solutions, identify funding sources, and share information.

There are no panaceas to the problems of water politics. The public must be welcome at the tables where important decisions are discussed, and experts of various sorts must reach out to local water users and embrace a wide range of cultural, social, and ethical concerns regarding fresh water and its management. While the challenges are great, the stakes of failure have never been greater. It is up to all of us to ensure we succeed, or at least try: future generations will be counting on us to do so.

SUMMARY

- A water-sensitive society will require major changes not only in decisions, but also in who gets to make them.
- Integrated water management and inclusive decision-making are essential to a new water politics paradigm.
- Ensuring access to water decisions regardless of gender, ethnicity or station in life is essential to reform.

RECOMMENDED READING

- A good account of gender and water is found in B. Van Koppen, A Gender Performance Indicator for Irrigation: Concepts, Tools, and Applications (2002).
- The issue of appropriate spatial governance of water problems is treated by E. Norman, K. Bakker, & C. Cook, "Introduction to the Themed Section: Water Governance and the Politics of Scale," *Water Alternatives* (2012).

WEBSITES

- http://www.un.org/waterforlifedecade/gender.shtml UN Water – Gender and Water (2014).
- http://www.un.org/womenwatch/daw/cedaw/ Convention on the Elimination of All Forms of Discrimination against Women.

Glossary

Adaptive management: approaches to water management that impose few permanent, large-scale changes to the water environment, and that emphasize small-scale approaches based on trial and error and social learning.

Aquifer: another name for a groundwater basin, or underground reservoir; usually a rock-laden formation containing freshwater.

Demand-management: efforts by water providers to encourage conservation and reduced water use through metering, rates structures, and public education and outreach.

Desalination: while usually applied to efforts to remove salt and brine from seawater to provide drinkable freshwater, it may also be used in estuaries or inland seas or rivers which have become contaminated with salts.

Diversion: moving or transferring water from one basin to another, often deemed moving it from a "basin of origin" to a "basin of destination."

Natural pollutant attenuation: letting natural biological or chemical processes within lagoons, wetlands, or other water bodies purify fresh water of pollutants injurious to human and ecological health.

Non-point pollution: water contamination resulting from runoff over a land surface, whether paved or unpaved. It may also include pollution deposited on water from atmospheric pollutants settling out of the air.

Over-drafting: drawing more water from an aquifer or groundwater basin than can be replenished by precipitation.

Point-source pollution: water contamination resulting from a single, identifiable outlet such as a discharge pipe into a river, stream, estuary, or other water body.

Rainwater harvesting: collecting precipitation in ponds, lagoons, or wetlands and using it for various domestic purposes.

Wastewater reuse: treating wastewater for domestic, agricultural, or commercial re-use.

References

AEA Technology (2012) Support to the identification of potential risks for the environment and human health arising from hydrocarbons operations involving hydraulic fracturing in Europe. Prepared for the European Commission – DG Environment. AEA/R/ED57281. October 8.

Aghakouchak, A., Feldman, D. L., Hoerling, M., Huxman, T. E., and Lund, J. (2015) Water and Climate: Recognize Anthropocentric Drought. *Nature* 524, 409–11.

American Wind Energy Association (2015) Wind Energy Conserving Water. Available at: http://www.awea.org/windandwater

Anderson, C. W. (1979) The Place of Principles in Policy Analysis. *American Political Science Review* 73, 711–23.

Arbues, F., García-Valiñas, M. Á., and Espiñeira, R. M. (2003) Estimation of Residential Water Demand: A State-of-the-Art Review. *Journal of Socio-Economics* 32, 81–102.

Arizona Department of Water Resources (2015) History of Water Management in Arizona. ADWR, Phoenix. Available at: http://www.azwater.gov/AzDWR/PublicInformationOfficer/history.htm

Arnold, C. A. (2005) Privatization of Public Water Services: The States' Role in Ensuring Public Accountability. *Pepperdine Law Review* 32, 561–604.

Australian Bureau of Statistics (2012) 1301.0 – 1986 Special Article – The Snowy Mountains Hydro-Electric Scheme, November. Available at: http://www.abs.gov.au/ausstats/abs@.nsf/0/FDE81AE268C76207CA2569DE00274C14?

Australian Government – National Water Market (2015) Department of the Environment, Canberra. Available at: http://www.nationalwatermarket.gov.au/about/

Australian Public Service Commission (2007) *Tackling Wicked Problems – A Public Policy Perspective*. Canberra: Australian Government.

Baer, M. (2008) The Global Water Crisis, Privatization, and the Bolivian Water War. In Whitely, J. M., Ingram, H., and Perry, R. W. (eds.) *Water, Place, and Equity*. Cambridge, MA: MIT Press, pp. 195–224.

Baer, M. (2015) From Water Wars to Water Rights: Implementing the Human Right to Water in Bolivia. *Journal of Human Rights* 14, 353–76.

Bakker, K. (2009) Water Security: Canada's Challenges. *Options Politiques*, July–August, 16–20.

Bakker, K. (2010) *Privatizing Water: Governance Failure and the World's Urban Water Crisis*. Ithaca, NY: Cornell University Press.

Bakker, K. (2013) Constructing 'Public' Water: The World Bank, Urban Water Supply, and the Biopolitics of Development. *Environment and Planning D: Society and Space* 31, 280–300.

Balana, B. (2016) Three Lessons from Ghana on Women's Access to Land and Water. Thrive: The Future of Our Food, Water, and the Environment. Research program on Water, Land and Ecosystems. CGIAR, February. Available at: https://wle.cgiar.org/thrive/2016/02/15/3-lessons-ghana-womens-access-land-and-water

Barclay, E. (2010) China Takes Another Stab at Resettlement with $62 Billion Water Plan. *National Geographic News*, August 29.

Barlow, M. (2009) *Blue Covenant: The Global Water Crisis and the Coming Battle for the Right to Water*. New York: New Press.

Barlow, M. and Clarke, T. (2002) *Blue Gold: the Fight to Stop the Corporate Theft of the World's Water*. New York: New Press.

Barnes, D., Galgani, F., Thompson, R., Barlaz, M. (2009) Accumulation and Fragmentation of Plastic Debris in Global Environments. *Phil. Trans. R. Soc. B* 364, 1985–98.

Bartels, L. (2015) Sen. Jerry Sonnenberg: No rain barrels for you, *Denver Post*, May 6. Available at: http://blogs.denverpost.com/thespot/2015/05/06/sen-jerry-sonnenberg-no-rain-barrels-for-you/119911/

Bauer, C. J. (1998) Slippery Property Rights: Multiple Water Uses and the Neoliberal Model in Chile, 1981–1995. *Natural Resources Journal* 38, 109–55.

Bauer, C. J. (2005) In the Image of the Market: The Chilean Model of Water Resources Management. *International Journal of Water* 3, 146–65.

Beatley, T. (1994) *Ethical Land Use: Principles of Policy and Planning*. Baltimore, MD: Johns Hopkins University Press.

Benson, M. H. and Craig, R. K. (2014) The End of Sustainability. *Society & Natural Resources: An International Journal* 27, 777–82.

Bergmann, M. (1999) The Snowy Mountains Hydro-Electric Scheme: How Did It Manage Without an EIA? Australian National University, February.

Berke, P. R., MacDonald, J., White, N., Holmes, M., Line, D., Oury, K., and Ryznar, R. (2003) Greening Development to Protect Watersheds: Does New Urbanism Make a Difference? *Journal of the American Planning Association* 69, 397–413.

Biello, D. (2014) Can Fracking Clean China's Air and Slow Climate Change? *Scientific American*, January 27. Available at: http://www.scientificamerican.com/article/can-fracking-clean-chinas-air-and-slow-climate-change/

Biggert-Waters Flood Insurance Program Reform Act of 2012. Available at: https://www.independentagent.com/Products/Insurance/Flood/Pages/Documents/06-28-12%20sec-by-sec%20flood%20conference%20rpt%20(final).pdf

Bird, D., Ling, M., and Haynes, K. (2012) Flooding Facebook – The Use of Social Media during the Queensland and Victorian Floods. *Australian Journal of Emergency Management* 27, 27–33.

Blatter, J. and Ingram, H. (2001) *Reflections on Water*. Cambridge, MA: MIT Press.

Blomquist, W. and Schlager, E. (2005) Political Pitfalls of Integrated Water Management. *Society and Natural Resources* 18, 101–17.

Boatright, M. T., Gargola, D. J., and Talbert, T. A. (2004) *The Romans: From Village to*

Empire – A History of Ancient Rome from Earliest Times to Constantine. Oxford: Oxford University Press.

Boberg, J. (2005) Liquid Assets: How Demographic Changes and Water Management Policies Affect Freshwater Resources. Report-MG-358-CF. Santa Monica, CA: RAND Corporation.

Boelens, R. (2009) The Politics of Disciplining Water Rights. *Development and Change* 40, 307–31.

Boelens, R., Getches, D. and Guevara-Gil, A. (eds.) (2010) *Out of the Mainstream: Water Rights, Politics and Identity.* Washington, DC: Earthscan.

Bolding, A., Mollinga, P. and van Straaten, K. (1995) Modules for Modernisation: Colonial Irrigation in India and the Technological Dimension of Agrarian Change. *Journal of Development Studies,* 31, 805–44.

Bond, P. (2002) *Unsustainable South Africa: Environment, Development, and Social Protest.* London: Merlin Press.

Borrell, B. (2015) The Urban Water Crisis – And What We Can Do About It. *Nature Conservancy Magazine,* August/September, 44–9.

Boyd, D. (2012) *The Environmental Rights Revolution: A Global Study of Constitutions, Human Rights and the Environment.* Vancouver, BC: University of British Columbia Press.

Braemer, F., Geyer, B., Castel, C., and Abdulkarim, M. (2010) Conquest of New Lands and Water Systems in the Western Fertile Crescent (Central and Southern Syria). *Water History* 2, 91–114.

Brown, R. R., Keath, N., and Wong, T. H. F. (2009) Urban Water Management in Cities: Historical, Current, and Future Regimes. *Water Science & Technology,* 59, 847–55.

Bruninga, S. (2002) On 30th Anniversary of Water Act Passage; Successes Touted, But More Challenges Seen. *Special Report – Environmental Reporter* 33, 2279–82.

Buller, H. (1996) Towards Sustainable Water Management: Catchment Planning in France and Britain. *Land Use Policy* 13, 289–302.

Burns, M. J., Fletcher, T. D., Duncan, H. P., Hatt, B. E., Ladson, A. R., and Walsh, C. J. (2014) The Performance of Rainwater Tanks for Stormwater Retention and Water Supply at the Household Scale: An Empirical Study. *Hydrological Processes* 29, 152–60.

Burton, L. (1991) *American Indian Water Rights and the Limits of Law.* Lawrence, KS: University Press of Kansas.

Butler, L. L. (1990) Environmental Water Rights: An Evolving Concept of Public Property. *Virginia Environmental Law Journal* 9, 323–79.

California Oregon Power Company v. Beaver Portland Cement Company, 295 U.S. 142 (1935).

Carpenter, S., Walker, B., Anderies, J. M., and Abel, N. (2001) From Metaphor to Measurement: Resilience of What to What? *Ecosystems* 4, 765–81.

Cash, D. W., Clark, W. C., Alcock, F., Dickson, N., Eckley, N., Guston, D. H., Jäger, J., and Mitchell, R. B. H. (2003) Knowledge Systems for Sustainable Development. *Proceedings of the National Academy of Sciences* 100, 8086–91.

Center for Watershed Science (2012) Addressing Nitrate in California's Drinking

Water – With a Focus on Tulare Lake Basin and Salina Valley Groundwater. Davis, CA, Report for the State Water Resources Control Board.

Chen, T. P. (2015) Cities in China's North Resist Tapping Water Piped From South – Huge project transferring water from Yangtze River to drier regions runs into budgetary constraints. *Wall Street Journal*, April 23. Available at: http://www.wsj.com/articles/cities-in-chinas-north-resist-tapping-water-piped-from-south-1429781402

Chesapeake Bay Program (2010) A Watershed Partnership. Available at: http://www.chesapeakebay.net/

China Daily (2012) China's Water Diversion Project Carries Risks. Xinhua News Agency, September 19.

Chu, H. (2014) France's Fracking Ban under Pressure. *Los Angeles Times*, June 27, p. A1.

City of Los Angeles (2008) Securing L.A.'s Water Supply. Department of Water and Power, Los Angeles, CA.

Clayton, J. (2009) Market-Driven Solutions to Economic, Environmental, and Social Issues Related to Water Management in the Western USA. *Water* 1, 19–31.

Coarelli, F. (2007) *Rome and Environs – An Archeological Guide*. Berkeley, CA: University of California Press.

Cochran, B. and Logue, C. (2010) A Watershed Approach to Improve Water Quality: Case Study of Clean Water Services' Tualatin River Program. *Journal of the American Water Resources Association* 47, 29–38.

Conant, E. (2006) Return of the Aral Sea. *Discover* 27, 54–8.

Conca, K. (2006) *Governing Water – Contentious Transnational Politics and Global Institution Building*. Cambridge, MA: MIT Press.

Connolly, P. and Dodge, H. (1998) *The Ancient City: Life in Classical Athens and Rome*. London: Oxford University Press.

Cook, S., Fengrui, L., and Huilan, W. (2000) Rainwater Harvesting Agriculture in Gansu Province, People's Republic of China. *Journal of Soil and Water Conservation* 55, 112–14.

Copeland, C. (1999) Clean Water Act – A Summary of the Law. Congressional Research Service Report for Congress, January 20.

Corcoran, E., Nellemann, C., Baker, E., Bos, R., Osborn, D., and Savelli, H. (eds.) (2010) *Sick Water? The Central Role of Wastewater Management in Sustainable Development. A Rapid Response Assessment*. The Hague: UN-Habitat/UNEP/GRID-Arendal.

Coulomb, R. (2001) Speech presented by the vice president of the World Water Council at the Closing Session of the 11th Stockholm Water Symposium, World Water Council, 3rd World Water Forum.

Cretikos, M., Eastwood, K., Dalton, C., Merritt, T., Tuyl, F., and Winn, L. (2008) Household Disaster Preparedness and Information Sources: Rapid Cluster Survey after a Storm in New South Wales, Australia. *BMC Public Health* 8, 1–9.

Crow, B. and Singh, N. (2009) The Management of International Rivers as Demands Grow and Supplies Tighten: India, China, Nepal, Pakistan, Bangladesh. *India Review*, July. Available at: http://escholarship.org/uc/item/48n485pc

Crow, B. and Sultana, F. (2002) Gender, Class, and Access to Water: Three Cases in a Poor and Crowded Delta. *Society and Natural Resources* 15, 709–24.

Curran, R. (2015) How on Earth Are Two of the Most Water-Rich Nations Having H_2O Crises? *Fortune*, April 6. Available at: http://fortune.com/2015/04/06/brazil-california-water-crisis-drought/

Da Costa Silva, G. (2011) Assessing Environmental Justice of Community-Based Watershed Management: A Tool to Build Adaptive Capacity in Latin America? *Local Environment* 16, 445–60.

Davis, M. L. (1993) *Rivers in the Desert: William Mulholland and the Inventing of Los Angeles*. New York: HarperCollins.

Davis, S. K. (2001) The Politics of Water Scarcity in the Western States. *Social Science Journal* 38, 527–42.

Davis, S. (2014) Why Water Systems Fail Part 8: Community-Based Management. *Improve International*, August 18. Available at: https://improveinternational.word-press.com/author/improveinternational/

De Clercq, G. (2014) Paris's Return to Public Water Supplies Makes Waves beyond France. Reuters, July 8. Available at: http://in.reuters.com/article/2014/07/08/water-utilities-paris-idINL6N0PE57220140708

Defense Intelligence Agency (2012) Global Water Security. Intelligence Community Assessment. ICA 2012-08, February 2. Available at: http://www.dni.gov/files/documents/Special%20Report_ICA%20Global%20Water%20Security.pdf

Delfino, J. (2001) Stockholm Water Symposium. Report by Comtech Regional Vice President for North America. Environmental Engineering and the World Water Vision. Available at: https://peer.asee.org/environmental-engineering-and-the-world-water-vision.pdf

Dellapenna, J. W. (1996) Rivers as Legal Structures: The Examples of the Jordan and the Nile. *Natural Resources Journal* 36, 217–50.

Dellapenna, J. W. and Gupta, J. (2009) The Evolution of Global Water Law. In Dellapenna, J. W. and Gupta, J. (eds.) *The Evolution of the Law and Politics of Water*. Delft: Springer, pp. 3–20.

Diaz, H. F. and Wahl, E. R. (2015) Recent California Water Year Precipitation Deficits: A 440 Year Perspective. *Journal of Climate* 28, 4637–52.

Dickinson, D. (2005) Eco-Islam Hits Zanzibar Fishermen. *BBC News*, February 17.

Dicochea, P. R. (2010) Between Borderlands and Bioregionalism: Life-Place Lessons along a Polluted River. *Journal of Borderlands Studies* 25, 19–36.

Dietz, T., Ostrom, E., and Stern, P. (2003) The Struggle to Govern the Commons. *Science* 302, 1907–12.

Dinar, A. (2013) The Development and Application of International Water Law. In Dinar, A., Dinar, S., McCaffrey, S., and McKinney, D. (eds.) *Bridges over Water: Understanding Transboundary Water Conflict, Negotiation, and Cooperation*. Singapore: World Scientific Publishing.

Dinar, A. (2016) Dealing with Prolonged Drought & Water Scarcity: Water Policy Reforms that Took Israel from a Water Scarce to a Water Abundant Nation. Public talk, University of California, Irvine, February.

Doig, W. (2012) The Impending Urban Water Crisis. Salon.com, March 31.

Available at: http://www.salon.com/2012/03/31/the_impending_urban_water_crisis/

Dolnicar, S., Hurlimann, A., and Nghiem, L. (2010) The Effect of Information on Public Acceptance – The Case of Water from Alternative Sources. *Journal of Environmental Management* 91, 1288–93.

Dowling, J. (2013) Is the Wally Back? Melbourne Water Use Surges. *The Age*, January 18. Available at: http://www.theage.com.au/victoria/is-the-wally-back-melbourne-water-use-surges-20130117-2cwan.html

Downs, T. J., Mazari-Hiriart, M., Domínguez-Mora, R., and Suffet, I. H. (2000) Sustainability of Least Cost Policies for Meeting Mexico City's Future Water Demand. *Water Resources Research* 36, 2321–39.

Dublin Statement on Water and Sustainable Development (1992) Available at: http://www.cawater-info.net/library/eng/l/dublin.pdf

Economist (2014) A Canal Too Far – The World's Biggest Water-Diversion Project Will Do Little to Alleviate Water Scarcity. *The Economist*, September 14.

Economy, E. C. (2010) *The River Runs Black – the Environmental Challenge to China's Future*. Ithaca, NY: Cornell University Press.

EcoPeace Middle East (2009) Water Being Held Hostage to the Conflict. Available at: http://foeme.org/www/?module=media_releases&record_id=68

Ecumenical Water Network (2008) Let Justice Roll Down Like Waters: Faith-Based Advocacy and Water for All. Report, April 21–28.

Edgecumbe, L. (2013) Spain's Troubled Waters. *El Pais*, March 22. Available at: http://blogs.elpais.com/trans-iberian/2013/03/spains-troubled-waters.html

Ehrenreich, B. (2011) Drip, Jordan – Israel's Water War with Palestine. *Harper's Magazine*, December, 52–61.

Electric Power Research Institute (2003) Use of Degraded Water Sources as Cooling Water in Power Plants. Technical Report 1005359. Palo Alto, CA: EPRI.

Elimelech, M. and Phillip, W. A. (2011) The Future of Seawater Desalination: Energy, Technology, and the Environment. *Science* 333, 712–17.

Entekhabi, D. (2013) The Water–Energy–Food Nexus. Paper presented at MIT Research & Development Conference, Ralph M. Parsons Laboratory for Environmental Science and Engineering, November 13.

Environmental Justice Coalition for Water (2005) *Thirsty For Justice: A People's Blueprint for California*. Oakland, CA: Environmental Justice Coalition for Water.

Environmental Protection Division, Watershed Protection Branch (2007) Coastal Georgia Water & Wastewater Permitting Plan for Managing Salt Water Intrusion, March. Available at: http://www.gadnr.org/cws/Documents/Coastal_Permitting_2007.pdf

ERCIP (European River Corridor Improvement Plans) (2014) Available at: www.ercip.eu

Ernst, H. R. (2003) *Chesapeake Bay Blues: Science, Politics, and the Struggle to Save the Bay*. New York: Rowman & Littlefield.

European Wind Energy Association (2014) *Saving Water with Wind Energy*. Brussels: EWEA.

FAO (Food and Agriculture Organization of the United Nations) (2006) World

Agriculture: Towards 2030/2050. Interim Report, Prospects for Food, Nutrition, Agriculture and Majority Commodity Groups. Rome, FAO.

Farrelly, M. K. and Brown, R. (2011) Rethinking Urban Water Management: Experimentation as a Way Forward? *Global Environmental Change* 21, 721–32.

Feldman, D. L. (1991) The Great Plains Garrison Diversion Unit and the Search for an Environmental Ethic. *Policy Sciences* 24, 41–64.

Feldman, D. L. (2015) California tackles water-energy interdependence by getting decision-makers to talk. *The Conversation*, June 24. Available at: http://theconversation.com/california-tackles-water-energy-interdependence-by-getting-decision-makers-to-talk-43040

Feldman, D. L. (2016) The West's Water – Multiple Uses, Conflicting Values, Interconnected Fates. In Miller, K., Harnlet, A., Kenney, D. and Redmond, K. (eds) *Western Water Policy in a Variable and Changing Climate*. Boca Raton, FL: CRC Press.

Feldman, D. L. and Ingram, H. (2009) Climate Forecasts, Water Management, and Knowledge Networks: Making Science Useful to Decision-Makers. *Weather, Climate, and Society* 1, 1022–33.

Feldman, D. L., Sengupta, A., Stuvick, L., Stein, E., Pettigrove, V., and Arora, M. (2015) Governance Issues in Developing and Implementing Offsets for Water Management Benefits: Can Preliminary Evaluation Guide Implementation Effectiveness? *WIRES Water* 2015, 121–30.

Feldman, D., Contreras, S., Karlin, B., Basolo, V., Matthew, R., Sanders, B., Houston, D., Cheung, W., Goodrich, K., Reyes, A., Serrano, K., Schubert, J., and Luke, A. (2016) Communicating Flood Risk: Looking Back and Forward at Traditional and Social Media Outlets. *International Journal of Disaster Risk Reduction* 15, 43–51.

Ferejohn, J. (1974) *Pork Barrel Politics: Rivers and Harbors Legislation, 1947–1968*. Stanford, CA: Stanford University Press.

Fleishman, J. and Linthicum, K. (2010) On the Nile, Egypt Cuts Water Use as Ethiopia Dams for Power. *Los Angeles Times*, September 12. Available at: http://articles.latimes.com/2010/sep/12/world/la-fg-nile-battle-20100912

Fogelson, R. (1993) *The Fragmented Metropolis: Los Angeles, 1850–1930*. Berkeley, CA: University of California Press.

Fort, D. and Nelson, B. (2012) Pipe Dreams: Water Supply Pipeline Projects in the West. Natural Resources Defense Council, New York, June.

Fox, I. K. (1966) Policy Problems in the Field of Water Resources. In Kneese, A. V. and Smith, S. C. (eds.) *Water Research*. Baltimore, MD: Johns Hopkins University Press.

Freeman, J. L. (1965) *The Political Process: Executive Bureau, Legislative Committee Relations*. New York: Random House.

Gad, A. (2008) Water Culture in Egypt. In El Moujabber, M., Shatanawi, M., Trisorio-Liuzzi, G., Ouessar, M., Laureano, P., and Rodríguez R. (eds.) *Water Culture and Water Conflict in the Mediterranean Area/Options Méditerranéennes*, Paris: CIHEAM, pp. 85–96.

Gallardo, M. C. (2016) Socio-Ecological Inequality and Water Crisis: Views of Indigenous Communities in the Alto Loa Area. *Environmental Justice* 8, 9–14.

Gardner, T. (2016) US House passes bill requiring EPA actions on lead-laced water. Reuters.com, February 10. Available at: http://www.reuters.com/article/michigan-water-house-idUSL2N15P32N

Garrido, A. and Llamas, M. R. (eds.) (2009) *Water Policy in Spain*. Boca Raton, FL: CRC Press.

Gillilan, D. M. and Brown, T. C. (1997) *Instream Flow Protection: Seeking a Balance in Western Water Use*. Washington, DC: Island Press.

Gilmartin, D. (1995) Models of the Hydraulic Environment: Colonial Irrigation, State Power and Community in the Indus Basin. In Arnold, D. and Guha, R. (eds.) *Nature, Culture, Imperialism: Essays on the Environmental History of South Asia*. New Delhi: Oxford University Press.

Gils, J. V. and Bendow, J. (2000) The Danube Water Quality Model and its Role in the Danube River Basin Pollution Reduction Programme. Technical Working Group, ICPDR.

Glaeser, E. (2011) *Triumph of the City: How Our Greatest Invention Makes us Richer, Smarter, Greener, Healthier, and Happier*. New York: Penguin Press.

Glantz, M. H. (2007) Aral Sea Basin: A Sea Dies, a Sea Also Rises. Ambio 36, 323–7.

Glassmeyer, S. T. (2007) The Cycle of Emerging Contaminants. *Water Resources Impact* 9, 5–7.

Gleick, P. H. (2003) Water Use. *Annual Review of Environmental Resources* 28, 275–314.

Gleick, P. H. and Heberger, M. (2012) The Coming Mega Drought. *Scientific American* 306, pp. 1–14.

Global Water Partnership – Southern Africa (2013) Unpacking the Water, Food, and Energy Nexus. Available at: http://www.gwp.org/GWP-SouthernAfrica/GWP-SA-IN-ACTION/News/Unpacking-the-water-food-and-energy-nexus/

Golden, M. and Min, B. (2013) Distributive Politics around the World. *Annual Review of Political Science* 16, 73–99.

Goosen, M., Hacene, M., Noreddine, G., and Shyam S. (2011) Application of Renewable Energies for Water Desalination. In Schorr, M. (ed.) *Desalination, Trends and Technologies*. New York: Intech.

Govardhan Das, S. V. and Burke, J. (2013) Smallholders and Sustainable Wells. A Retrospect: Participatory Groundwater Management in Andhra Pradesh (India). Rome, FAO. Available at: http://www.fao.org/docrep/018/i3320e/i3320e.pdf

Government of Canada (2016) Project Profile: Artibonite River Watershed Rehabilitation. Foreign Affairs, Trade and Development Canada, February 24. Available at: http://www.acdi-cida.gc.ca/cidaweb/cpo.nsf/projen/A031937001

Grafton, R. Q. and Hussey, K. (2011) *Water Resources Planning and Management*. Oxford: Oxford University Press.

Grant, S. B., Fletcher, T. D., Feldman, D. L., and Saphores, J. D. (2013) Adapting Urban Water Systems to a Changing Climate: Lessons from the Millennium Drought in Southeast Australia. *Environmental Science & Technology* 47, 10727–34.

Gronewold, N. (2009) Haiti: Environmental Destruction, Chaos Bleeding across Border. Greenwire, December 14. Available at: http://www.eenews.net/stories/85634

Grover, P. K. (2014) Impact of Verdict on Kishanganga Project. *Hindustan*

Times, January 28. Available at: http://www.hindustantimes.com/chandigarh/impact-of-verdict-on-kishanganga-project/story-A7t55uqlwMDmFnfqyM1V3O.html

Groves, D. G., Lempert, R. J., Knopman, D., and Berry, S. H. (2008) Preparing for an Uncertain Future Climate in the Inland Empire – Identifying Robust Water Management Strategies (Report –DB-0550-NSF). RAND Corporation, Santa Monica, CA.

Grubb, M., Koch, A. Munson, F., and Sullivan, K. (1993) *The Earth Summit Agreements: A Guide and Assessment – An Analysis of the Rio '92 UN Conference on Environment and Development*. London: Earthscan Publications.

Gruen, G. (1993) Recent Negotiations Over the Waters of the Euphrates and Tigris. In *Proceedings of the International Symposium on Water Resources in the Middle East: Policy and Institutional Aspects*. Urbana, IL, October 24–27.

Guston, D. H. (2001) Boundary Organizations in Environmental Science and Policy: An Introduction. *Science, Technology, and Human Values* 26, 399–408.

Hammer, C. (2010) *The River: A Journey through the Murray-Darling Basin*. Melbourne: University of Melbourne Press.

Hamner, J. H. and Wolf, A. T. (1998) Patterns in International Water Resource Treaties: The Transboundary Freshwater Dispute Database. *Colorado Journal of International Environmental Law and Policy* 158, 157–77.

Hanak, E., Lund, J., Dinar, A., Gray, B., Howitt, J., Mount, J., Moyle, P., and Thompson, B. (2011) *Managing California's Water: From Conflict to Reconciliation*. San Francisco, CA: Public Policy Institute of California.

Harrington, C. (2014) Water Wars? Think Again: Conflict Over Freshwater Structural Rather Than Strategic. New Security Beat. Wilson Center, April 15. Available at: http://www.newsecuritybeat.org/2014/04/water-wars/

Hart, H. C. (1957) *The Dark Missouri*. Madison, WI: University of Wisconsin Press.

Hasnain, K. (2014) India Agrees to Re-Examine Objections to Kishanganga Dam Design. *DAWN – Pakistan*, August 27.

Heather, P. (2006) *The Fall of the Roman Empire – A New History of Rome and the Barbarians*. Oxford: Oxford University Press.

Hennessy-Fiske, M. (2016) A Water Crisis in a City of Crises. *Los Angeles Times*, January 15, p.A9.

Henry, L. A. and Douhovnikoff, V. (2008) Environmental Issues in Russia. *Annual Review of Environment and Resources* 33, 437–60.

Highsmith, A. R. (2016) Failing Flint. *Los Angeles Times*, January 31, p.A26.

Hoekstra, A. Y. (2010) The Relation between International Trade and Water Scarcity – Draft. Staff Working Paper ERSD-2010-05. World Trade Organization, Economic Research and Statistics Division, January.

Hoekstra, A. Y. and Chapagain, A. K. (2007) Water Footprints of Nations: Water Use by People as a Function of Their Consumption Pattern. *Water Resources Management* 21, 35–48.

Hoekstra, A. Y. and Chapagain, A. K. (2008) *Globalization of Water: Sharing the Planet's Freshwater Resources*. Oxford: Blackwell Publishing.

Hoffman, J. (2010) Using the Water Bill to Foster Conservation. *On Tap*, Winter,

18–22. Available at: http://www.nesc.wvu.edu/pdf/dw/publications/ontap/magazine/OTWI10_features/water_bill_foster_conservation.pdf

Holland, J. (2012) *Dam Busters: The True Story of the Inventors and Airmen Who Led the Devastating Raid to Smash the German Dams in 1943*. New York: Grove Press.

Homer-Dixon, T. (2000) *Environment, Society, and Violence*. Princeton, NJ: Princeton University Press.

Hooper, B. P. (2005) *Integrated River Basin Governance: Learning from International Experience*. London: IWA Publishing.

Hoornbeek, J. A. (2011) *Water Pollution Policies and the American States – Runaway Bureaucracies or Congressional Control?* Albany, NY: SUNY Press.

Howe, C. A., Vairavamoorthy, K., and van der Steen, N. P. (2011) SWITCH – Sustainable Water Management in the City of the Future – Findings from the SWITCH project, 2006–2011. The Netherlands: European Commission's 6th Framework Programme and SWITCH Consortium partners.

Hughes, S. and Pincetl, S. (2014) Evaluating Collaborative Institutions in Context: The Case of Regional Water Management in Southern California. *Environment and Planning C: Government and Policy* 32, 20–38.

Huisman, P. (2000) Transboundary Cooperation in Shared River Basins: Experiences from the Rhine, Meuse and North Sea. *Water Policy* 2, 83–97.

Huitema, D., Mostert, E., Egas, W., Moellenkamp, S., and Pahl-Wostl, C. (2009) Adaptive Water Governance: Assessing the Institutional Prescriptions of Adaptive (Co-)Management from a Governance Perspective and Defining a Research Agenda. *Ecology and Society* 14, art. 26.

Hundley, N. Jr. (2009) *Water and the West – the Colorado River Compact and the Politics of Water in the American West*, 2nd edn. Berkeley, CA: University of California Press.

Hunt, T. (2015) *Ten Cities that Made an Empire*. London: Penguin.

Ingram, H. and Oggins, C. R. (1992) The Public Trust Doctrine and Community Values in Water. *Natural Resources Journal* 32, 515–37.

Ingram, H., Laney, N., and McCain, J. R. (1980) *A Policy Approach to Political Representation: Lessons from the Four Corners States*. Baltimore, MD: Johns Hopkins University Press for Resources for the Future.

Instituto Mexicano de Tecnología del Agua (1987) Overview of the Infrastructure for Cutzamala System. Visita al Sistema Cutzamala. Boletín No. 2. México.

ICLEI (International Council of Local Environmental Initiatives for Sustainability) (1995) Municipal leaders' communiqué to the Conference of the parties to the UN Framework Convention on Climate Change, Berlin, March.

ICLEI (International Council of Local Environmental Initiatives for Sustainability) (2006) South Australia Water Campaign Launched. Available at: http://www.iclei.org/details/article/south-australia-water-campaign-launched.html

ICLEI (International Council of Local Environmental Initiatives for Sustainability) (2007) ICLEI's Climate Resilient Communities Program Addresses Adaptation, Vulnerabilities, April 11.

ICPDR (International Commission for Protection of the Danube River) (2005) The Danube River Basin District, Part A – basin wide overview. ICPDR, Vienna. Available at: http://www.icpdr.org/main/search/basin%20wide%20overview%202005

International Water Association (2013) Montreal Declaration on Cities of the Future. Available at: http://www.iwa-network.org/programs/cities-of-the-future/

IWMI (International Water Management Institute) (2011) Innovative Electricity Scheme Sparks Rural Development in India's Gujarat State. Available at: http://www.iwmi.cgiar.org/Publications/Success_Stories/PDF/2011/Issue_9-Innovative%20electricity%20scheme%20sparks.pdf

Jacobs, K. L., Garfin, G. M., and Lenart, M. (2005) More Than Just Talk: Connecting Science and Decision-Making. *Environment* 47, 6–22.

Jacobson, E. M., Hoag, D. L. and Danielson, L. E. (1994) *The Tar-Pamlico River Basin Nutrient Trading Program*. Raleigh, NC: Cooperative Extension Service, Department of Agricultural and Resource Economics, NCSU.

Jägermeyr, J., Gerten, D., Schaphoff, S., Heinke, J., Lucht, W., and Rockström, J. (2016) Integrated Crop Water Management Might Sustainably Halve the Global Food Gap. *Environmental Research Letters* 11, 025002.

Jansen, G. (2000) Urban Water Transport and Distribution. In Wikander, Ö. (ed.) *Handbook of Ancient Water Technology*. Leiden: Brill, pp. 103–25.

Jennings, R. (2015) Taiwan Aims to Rein in Water Use. *Los Angeles Times*, May 10, p. A5.

Jiménez-Bello, M. A., Martínez Alzamora, F., Bou Soler, V., and Bartolí Ayala, H. J. (2010) Methodology for Grouping Intakes of Pressurized Irrigation Networks into Sectors to Minimize Energy Consumption. *Journal of Biosystems Engineering* 105, 429–38.

Jones, K. R. and Wills, J. (2009) *The American West: Competing Visions*. Edinburgh: Edinburgh University Press.

Kahneman, D., Slovic, P., and Tversky, A. (eds.) (1982) *Judgment Under Uncertainty: Heuristics and Biases*. Cambridge: Cambridge University Press.

Kahrl, W. M. (1982) *Water and Power: The Conflict over Los Angeles' Water Supply in the Owens Valley*. Berkeley, CA: University of California Press.

Kallis, G., Kiparsky, M., and Norgarrd, R. (2009) Collaborative Governance and Adaptive Management: Lessons from California's CALFED Water Program. *Environmental Science & Policy* 12, 631–43.

Kamash, Z. (2012) An Exploration of the Relationship between Shifting Power, Changing Behaviour and New Water Technologies in the Roman Near East. *Water History* 4, 79–93.

Kedward, J. (2012) Really, Rain Barrels Illegal? Pueblo Pulp, July. Available at: http://pueblopulp.com/really-rain-barrels-illegal

Keenan, S. P., Kranich, R. S., and Walker, M. S. (1999) Public Perceptions of Water Transfers and Markets: Describing Differences in Water Use Communities. *Society and Natural Resources* 12, 279–92.

Kenney, D. S., McAllister, S. T., Caile, W. H., and Peckham, J. S. (2000) *The New Watershed Source Book – A Directory and Review of Watershed Initiatives in the Western U.S.* Boulder, CO: Natural Resources Law Center, University of Colorado School of Law.

Keremane, G., McKay, J., and Wu, Z. (2011) Not Stormwater in My Teacup: An Internet Survey of Residents in Three Australian Cities. *Water*, April, 118–24.

Kershner, I. (2015) Aided by the Sea, Israel Overcomes an Old Foe: Drought. *New York Times*, May 29. Available at: http://www.nytimes.com/2015/05/30/world/middleeast/water-revolution-in-israel-overcomes-any-threat-of-drought.html

Kiderra, I. (2014) Too many people, not enough water; Now and 2,700 years ago. UC San Diego News Center, November 10. Available at: http://ucsdnews.ucsd.edu/pressrelease/too_many_people_not_enough_water_now_and_2700_years_ago

Kings, S. (2012) Carolina's Water Woes Indicate Larger Structural Problems. *Mail-Guardian (S.A.)*, July 19. Available at: http://mg.co.za/article/2012-07-19-carolina-water-woes-structural-problems

Kiparsky, M. and Hein, J. F. (2013) Regulation of Hydraulic Fracturing in California: A Wastewater and Water Quality Perspective. Center for Law, Energy and the Environment, Berkeley, CA.

Kiparsky, M., Sedlak, D. L., Thompson, Jr., B. H., and Truffer, B. (2013) The Innovation Deficit in Urban Water: The Need for an Integrated Perspective on Institutions, Organizations, and Technology. *Environmental Engineering Science* 30, 395–408.

Knopman, D. S. (2006) Success Matters: Recasting the Relationship among Geophysical, Biological, and Behavioral Scientists to Support Decision Making on Major Environmental Challenges. *Water Resources Research* 42, W03S09.

Koeppel, G. T. (2000) *Water for Gotham: A History*. Princeton, NJ: Princeton University Press.

Koloski-Ostrow, A. O. (2015) Talking Heads: What Toilets and Sewers Tell Us about Ancient Roman Sanitation. *The Conversation*, November 19. Available at: https://theconversation.com/talking-heads-what-toilets-and-sewers-tell-us-about-ancient-roman-sanitation-50045

Koontz, T. M., Steelman, T. A., Carmin, J., Korfmacher, K. S., Moseley C., and Thomas, C. W. (2004) *Collaborative Environmental Management: What Roles for Government?* Washington, DC: Resources for the Future.

Kornfeld, I. E. (2009) Mesopotamia: A History of Water and Law. In Dellapenna, J. W. and Gupta, J. (eds.) *The Evolution of the Law and Politics of Water*. Delft: Springer, pp. 21–36.

Kozacek, C. (2015) Sao Paulo Drought Perception Impedes Government Action – Transparency, Accountability, and Civic Participation Are Key to Improving Sao Paulo's Water Security. Circle of Blue, May 4. Available at: http://www.circleofblue.org/waternews/2015/world/sao-paulo-drought-perception-impedes-government-action/

Kumar, D. (2010) *Managing Water in River Basins*. Oxford: Oxford University Press.

Lal, R. (2004) Carbon Emission from Farm Operations. *Environment International* 30, 981–90.

Laster, R., Aronovsky, D., and Livney, D. (2008) Water in the Jewish Legal Tradition. In Dellapenna, J. W. and Gupta, J. (eds.) *The Evolution of the Law and Politics of Water*. Delft: Springer, pp. 53–66.

Lautze, J. and Giordano, M. (2005) Transboundary Water Law in Africa: Development, Nature, and Geography. *Natural Resources Journal* 45, 1053–87.

Lebel, L., Anderies, J. M., Campbell, B., Folke, C., Hatfield-Dodds, S., Hughes, T. P., and Wilson, J. (2006) Governance and the Capacity to Manage Resilience in Regional Social-Ecological Systems. *Ecology and Society* 11, 19–38.

Lemos, M. C. and de Oliveira, J. L. F. (2004) Can Water Reform Survive Politics? Institutional Change and River Basin Management in Ceará, Northeast Brazil. *World Development* 32, 2121–37.

Lemos, M. C. and de Oliveira, J. L. F. (2005) Water Reform Across the State/Society Divide: The Case of Ceará, Brazil. *International Journal of Water Resources Development* 21, 93–107.

Li, J. and Liu, J. (2009) Quest for Clean Water: China's Newly Amended Water Pollution Control Law. Wilson Center. Available at: http://www.wilsoncenter.org/publication/quest-for-clean-water-chinas-newly-amended-water-pollution-control-law

Linton, J. (2010) *What is Water? The History of a Modern Abstraction.* Vancouver, BC: University of British Columbia Press.

Little, A. (2015) How Israel Found Too Much Water. *Bloomberg Businessweek,* January 12–18, pp. 49–53.

Lockwood, H. and Smits, S. (2011) *Supporting Rural Water Supply: Moving Towards a Service Delivery Approach.* Rugby: Practical Action Publishing.

Loomis, B. (2015) As Colorado River Runs Dry, Arizona's Water-Resources Staff Has Been Depleted, Too. *Arizona Republic,* November 9. Available at: http://www.azcentral.com/story/news/arizona/investigations/2015/11/09/arizona-water-resources-staff-depleted/75321606/

Los Angeles Department of Water and Power (2010) *The Story of the Los Angeles Aqueduct.* Available at: http://wsoweb.ladwp.com/Aqueduct/historyoflaa/

Low, K. G., Feldman, D. L., Grant, S. B., Hamilton, A. J., Gan, K., Saphores, J. D., and Arora, M. (2015) Fighting Drought with Innovation: Melbourne's Response to the Millennium Drought in Southeast Australia. *WIRES Water* 2, 315–28.

Lowi, M. (1991) West Bank Water Resources and the Resolution of Conflict in the Middle East. Paper presented for the project on Environmental Change and Acute Conflict, June 15–17.

Lu, F., Ocampo-Raeder, C., and Crow, B. (2014) Equitable Water Governance: Future Directions in the Understanding and Analysis of Water Inequities in the Global South. *Water International* 39, 129–42.

Lundqvist, J., Turton, A., and Narain, S. (2001) Social, Institutional and Regulatory Issues. In Maksimovic, C. and Tejada-Guilbert, J. A. (eds.) *Frontiers in Urban Water Management: Deadlock or Hope.* London: IWA Publishing, pp. 344–98.

McConnell, G. (1966) *Private Power and American Democracy.* New York: Vintage.

MacDonnell, L. J. and Fort, D. (2008) Policy Report – A New Western Water Agenda: Opportunities for Action in an Era of Growth and Climate Change. University of New Mexico Law School, Albuquerque, NM.

McGinnis, M. (ed.) (1998) *Bioregionalism.* New York: Routledge.

McGinnis, M. (2005) Costs and Challenges of Polycentric Governance, Department of Political Science and Workshop in Political Theory and Policy Analysis,

Indiana University, Bloomington, Prepared for Workshop on Analyzing Problems of Polycentric Governance in the Growing EU, Humboldt University, Berlin, June 16–17.

Macknick, J., Newmark, R., Heath, G., and Hallett, K. C. (2011) A Review of Operational Water Consumption and Withdrawal Factors for Electricity Generating Technologies. Prepared under Task No. DOCC.1005, National Renewable Energy Lab.

McLaughlin, D. (2013) Water and Food Security. Paper presented at MIT Research & Development Conference, Ralph M. Parsons Laboratory for Environmental Science and Engineering, November 13.

Mann, D. (1985) Democratic Politics and Environmental Policy. In Kaminiecki, S. (ed.) *Controversies in Environmental Policy*. Albany, NY: SUNY Press.

Martin, S. O. (2010) Maryland's Second Generation of Smart Growth. *Planning* 76, 20–4.

Medellín-Azuara, J., Mendoza-Espinosa, L., Pells, C., and Lund, J. R. (2013) Pre-Feasibility Assessment of a Water Fund for the Ensenada Region – Infrastructure and Stakeholder Analyses. Center for Watershed Sciences, UC Davis and Nature Conservancy, Davis, CA.

Melvin, J. (2014) Tap Water 'Polluted' for 1.5 Million in France. *The Local, France's News in English*, February 26. Available at: http://www.thelocal.fr/20140226/15-million-french

Miller, G. W. (2006) Integrated Concepts in Water Reuse: Managing Global Water Needs. *Desalination* 187, 65–75.

Ministère de l'Amenagement du Territoire et de l'Environnement (1999) The Water Resources Department, Dialogue at the Local Level, and State-Supervised and Jointly-Supervised Agencies, Government of France.

Mirosa, O. and Harris, L. M. (2012) Human Right to Water: Contemporary Challenges and Contours of a Global Debate. *Antipode* 44, 932–49.

Mitchell, R. B. (2009) *International Politics and the Environment*. Beverly Hills, CA: Sage Publications.

Moehring, E. P. and Green, M. S. (2005) *Las Vegas: A Centennial History*. Reno, NV: University of Nevada Press.

Mono Lake Newsletter (2014) Special Report for Mono Lake Committee Members. March.

Morgan, B. (2012) *Water on Tap – Rights and Regulation in the Transnational Governance of Urban Water Services*. Cambridge: Cambridge University Press.

Moriarty, P., Batchelor, C., Abd-Alhadi, F. T., Laban, P., and Fahmy, H. (2007) The EMPOWERS Approach to Water Governance: Guidelines, Methods and Tools. Amman, Jordan, Inter-Islamic Network on Water Resources Development and Management (INWRDAM)/EMPOWER Partnership.

Morse, R. (2008) Environmental Justice through the Eye of Hurricane Katrina. Joint Center for Political and Economic Studies, Heath Policy Institute, Washington, DC.

Mosse, D. (2008) Epilogue: The Cultural Politics of Water – A Comparative Perspective. *Journal of Southern African Studies* 34, 939–48.

Mostaghim, R. and Sandels, A. (2014) Dying Lake Reflects Crisis. *Los Angeles Times*, April 21.

Mostert, E. (2009) International Co-operation on Rhine Water Quality 1945–2008: An Example to Follow? *Physics and Chemistry of the Earth, Parts A/B/C* 34, 142–9.

Mtisi, S. and Nicol, A. (2003) Water Points and Water Policies: Decentralisation and Community Management in Sangwe Communal Area, Zimbabwe. Sustainable Livelihoods in Southern Africa: Institutions, Governance and Policy Processes. Available at: http://www.ids.ac.uk/publication/water-points-and-water-policies-de centralisation-and-community-management-in-sangwe-communal-area-zimbabwe

Mulholland, C. (2002) *William Mulholland and the Rise of Los Angeles*. Berkeley, CA: University of California Press.

Mulvaney, D. (2014) Solar Energy Isn't Always as Green as You Think – Do Cheaper Photovoltaics Come with a Higher Environmental Price Tag? *IEEE Spectrum*, August 26. Available at: http://spectrum.ieee.org/green-tech/solar/solar-energy-isnt-always-as-green-as-you-think

Mumme, S. P. (2016) Scarcity and Power in US–Mexico Transboundary Water Governance: Has the Architecture Changed since NAFTA? *Globalizations*, DOI: 10.1080/14747731.2015.1129710

Naidoo, R., Balmford, A., Ferraro, P. J., Polasky, S., Ricketts, T. H., and Rouget, M. (2006) Integrating Economic Costs into Conservation Planning. *Trends in Ecology & Evolution* 21, 681–7.

Naff, T. A. (2008) Islamic Law and the Politics of Water. In Dellapenna, J. W. and Gupta, J. (eds.) *The Evolution of the Law and Politics of Water*. Delft: Springer, pp. 37–52.

Naff, T. A. and Dellapenna, J. W. (2002) Can There Be Confluence? A Comparative Consideration of Western and Islamic Fresh Water Law. *Water Policy* 4, 465–89.

National Academy of Sciences (2014) *Reducing Coastal Risk on the East and Gulf Coasts*. Washington, DC: National Academy of Sciences.

National Reclamation Act of 1902. Public Law 57–161, as amended.

NRC (National Research Council) (2008) *Water Implications of Biofuels Production in the United States*. Washington, DC: National Academies Press.

NRC (National Research Council) (2012) *Water Reuse: Potential for Expanding the Nation's Water Supply Through Reuse of Municipal Wastewater*. Washington, DC: National Academies Press.

National Water Resources Strategy (2013) *National Development Plan – South Africa*. Available at: https://www.dwa.gov.za/nwrs/

Neslen, A. (2015) Poland's Shale Gas Revolution Evaporates in Face of Environmental Protests. *The Guardian*, January 12. Available at: http://www.theguardian.com/ environment/2015/jan/12/polands-shale-gas-revolution-evaporates-in-face-of-envir onmental-protests

Newson, M. (1997) *Land, Water and Development: Sustainable Management of River Basin Systems*, 2nd edn. New York: Routledge.

New York City (2011) History of New York City Water Supply. Available at: http:// www.nyc.gov/html/dep/html/drinking_water/history.shtml

Nieswiadomy, M. L. (1992) Estimating Urban Residential Water Demand: Effects of Price Structure, Conservation, and Education. *Water Resources Research* 28, 609–15.

Nieswiadomy, M. L. and Molina, D. J. (1989) Comparing Residential Water Demand Estimates under Decreasing and Increasing Block Rates Using Household Data. *Land Economics* 65, 280–9.

Nijhuis, M. (2015) Harnessing the Mekong or Killing it? *National Geographic* 227, 102–29.

Nile Basin Initiative Secretariat (2014) Entebbe, Uganda. Available at: http://www.nilebasin.org/

Nile Basin Initiative (2016) Eastern Nile Technical Regional Office. Available at: http://nilebasin.org/index.php/about-us/nile-basin-initiative/2-about-us/21-eastern-nile-technical-regional-office

Norman, E., Bakker, K., and Cook, C. (2012) Introduction to the Themed Section: Water Governance and the Politics of Scale. *Water Alternatives* 5, 52–61.

North Carolina, Dept. of Environment and Natural Resources (2014) Tar-Pamlico Nutrient Trading. Available at: http://portal.ncdenr.org/web/wq/ps/nps/tarpam-nutrienttrade

Nugent, W. (2001) *Into the West – The Story of its People*. New York: Vintage.

Nye, J. S. Jr. (2004) *Soft Power: The Means to Succeed in World Politics*. New York: Perseus Books.

O'Connor, R., Yarnal, B., Dow, K., Jocoy, C. L., and Carbone, G. J. (2005) Feeling At-Risk Matters: Water Managers and the Decision to Use Forecasts. *Risk Analysis* 25, 1265–75.

Office of the Secretary, US Department of the Interior (2012) Salazar Announces Improvements to Glen Canyon Dam Operations to Restore High Flows and Native Fish in Grand Canyon: Adaptive management strategy meets water and power supply needs. Washington, DC, May 23.

Ojos Negros Research Group (2012) Sustainable Management of Water in the Ojos Negros Valley, Baja California, Mexico. San Diego State University/Universidad Autónoma de Baja California/Instituto Nacional de Investigaciones Agrícolas, Forestales y Pecuarias. Available at: http://ponce.sdsu.edu/ojosnegrosreportex-ecutivesummary.html

One Drop (2014) Project Honduras. Available at: https://www.onedrop.org/en/project/honduras/

Oren, M. B. (2003) *Six Days of War: June 1967 and the Making of the Modern Middle East*. New York: Random House.

OECD (Organization for Economic Cooperation and Development) (1999) *Environmental Performance Review: Russian Federation*. Paris: OECD, Center for Cooperation with Non-Members.

Orlowski, A. (2015) Water Source of Last Resort: the Desert. *Orange County Register*, June 7, pp. 1, 6–7.

Ostrom, E. (2010) Beyond Markets and States: Polycentric Governance of Complex Economic Systems. *American Economic Review* 100, 1–33.

Pacific Institute (2014) *Issue Brief: The Untapped Potential of California's Water Supply: Efficiency, Reuse, and Stormwater*. Oakland, CA: Pacific Institute.

Palmer, M. A., Liu, J., Matthews, J. H., Mumba, M., and D'Odorico, P. (2015) Water Security: Gray or Green? *Science* 349, 584–5.

Palomar, P. and Losada, I. J. (2011) Impacts of Brine Discharge on the Marine Environment: Modeling as a Predictive Tool. In Schorr, M. (ed.) *Desalination, Trends and Technologies*. New York: Intech.

Parenteau, P. (2016) What Scalia's Death Means for Environment and Climate. *The Conversation*, February 18.

Pearce, M. (2016) A 'Man-made' Disaster in Flint. *Los Angeles Times*, January 23, p.A10.

Peters, P. E. (1994) *Dividing the Commons: Politics, Policy, and Culture in Botswana*. Charlottesville, VA: University Press of Virginia.

Petersen, D., Minkler, M., Vasquez, V. B., and Baden, A. C. (2006) Community-Based Participatory Research as a Tool for Policy Change: A Case Study of the Southern California Environmental Justice Collaborative. *Review of Policy Research* 23, 339–54.

Pfeiffer, E. and Leentvaar, J. (2013) Knowledge Leads, Policy Follows? Two Speeds of Collaboration in River Basin Management. *Water Policy* 15, 282–99.

Phillips, F. M., Hall, G. E., and Black, M. E. (2011) *Reigning in the Rio Grande: People, Land, and Water*. Albuquerque, NM: University of New Mexico Press.

Pitzer, G. (2009) The Water–Energy Nexus in the Colorado River Basin. Colorado River Project: River Report. Sacramento, CA: Water Education Foundation.

Pitzer, P. (1994) *Grand Coulee: Harnessing a Dream*. Pullman, WA: Washington State University Press.

Po, M., Nancarrow, B. E., Leviston, Z., Porter, N. B., Syme, G. J., and Kaercher, J. D. (2005) *Predicting Community Behaviour in Relation to Wastewater Reuse: What Drives Decisions to Accept or Reject?* Water for a Healthy Country National Research Flagship. Perth: CSIRO Land and Water.

Podolosky, L. (2012) Barriers to Low Impact Development. Prepared by the Local Government Commission for the Southern California Stormwater Monitoring Coalition, Sacramento, CA.

Pomeroy, E. (1955) Toward a Reorientation of Western History: Continuity and Environment. *Mississippi Valley Historical Review* XLI, 579–99.

Post, A. (2009) The Paradoxical Politics of Water Metering in Argentina. In: *Poverty in Focus – International Policy Centre for Inclusive Growth No. 18*. Poverty Practice, Bureau for Development Policy, UNDP, pp.16–18.

Postel, S. (2000) Entering an Era of Water Scarcity: The Challenges Ahead. *Ecological Applications* 10, 941–8.

Powers, A. (1999) The Current Controversy Regarding TMDLs: Pollutant Trading. *Vermont Journal of Environmental Law* 4, 10–41.

Purcell, N. (1994) The Arts of Government. In Boardman, J., Griffin, J., and Murray, O. (eds.) *The Roman World*. Oxford: Oxford University Press, pp.150–81.

Purdy, J. M. (2012) A Framework for Assessing Power in Collaborative Governance Processes. *Public Administration Review* 72, 409–17.

Rabe, B. G. (2004) *Statehouse and Greenhouse: The Emerging Politics of American Climate Change Policy*. Washington, DC: Brookings Institution.

Rai, S. (2003) Protests in India Deplore Soda Makers' Water Use. *New York Times*, May 21. Available at: http://www.nytimes.com/2003/05/21/business/protests-in-india-deplore-soda-makers-water-use.html

Ray, A., Garfin, G. M., Lenart, M., Wilder, M., Vasquez-Leon, M., and Comrie, A. C. (2007) Applications of Monsoon Research: Opportunities to Inform Decision Making and Reduce Regional Vulnerability. *Journal of Climate* 20, 1608–27.

Rijke, J., Brown, R., Zevenbergen, C., Ashley, R., Farrelly, M., Morison, P., and van Herk, S. (2012) Fit-for-Purpose Governance: A Framework to Make Adaptive Governance Operational. *Environmental Science & Policy* 22, 73–84.

Rittel, H. and Weber, M. (1973) Dilemmas in a General Theory of Planning. *Policy Sciences* 4, 155–69.

Robinson, J. (2013) *Contested Water: The Struggle Against Water Privatization*. Cambridge, MA: MIT Press.

Rochman, C. and Kross, S. (2015) Tiny Beads, Big Problem, Easy Fix: Why Scientific Evidence Supports a Ban on Microbeads. *The Conversation*, June 4. Available at: https://theconversation.com/tiny-beads-big-problem-easy-fix-why-scientific-evidence-supports-a-ban-on-microbeads-42511

Rodriguez, A. (2010) Levee Breaches Blamed on the Rich. *Los Angeles Times*, September 12, p. A12.

Romney, L. (2015) The Source of their Concern – A Bottling Plant Will Bring Jobs to Mount Shasta, But Some Object to Exporting a Dwindling Resource. *Los Angeles Times*, May 10, pp. A1–A14.

Rotman, M. (2015) Cuyahoga River Fire. Cleveland Historical. Available at: http://clevelandhistorical.org/items/show/63

Ruhl, J. B. (2005) Water Wars, Eastern Style: Divvying Up the Apalachicola-Chattahoochee-Flint River Basin. *Journal of Contemporary Water Research & Education* 131, 47–54.

Sadoff, C., Greiber, T., Smith, M., and Bergkamp, G. (2008) Share: Managing Water across Boundaries. International Union for the Conservation of Nature, Gland, Switzerland.

Salman, M. A. and Uprety, K. (2003) *Conflict and Cooperation on South Asia's International Rivers: A Legal Perspective*. Washington, DC: World Bank.

Salzman, J. (2012) *Drinking Water: A History*. New York: Overlook Books.

Samson, S. A. and Bacchus, S. (2000) Point-Water Marketing: The Other Side of the Coin. *Water Resources Impact* 2, 15–16.

Santa Cruz Declaration on the Global Water Crisis (2014) *Water International* 39, 246–61.

Sarewitz, D. and Pielke Jr., R. A. (2007) The Neglected Heart of Science Policy: Reconciling Supply of and Demand for Science. *Environmental Science and Policy* 10, 5–16.

Satterthwaite, D. (2000) Will Most People Live in Cities? *British Medical Journal* 321, 1143–5.

Schneider, J. (1987) *World Public Order of the Environment: Towards an International Ecological Law and Organization*. Toronto: University of Toronto Press.

Schragger, R. (2016) Flint Wasn't Allowed Democracy: That's Part of the Reason

Nobody Acted When Its Water Was Poisoned. Slate, February 8. Available at: http://www.slate.com/articles/news_and_politics/jurisprudence/2016/02/a_big_reason_for_the_flint_water_crisis_no_democracy_there.html

Schulte-Wülwer-Leidig, A. (ed.) (2008) *The Rhine: A River and its Relations*. Koblenz: IKSR-CIPR-CIBR.

Schultz, C. (2014) ISIS is Cutting Off Water to Uncooperative Villages – In Parched Syria and Iraq, Water Is a Weapon. Smithsonian.com, October 7. Available at: www.smithsonianmag.com/smart-news/isis-cutting-water-uncooperative-villages

Scott, C. A., Varady, R. G., Meza, F., Montaña, E., de Raga, G. B., Luckman, B., and Martius, C. (2012) Science-Policy Dialogues for Water Security: Addressing Vulnerability and Adaptation to Global Change in the Arid Americas. *Enviroment* 54, 30–42.

Selby, J. (2013) Cooperation, Domination and Colonisation: The Israeli-Palestinian Joint Water Committee. *Water Alternatives* 6, 1–24.

Selin, H. and VanDeveer, S. D. (2009) *Changing Climates in North American Politics – Institutions, Policymaking, and Multilevel Governance*. Cambridge, MA: MIT Press.

Selman, M., Greenhalgh, S., Branosky, E., Jones, C., and Guiling, J. (2009) Water Quality Trading Programs: An International Overview. WRI Issue Brief: Water Quality Trading no. 1. World Resources Institute, March.

Shah, T. and Verma, S. (2008) Co-Management of Electricity and Groundwater: An Assessment of Gujarat's Jyotigram Scheme. *Economic and Political Weekly* 43, 59–66.

Shamir, U. (1998) Water Agreements between Israel and Its Neighbors. In Albert, J., Bernhardson, M., and Kenna, R. (eds) *Transformations of Middle Eastern Natural Environments: Legacies and Lessons*. Number 103, Bulletin Series, Yale School of Forestry and Environmental Studies, pp. 274–96.

Shaughnessy, E. L. (2000) *China: Empire and Civilization*. Oxford: Oxford University Press.

Sheridan, K. (2014) No Matter How Many Water Protesters Turn Out in Dublin, Complex Problems Will Remain. *The Irish Times*, December 10. Available at: http://www.irishtimes.com/opinion/no-matter-how-many-water-protesters-turn-out-in-dublin-complex-problems-will-remain-1.2031643

Shiva, V. (2009) *Water Wars: Privatization, Pollution, and Profit*. London: Pluto Press.

Shrank, S. and Fahramand, F. (2011) Biofuels Regain Momentum. Vital Signs, Worldwatch Institute. Available at: http://vitalsigns.worldwatch.org/vs-trend/biofuels-regain-momentum

Sivakumar, B. (2011) Global Climate Change and Its Impacts on Water Resources Planning and Management: Assessment and Challenges. *Stochastic Environmental Research and Risk Assessment* 25, 583–600.

Smith, M. A. (2006) Russian Environmental Problems. Conflict Studies Research Centre, Russian Series 06/41, September. London: Defence Academy of the United Kingdom.

Smith, M. (2016) Flint Wants Safe Water and Someone to Answer for Its Water Crisis. *New York Times*, January 9. Available at: http://www.nytimes.com/2016/01/10/us/flint-wants-safe-water-and-someone-to-answer-for-its-crisis.html

Smith, A. and Stirling, A. (2010) The Politics of Social-Ecological Resilience and Sustainable Sociotechnical Transitions. *Ecology and Society* 15, 11–23.

Smythe, W. E. (1900) *The Conquest of Arid America*. London: Harper and Brothers.

Sofoulis, Z. and Williams, C. (2008) From Pushing Atoms to Growing Networks: Cultural Innovation and Co-Evolution in Urban Water Conservation. *Social Alternatives* 27, 50–7.

Sproule-Jones, M. (1982) Public Choice Theory and Natural Resources: Methodological Explication and Critique. *American Political Science Review* 76, 790–804.

Star, S. L. and Griesemer, J. (1989) Institutional Ecology, Translations and Boundary Objects: Amateurs and Professionals in Berkeley's Museum of Vertebrate Zoology. *Social Studies of Science* 19, 387–420.

Starr, K. (1990) *Material Dreams: Southern California through the 1920s*. New York: Oxford University Press.

Stockholm Environment Institute (2011) Bonn 2011 Conference: The Water, Energy and Food Security Nexus – Solutions for the Green Economy, November 16–18.

Sule, S. (2003) *Understanding Our Civic Issues: Mumbai's Water Supply*. Mumbai: The Bombay Community Public Trust.

Supski, S. and Lindsay, J. (2013) Australian Domestic Water Use Cultures: A Literature Review. Monash University, Cooperative Research Centre for Water Sensitive Cities.

Swyngedouw, E. (2004) *Social Power and the Urbanisation of Water: Flows of Power*. Oxford: Oxford University Press.

Swyngedouw, E. (2005) Dispossessing H_2O: The Contested Terrain of Water Privatization. *Capitalism, Nature, Socialism* 16, 81–98.

Swyngedouw, E. (2007) Water, Money, and Power. *Socialist Register* 43, 195–212.

Swyngedouw, E. (2013) UN Water Report 2012: Depoliticizing Water. *Development and Change* 44, 823–35.

Tanoli, Z. (2015) Kishan Ganga Dam: Pakistan Decides to Opt for a 'Neutral Expert'. *The Express Tribune – Pakistan*, October 15. Available at: http://tribune.com.pk/story/973130/kishan-ganga-dam-pakistan-decides-to-opt-for-a-neutral-expert/

Tarlock, A. D. (1997) *Law of Water Rights and Resources*. Deerfield, IL: Clark, Boardman and Callaghan (updated 1998).

Tarlock, A. D., Corbridge, Jr., J. N., and Getches, D. H. (1993) *Water Resource Management: A Casebook in Law and Public Policy*, 4th edn. Westbury, NY: The Foundation Press.

The Aral Sea Crisis (2008) Available at: http://www.columbia.edu/~tmt2120/introduction.htm

The Kolontar Report: Causes and Lessons from the Red Mud Disaster (2011) Budapest: The Greens/European Free Alliance Parliamentary Group in the European Parliament and LMP – Politics Can Be Different, March.

The Nature Conservancy (2015) California – Saving Salmon in the Lassen Foothills. Available at: http://www.nature.org/ourinitiatives/regions/northamerica/unitedstates/california/explore/saving-salmon-in-the-lassen-foothills.xml

The Parliamentary Committee of Inquiry on the Israeli Water Sector (2002) Jerusalem, Israel.

Tir, J. and Ackerman, J. T. (2009) Politics of Formalized River Cooperation. *Journal of Peace Research* 46, 623–40.

Tirmizi, F. (2011) Rare Victory: Pakistan Wins Stay Order Against Indian Dam. *The Express Tribune*, September 25. Available at: http://tribune.com.pk/story/259650/court-of-arbitration-halts-construction-of-Kisheganga-dam/

Tisdell, J. G. (2003) Equity and Social Justice in Water Doctrines. *Social Justice Research* 16, 401–16.

Tokyo Waterworks Bureau (2013) Outline of the Tokyo Waterworks Bureau, Japan.

UNEP (United Nations Environment Program) (2013) Haiti – Dominican Republic Environmental Challenges in the Border Zone, June. Available at: http://postconflict.unep.ch/publications/UNEP_Haiti-DomRep_border_zone_EN.pdf

UNESCO-IHE – Institute for Water Education (2011) *Water Solutions – UNESCO-IHE in Partnership*. Delft: UNESCO.

United Nations Division for Sustainable Development (1992) UN Conference on Environment & Development, Rio de Janeiro, Brazil, 3–14 June 1992. Agenda 21. Available at: https://sustainabledevelopment.un.org/content/documents/Agenda21.pdf

United Nations Human Settlements Programme (2011) *Cities and Climate Change: Global Report on Human Settlements, 2011*. London: Earthscan.

UN Water (2012) *Managing Water under Uncertainty and Risk – The United Nations World Water Development Report 4, Volume 1*. Paris: United Nations Educational, Scientific, and Cultural Organization. Available at: http://www.unesco.org/new/fileadmin/MULTIMEDIA/HQ/SC/pdf/WWDR4%20Volume%201-Managing%20Water%20under%20Uncertainty%20and%20Risk.pdf

UN Water (2014a) Water and Urbanization. United Nations Inter-Agency Mechanism on all Freshwater related Issues, Including Sanitation. Available at: http://www.unwater.org/topics/water-and-urbanization/en/

UN Water (2014b) Gender and Water. Available at: http://www.un.org/waterforlifedecade/gender.shtml

UN Water (2014c) Water and Cities. Available at: http://www.un.org/waterforlifedecade/water_cities.shtml)

UN Water (2014d) Water and Energy. Available at: http://www.un.org/waterforlifedecade/water_and_energy.shtml

UN Water (2015) Water for a Sustainable World. United Nations World Water Development 2015. Paris: United Nations Educational, Scientific, and Cultural Organization.

UN Women (2009) Convention on the Elimination of all forms of Discrimination against Women. United Nations Entity for Gender Equality and the Empowerment of Women. Available at: http://www.un.org/womenwatch/daw/cedaw/

UN World Water Assessment Programme (2003) *Water for People, Water for Life: The United Nations World Water Development Report*. Barcelona: UNESCO and Berghahn Books.

UNWWDR (United Nations World Water Development Report) (2006) *Water – A Shared Responsibility*. World Water Assessment Programme Report No. 2. Paris: UNESCO. Available at: http://www.unesco.org/new/en/natural-sciences/environment/water/wwap/wwdr/wwdr2-2006/

US Bureau of Reclamation (2008) Lower Colorado Basin: The Law of the River. Available at: http://www.usbr.gov/lc/region/g1000/lawofrvr.html

US Bureau of Reclamation (2012) Colorado River Basin Water Supply and Demand Study – Report. Washington, DC: USBR.

US Bureau of Reclamation (2014) Glen Canyon Dam: Adaptive Management Program. Available at: http://www.usbr.gov/uc/rm/amp/

US Department of Energy (2006) Energy Demands on Water Resources. Report to Congress on the Interdependence of Energy and Water.

US Department of Energy (2014) The Water–Energy Nexus: Challenges and Opportunities. Washington, DC: DOE. Available at: http://www.energy.gov/sites/prod/files/2014/07/f17/Water%20Energy%20Nexus%20Full%20Report%20July%202014.pdf

US Department of Energy/Energy Efficiency and Renewable Energy (2008) *20% Wind Energy by 2030: Increasing Wind Energy's Contribution to US Electricity Supply*. Oak Ridge, TN: Department of Energy.

US Environmental Protection Agency (2012) Chapter 3 – Development and Implementation of The TMDL – Guidance for Water Quality-Based Decisions: The TMDL Process (March 2012 update).

US Environmental Protection Agency (2015) Persistent Organic Pollutants: A Global Issue, A Global Response. Available at: http://www.epa.gov/international-cooperation/persistent-organic-pollutants-global-issue-global-response

US Government Accountability Office (2015) Technology Assessment – Water in the Energy Sector: Reducing Freshwater Use in Hydraulic Fracturing and Thermoelectric Power Plant Cooling. GAO-15-545. Washington, DC: GAO.

van de Meene, S., Brown, R. R., and Farrelly, M. A. (2011) Towards Understanding Governance for Sustainable Urban Water Management. *Global Environmental Change* 21, 1117–27.

Vandersypen, K., Keita, A., Coulibaly, Y., Raes, D., and Jamin, J.-Y. (2007) Formal and Informal Decision Making on Water Management at the Village Level: A Case Study from the Office du Niger Irrigation Scheme (Mali). *Water Resources Research* 43, W06419.

Van Koppen, B. (2002) A Gender Performance Indicator for Irrigation: Concepts, Tools, and Applications. Research Report 59. Colombo, Sri Lanka: International Water Management Institute.

Van Koppen, B. (2008) Redressing Inequities of the Past from a Historical Perspective: The Case of the Olifants Basin, South Africa. *Water SA* 34, 432–8.

Van Koppen, B., Giordano, M., Butterworth, J., and Mapedza, E. (2007) Community-Based Water Law and Water Resource Management Reform in Developing Countries. Wallingford, Oxon: CABI.

Vasek, L. and Wilson, L. (2012) 'Long Overdue' Murray-Darling Basin Plan Becomes Law. *The Australian*, November 22.

Victorian Water Industry Association (2007) Recycled Water Returned to Stream for Environmental Flows. Position Paper, VicWater Working Group, June.

Vidal, J. (2014) Water Supply Key to Outcome of Conflicts in Iraq and Syria, Experts Warn. *The Guardian*, July 2. Available at: http://www.theguardian.com/environment/2014/jul/02/water-key-conflict-iraq-syria-isis

Waggoner, P. E. (ed.) (1990) *Climate Change and US Water Resources*. New York: John Wiley & Sons.

Walton, J. (1993) *Western Times and Water Wars – State, Culture, and Rebellion in California*. Berkeley, CA: University of California Press.

Wang, U. (2014) New Technology Tools Aim to Reduce Water Use. *The Wall Street Journal*, May 18. Available at: http://online.wsj.com/news/articles/SB10001424052702303647204579543781303147754

Water for People (2014) RIR – Honduras, June 1. Available at: https://www.waterforpeople.org/where-we-work/honduras

Waterbury, J. (1979) *Hydropolitics of the Nile Valley*. New York: Syracuse University Press.

Waterbury, J. (2002) *The Nile Basin – National Determinants of Collective Action*. New Haven, CT: Yale University Press.

Water in the West (2013) *Water and Energy Nexus: A Literature Review*. Stanford, CA: A joint program of Stanford Woods Institute for the Environment and Bill Lane Center for the American West.

Weber, M. (2001) *From Max Weber: Essays in Sociology* (eds Gewirth, H. H. and Wright Mills, C. London: Routledge and Kegan Paul.

Western Water (2010) *Regional Environmental Improvement Plan: Western Water's Recycled Water Schemes*. Southbank, Victoria: URS Australia Pty Ltd.

Western Water (2013) *Annual Report 2012/13 – Optimising local resources*. Sunbury, Victoria: Western Water.

WHO (World Health Organization) (2008) *Safer Water, Better Health: Costs, Benefits and Sustainability of Interventions to Protect and Promote Health*. Geneva: WHO.

Wilkinson, C. F. (1992) *Crossing the Next Meridian: Water, Power, and the Future of the American West*. Washington, DC: Island Press.

Winemiller, K. O. and multiple authors (2016) Balancing Hydropower and Biodiversity in the Amazon, Congo, and Mekong. *Science* 351, 128–9.

Winters v. United States, 207 U.S. 564 (1908).

Wittfogel, K. A. (1957) *Oriental Despotism: A Comparative Study of Total Power*. New Haven, CT: Yale University Press.

Wolf, A. T. and Newton, J. (2007a) Case Study of Transboundary Dispute Resolution: The Tigris-Euphrates Basin. Program in Water Conflict Management and Transformation, Institute for Water and Watersheds, Oregon State University. Available at: http://www.transboundarywaters.orst.edu/research/case_studies/index.html

Wolf, A. T. and Newton, J. (2007b) Case Study of Transboundary Dispute Resolution: The La Plata Basin. Program in Water Conflict Management and Transformation, Institute for Water and Watersheds, Oregon State University. Available at: http://www.transboundarywaters.orst.edu/research/case_studies/La_Plata_New.htm

Wolf, A. T., Kramer, A., Carius, A., and Dabelko, G. D. (2005) *Water Can Be a Pathway To Peace, Not War*. Washington, DC: Global Policy Forum.

Wong, J. L. (2015) Food–Energy–Water Nexus: An Integrated Approach to Understanding China's Resource Challenges. The Water, Energy and Food Security Resource Platform. Nexus News, Bonn, Germany. Available at: https://cdn.americanprogress.org/wp-content/uploads/issues/2010/07/pdf/haqspring-2010final.pdf

Wong, S. (2007) China Bets on Massive Water Transfers to Solve Crisis. *International Rivers*, December 15. Available at: https://www.internationalrivers.org/resources/china-bets-on-massive-water-transfers-to-solve-crisis-1899.

Wong, T. H. and Brown, R. R. (2009) The Water Sensitive City: Principles for Practice. *Water Science & Technology* 60, 673–82.

World Bank Web (2014) South Africa Report, May 28.

World Civil Society Forum (2002) Strengthening International Cooperation, Geneva, Switzerland. Available at: http://www.worldcivilsociety.org/REPORT/EN/03/

World Resources Institute (WRI) (2005) Millennium Ecosystem Assessment: Ecosystems and Human Well-Being: Wetlands and Water Synthesis. Washington, DC: WRI.

Worster, D. (1979) *Dust Bowl: The Southern Plains in the 1930s*. New York: Oxford University Press.

Worster, D. (1985) *Rivers of Empire: Water, Aridity, and the Growth of the American West*. New York: Oxford University Press.

WWAP (World Water Assessment Program) (2009) *The United Nations World Water Development Report 3: Water in a Changing World*. Paris: UNESCO.

Yang, H., Flower, R. J., and Thompson, J. R. (2013) Shale-Gas Plans Threaten China's Water Resources. *Science* 340, 1288.

Yardley, W. (2015) Shrinking Colorado River a Growing Concern for Arizona. *Los Angeles Times*, July 26.

Young, O. (1989) *Compliance and Public Authority: A Theory with International Applications*. Baltimore, MD: Johns Hopkins University Press.

Young, O. (2002) Institutional Interplay: The Environmental Consequences of Cross-Scale Interactions. In Ostrom, E., Dietz, T., Dolsak, N., Stern, P. C., Stonich, S., and Weber, E. (eds.) *The Drama of the Commons*. Washington, DC: National Academy Press.

Zeitoun, M. (2007) The Conflict vs. Cooperation Paradox: Fighting Over or Sharing of Palestinian–Israeli Groundwater? *Water International* 32, 105–20.

Zeitoun, M. and Warner, J. (2006) Hydro-Hegemony – A Framework for Analysis of Trans-Boundary Water Conflicts. *Water Policy* 8, 435–60.

Zwarteveen, M. (2012) Seeing Women and Questioning Gender in Water Management. In Prakash, A., Singh, S., Goodrich, C. G., and Janakarajan, S. (eds.) *Water Resources Policies in South Asia: Analyzing Regional and Country Experiences*. New Delhi: Routledge, pp. 38–65.

Index